teacher guide

words for academic writing
vocabulary across curricula

Gail N. Adams, M.Ed.

Susan Van Zant, Ed.D.

Sopris West®
EDUCATIONAL SERVICES

A Cambium Learning Company

BOSTON, MA • LONGMONT, CO

ISBN 13-digit: 978-1-60218-217-2
ISBN 10-digit: 1-60218-217-5

Printed in the United States of America

Published and Distributed by

Sopris West®
EDUCATIONAL SERVICES

A Cambium Learning Company

4093 Specialty Place • Longmont, Colorado 80504
(303) 651-2829 • www.sopriswest.com

(160805/322/11-07)

Dedication

To the memory of Sheron Brown—author, colleague, friend, and reading specialist extraordinaire.

Acknowledgments

We would like express our appreciation to:

Dr. Anita Archer, our mentor and role model, for her inspiration, guidance, and friendship.

Our husbands, Larry Adams and Jerry Van Zant, for their unconditional support and patience.

We are grateful for the outstanding work in the field of vocabulary acquisition and development conducted by so many talented educators, including:

Richard Anderson, Scott Baker, Isabel Beck, Wesley Becker, Andrew Biemiller, Jeanne Chall, Linda Diamond, Kevin Feldman, Edward Kame'enui, Kate Kinsella, Linda Kucan, Margaret McKeown, William Nagy, Deborah Simmons, and Steven Stahl

Gail N. Adams

Susan Van Zant

About the Authors

Gail Adams holds a master's degree in education with an emphasis in reading and is certified in general education, special education, and as a reading specialist. A veteran teacher with more than 30 years' experience, Ms. Adams has worked with elementary and middle school students in both general and special education. As an educational consultant, she trains teachers all over the United States in cooperation with school districts, state departments, and professional organizations, and is a frequent conference presenter.

Adams was a contributing author and trainer for the materials developed under two California reading grants in 1999 and 2000: Struggling Reader Intervention Programs and Teaching Reading in Every Classroom. She has also published articles in *Principal* magazine and for Educational Research Service. Adams is coauthor of *The Six-Minute Solution: A Reading Fluency Program* for primary (K–grade 2), intermediate (grades 3–5), and secondary (grades 6–9) students (Sopris West, 2007).

Susan Van Zant is an educational consultant. She holds a master's degree in curriculum development from Northern Arizona University and a doctorate in educational administration from Alliant University. Dr. Van Zant taught reading in the elementary grades prior to her appointment as school principal. She served as an elementary and middle school principal for 27 years. Because she worked with her teachers to present a well-defined reading program—which led to increasingly higher achievement scores—three of the schools where she was principal were selected to be National Blue Ribbon Schools. In recognition for her achievements, Dr. Van Zant was selected to be a National Distinguished Principal and is the recipient of a Milken Educator Award.

Dr. Van Zant's interest in the development of academic vocabulary is based upon her commitment to help all children learn to read and write well. She trains and presents to educators throughout the United States. Dr. Van Zant has published articles in *Principal* magazine, *American School Board Journal*, and *Educational Leadership* journal.

Contents

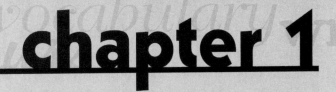
What is the *Words for Academic Writing: Vocabulary Across Curricula* program?

Words for Academic Writing is a supplementary vocabulary program designed to teach words frequently encountered in writing assignments. The program provides a research-based format for directly teaching writing vocabulary and offers multiple opportunities for students to both deeply process the meanings of the words and to practice using them. *Words for Academic Writing* is appropriate for general, special education, and English as a second language (ESL) students in grades 4–8 as well as for high school students in intervention programs. The *Words for Academic Writing* program can be implemented as:

- an introductory language arts unit, with a focus on generalizing the use of academic words commonly found in written assignments across curricula and in content areas including English, history, the sciences, and other courses in which written responses are expected;
- a daily "warm-up" activity to increase student understanding and use of academic words; or
- part of a language arts intervention program or summer school program.

What are "academic words"?

Academic words are those that are used in the classroom, in textbooks, and often included in tests. These words are different from those commonly used outside the classroom in terms of vocabulary, syntax, and grammar. Averil Coxhead (2000), from the School of Linguistics and Applied Language Studies at Victoria University of Wellington, New Zealand, compiled *The Academic Word List*. This list consists of 570 words that are grouped into ten sublists based on word frequency in academic texts.

Many English-only students—particularly struggling readers—with large social vocabularies often have trouble understanding words that are specifically used within a school setting. ESL students develop basic conversational skills well before they become proficient in academic language development. When students do not understand the language of school, they often do not fully comprehend what they have read and have difficulty participating in class discussions and responding appropriately to written assignments.

Isabel Beck and colleagues (Beck, McKeown, & Kucan, 2002) suggested that vocabulary words fall into three tiers, based on frequency of use. Tier 1 words (e.g., **boy**, **girl**, **dog**) are basic words that are already part of most students' lexicon and do not need to be taught. Tier 3 words (e.g., **tundra**, **isotope**, **lathe**) are limited to specific domains and should be taught to provide students with the knowledge needed to comprehend content-area material. Tier 2 words (e.g., **compare**, **contrast**, **analyze**), however, are found across a variety of domains that students are likely to encounter frequently. Tier 2 words—general-use by nature but not necessarily used at home—fall into the category of academic vocabulary and should, therefore, constitute the content of explicit vocabulary instruction. Rich knowledge of Tier 2 words can have a powerful impact on a student's verbal functioning (Beck et al., 2002).

Why should I teach academic words?

Instruction in the use of common academic writing words enables students to more fully understand concepts presented in class, be better prepared to participate in class discussions, and complete written assignments correctly. When students experience academic success, they develop self-confidence and the desire to achieve at higher levels. The importance of academic vocabulary use extends beyond the classroom as well. "Learning academic English is probably one of the surest, most reliable ways of attaining socioeconomic success in the United States today" (Scarcella, 2003).

There is an extensive research base that supports both the need for, and the importance of, explicit English vocabulary instruction. As cited below, a pervasive vocabulary gap exists:

- A gap in word knowledge persists through the elementary years (White, Graves, & Slater, 1990).
- The vocabulary gap between struggling readers and proficient readers grows each year (Stanovich, 1986).
- After the primary grades, the "achievement gap" among socioeconomic groups is a language gap (Hirsch, 2003).
- For ELL students, the "achievement gap" is primarily a vocabulary gap (Carlo et al., 2004).

A research base also points to a strong correlation between vocabulary knowledge and reading comprehension:

- Vocabulary instruction leads to gains in reading comprehension (Chall, Jacobs, & Baldwin, 1990; Scarborough, 1998; Stahl & Fairbanks, 1986).
- Instruction in specific word knowledge and concepts helps students develop a depth of knowledge that allows them to become better independent learners (Baumann & Kame'enui, 1991; Nagy, 1988).
- Vocabulary is related to overall school achievement (Anderson & Nagy, 1991; Becker, 1977).
- Vocabulary instruction can significantly improve students' comprehension (Stahl & Fairbanks, 1986).
- Instruction of specific words is particularly helpful for those words that are conceptually difficult or that are not part of students' everyday social conversation (Beck, McKeown, & Omanson, 1987).

What is "academic writing"?

Academic writing is analytical writing, the type that is expected in school. The general purpose of academic writing is to present information that demonstrates the writer's understanding of the subject. The specific purpose of academic writing will vary by assignment, as students may be asked to describe, explain, or persuade.

There are two basic kinds of writing structure: *narrative* and *expository*. Narrative writing is used to tell a story, while expository writing explains, informs, or persuades. Most students are more familiar with narrative writing, since they have often heard or seen stories on television and in movies before they enter school. Narrative text is usually a reflection of a daily routine in that it has a beginning, a middle, and an end. The focus of primary-grade writing instruction is usually narrative writing for which students are most often encouraged to use their creative imaginations.

As students progress through the grades, however, most of their writing will be expository. Expository writing is academic writing and reflects logical thinking. It employs deductive reasoning by stating the main idea and providing examples and details to support the main idea. Expository writing has a formal voice that avoids slang and colloquialisms and uses a third-person point of view. The ability to write clearly and accurately about topics in the content areas is a key component to academic success. Students with academic writing skills are able to effectively convey answers using facts and logic, and they can produce pieces that demonstrate an understanding of the inherent vocabulary of their assignment topics.

Since academic writing is challenging for many students, it is imperative that they be taught to use higher-level words effectively in oral and written assignments. *Words for Academic Writing* is designed to teach students academic words commonly found in writing assignments and to extend their knowledge of the words into expository writing assignments.

How do I use *Words for Academic Writing* to teach academic words?

This program is divided into four units (Chapter 3, Units 1–4), each consisting of six academic words (e.g., **contrast**, **analyze**), and an optional fifth unit (Chapter 3, Unit 5) that contains six academic writing terms (e.g., **sentence fluency**, **word choice**) that are frequently used to evaluate student writing. We selected the words and writing terms based on their frequency in writing assignments and as reported by teachers to be often misunderstood by students.

All units include a Pretest and a Posttest (refer to samples in *Appendix A*) in which students are asked to match academic words/writing terms with their definitions, to complete a cloze activity with academic words/writing terms, and to use a graphic organizer to form a written answer to a generative request. Additionally, all units include an optional Generative Assessment (refer to sample in *Appendix A*) to determine if students are able to generalize their academic-word/writing-term knowledge. Many vocabulary extension activities (refer to *Appendix B*) may also be used as generative assessments.

Vocabulary acquisition research (Beck & McKeown, 1991; Wolfe, 2001) indicates that new words are better learned when students can relate the word to both known words and personal experience. *Words for Academic Writing* activities are designed for students to personally interact with, and be actively engaged in, the lessons. Words are explicitly presented in the following research-based instructional format:

A. **Introduction and Pronunciation**. The teacher introduces the word, and students pronounce it. Pronouncing the word helps students make a connection to the word.

B. **Explanation**. The teacher provides a "student-friendly" explanation of the word rather than a dictionary definition.

C. **Example Sentences**. The teacher provides two example sentences, and students complete sentence stems with the target word.

D. **Checking for Understanding**. The teacher provides example and non-example sentences to which students respond in a "yes-no-why" manner. The teacher also prompts students to say or write generative responses (e.g., the teacher prompts a student by saying, "**Summarize** the events of your last birthday celebration").

E. **Vocabulary Words Table**. Students complete a table for each unit, listing each academic writing word, its meaning, and an example sentence.

F. **Word Forms Table**. Teacher and students add prefixes and suffixes to the target word to make word families. Students record the various forms of the word on the unit Word Forms Table.

G. **Cloze Exercise**. Students complete sentences using target word forms from the Word Forms Table.

H. **Informational Passage**. Students pair an academic writing word or term with an informational passage that provides essay-writing strategies.

I. **Framed Paragraph and Sentence Stems**. *(Optional, to be used in conjunction with items J and K, following.)* Paragraph topics and sentence stems provide students with various levels of scaffolding: topic sentences, transition words, and parts of supporting sentences. Paragraph frames help students to gradually learn academic writing structure and eventually use it in their own writing without assistance.

J. **Paragraph Starters**. Sentence stems serve as a way to begin writing sentences with academic vocabulary. Students complete the sentence stems and finish the paragraphs.

K. **Paragraph Topics**. General background knowledge provides students with ideas for writing.

How do I help students generalize academic writing words across settings?

Research suggests that students need to see a word about 12 times before they know it well enough to improve their comprehension (McKeown, Beck, Omanson, & Pople, 1985). Presumably, students would need the same amount of word exposure before they "own" the word well enough to use it in their daily language. Suggestions include:

- Provide visual reminders of newly introduced vocabulary words, and use the words repeatedly as part of daily classroom discussions to help students incorporate the words into their oral and written vocabularies.

- Add each new vocabulary word to a thematic classroom visual aid (e.g., an Academic Writing Word Wall), and provide students with a word notebook in which they can record the new words.

- Use extension games (e.g., "Jeopardy!," "Concentration," "Guess My Word") and Word Sort activities to enhance understanding and for informal assessment. Words can be sorted in a variety of ways (e.g., by parts of speech, similar meaning, prefixes, and suffixes).

- Teach students to use structural analysis to determine the meaning of related words.

- Encourage students to use the new words in oral and written language by providing word- and sentence-substitution activities.

- Teach students to use key words and mnemonic devices to remember the meanings of words.

How do I encourage students to actively participate in the lessons?

Struggling students often do not know how to approach learning or direct their own thinking process (McIntosh, Vaughn, Schumm, Haager & Lee, 1993). This program is designed to help ensure that students are provided with guided opportunities to enhance their understanding of academic words used in writing as well as to engage students in thoughtful responses to questions.

There is a strong correlation between student responses and achievement. Dr. Patricia Wolfe (2001), an educational consultant in the area of brain-based research, states, "No matter how well-planned, stimulating, relevant, exciting, and colorful the lesson, if the teacher does all of the interacting with material, the teacher's—not the student's—brain will grow." Clearly, students need to be actively involved in the process of learning in order for them to achieve at optimal levels.

The activities in *Words for Academic Writing* are based upon Dr. Anita Archer's model of instruction ("I do it. We do it. You do it.") and her recommended practices for increasing student participation by incorporating techniques such as choral responses, non-verbal responses, choral reading, cloze reading procedure, and use of peer partners.

- **Choral responses**. When the answer is short and the same, students respond as a group.

  Advantages: All students participate, and all students receive practice.

  Teaching Tips: Teach students a verbal and/or auditory signal, and require that they answer in "one voice." This requirement will discourage blurters and non-responders. Be sure to give students adequate thinking time prior to signaling for a response.

- **Non-verbal responses**. Students use a physical gesture (e.g., touch the directions, use hand signals, write) to respond to questions.

  Advantages: Nonverbal and written responses keep students actively involved. Touching directions or items encourages students to attend to the task at hand. These activities discourage off-task behavior.

  Teaching Tips: When requiring a nonverbal response such as touching an item, wait for all students to comply. When requiring a written response, tell students to keep writing until you ask them to stop.

- **Choral reading**. The whole class reads aloud from the same selection.

  Advantage: All students participate.

  Teaching Tips: Read at a moderate rate. Instruct students to "Keep your voice with mine." In order to be effective, choral reading should sound like one voice. Some students may need practice in this skill.

- **Cloze reading procedure**. Teacher reads material to students, using a moderate rate of speed. Then, the teacher intentionally deletes meaningful words by pausing and having students say the word.

  Advantages: Assists students in reading difficult material. Provides group practice and maintains attention.

  Teaching Tip: Make sure to delete meaningful words such as key vocabulary or target words.

- **Peer partners**. Students work with a partner to respond to questions and/or solve problems. Using peer partners is perhaps the easiest and most effective way to involve students in learning.

    Advantages: Responding to a peer is less threatening than responding to a larger group. Students receive support, clarification, and feedback from peers. Students have more time to think and rehearse, leading to reflection, thoughtfulness of response, and self-confidence.

    Teaching Tips: Circulate throughout the classroom, and monitor students as they interact with peers. This active supervision helps to maintain on-task behavior and allows the teacher to informally evaluate student progress.

Many partner activities in the *Words for Academic Writing* program are also based on the Think-Pair-Share model. Students are posed questions and asked to first think about their responses. They then write down their responses and finally share their ideas with their partners. The teacher then selects a few students to share their responses with the entire class. McTighe and Lyman (1988) found that the Think-Pair Share method helped to ensure active student involvement and high levels of attention, and promoted and increased verbal interactions.

What components are included in the *Words for Academic Writing* program?

The following components comprise this program:
- *Teacher Guide,* which includes lesson plans with step-by-step instructions for teaching 24 academic writing words and six academic writing terms;
- Pretest, Posttest, and Generative Assessment for each unit (CD-ROM);
- Pretest and Posttest answer keys (Appendix D);
- Extension activities (e.g., word games, word sorts) (Appendix B);
- Graphic organizers (Appendix C and CD-ROM);
- Glossary; and
- *Student Book.*

The *Student Book* is comprised of activities that introduce and reinforce acquisition of the 24 academic writing words and six academic writing terms. Each word or term is paired with an informational passage that provides essay-writing strategies. Most activities are teacher-directed and can be used with whole-group or small-group instruction. Some activities are designed for partner practice, while the two activities at the end of each lesson can be completed as independent practice.

Units 1–4 of the *Student Book* contain two tables: a unit Vocabulary Words Table for students to list each academic word, its critical attributes, and an example or illustration of the word; and a unit Word Forms Table for students to sort each academic word and its related word forms by parts of speech. Optional Unit 5, which covers academic terms, contains a unit Writing Terms Table in which students list each term, its attributes, and an example or illustration of the term. Once the *Student Book* is completed, the Vocabulary Words Tables, the Word Forms Tables, the Writing Terms Table, and the informational passages serve as reference materials for each unit.

Optional Generative Assessments are designed to provide a practical connection to the curriculum and its instruction. Presented after each unit is covered, these assessments ask students to apply specific academic words and writing terms to their personal experiences and background knowledge in the form of short written responses.

All five units in *Words for Academic Writing* include a Pretest, a Posttest, an optional Generative Assessment, and detailed lessons for teaching each academic writing word and/or writing term. All unit lessons in the Words for Academic Writing program follow this same research-based format.

Unit Pretest

Objective	To determine students' prior knowledge of academic words or writing terms that will be taught in the unit
Materials needed	For each student, one copy of the unit's Pretest
Time allotment	20 minutes (Part A, 10 minutes; Part B, 10 minutes)

Instructional Procedure

Step 1 Explain to students that the reason for taking the Pretest is to determine their level of knowledge of the six academic words or writing terms they will be learning in the unit.

- Inform students that they will take a Posttest after each unit is completed to measure how well they have learned the unit's words or writing terms.
- One part of the Posttest (Units 2–4 only) will include academic words that were covered in previous units. Another part of the Posttest will require them to make a graphic organizer, which they will use to form a written response.
- At this point, you may choose to explain the optional Generative Assessment, a separate supplemental element of the Posttest (see "Unit Generative Assessment" section, following). The Generative Assessment will ask students to demonstrate their understanding of the target words or writing terms by using them in short written examples based on their personal knowledge and experiences. Students will make their own graphic organizers to form their written responses.
- Inform students that only Posttest scores will be recorded as part of their grade.

Note: Teachers may choose to use each unit's optional Generative Assessment as the sole assessment measure for the unit (i.e., omit the Pretest and Posttest).

Step 2 Review the directions in the Pretest.

Step 3 Administer the Pretest.

Lesson Format

Note: These vocabulary lessons are designed for active student participation. Divide students into partnerships, and assign students as Partner 1 and Partner 2.

Objective   To enable students to deeply process and learn the
                           meanings of six academic vocabulary words in each unit

Materials needed   *Teacher Guide*, one *Student Book* for each student

Instructional Procedure

   A. Introduction and Pronunciation
- Explicitly introduce each academic word using the following format:
  - Tell students the word: "This word is _____."
  - Say the word in parts.
  - Ask students to repeat the word in parts and then say the whole word.

   B. Explanation
- Give students an explanation of the academic word in easily understood language (e.g., say: "**Compare** means *to tell or show how two or more things are the same or different*").
- Ask students to repeat the explanation.
- Direct Partner 1s to say the explanation to Partner 2s.
- Direct Partner 2s to tell Partner 1s if their explanation was correct.

   C. Example Sentences
- Ask the class to choral-read two example sentences (e.g., "Tomas was asked to **explain** the reason for his late arrival at school").
- Pose a question about each sentence (e.g., "When Tomas gave the reason for his late arrival at school, what was he doing?").
- Use a sentence stem to elicit a form of the academic word in the answer (e.g., "Tomas was _____ [**explaining**] the reason").
- Have students say the answer sentence to their partners.

   D. Checking for Understanding
- Stress to students that it is important to understand the meaning of an academic word when it is used in different ways.
- For this activity, tell students that they will (1) read sentences; (2) think, say, or write responses; and (3) explain their responses.
- Direct students to respond to their partners (e.g., say: "Partner 2s, read and respond to the first sentence. Partner 1s, tell your partner if you agree or disagree with the response").
Note: While students are responding, monitor their exchanges. Ask two or three students to share their responses with the class.

   E. Vocabulary Words Table
- Direct students to complete a Vocabulary Words Table for the new academic word.
- Instruct students to write an explanation of the word, then write their own sentence, give an example, or draw a picture to represent the word.

F. Word Forms Table
- Tell students that once they learn a new academic word, it is easy to learn other forms of the word. For instance: (1) Adding a prefix or a suffix makes a new but related word; (2) Word forms usually have similar spellings, pronunciations, and meanings; (3) Word forms are often different parts of speech.
- Say: "It is important to understand parts of speech: nouns, verbs, adjectives, and adverbs:
  - "We all know that a **noun** is a word that represents a person, place, thing, or idea. In school assignments, nouns are words that tell you *what you are asked to make* for an assignment or a test. For example, you might be asked to make a *comparison* between two books, three ideas, or four points of view.
  - "**Verbs** are words that represent actions, experiences, or states. In school assignments and tests, verbs tell you *what you are to do* for the assignment. For example, you might be asked to *compare* dinosaurs to animals of today.
  - "**Adjectives** are words that describe nouns or pronouns. In school assignments, adjectives *give a specific type of information* about the assignment. For example, you might be asked to make a *comparable* judgment between two or more ideas.
  - "**Adverbs** are words that add meaning to a verb, an adjective, another adverb, or a sentence. In school assignments, adverbs tell you *how you should do* the assignment. You might be asked to look *comparatively* at three parts of an issue."
- Direct students to the unit Word Forms Table and note that it is divided into four columns. Instruct students to add forms of the targeted academic word to the chart.

G. Cloze Exercise
- Direct students to use their new word forms to complete the cloze exercise with their partners. Provide adequate time for them to do so.
- Then ask students to follow along as you read the sentences to determine if their answers are correct.

H. Informational Passage
- Tell students that each academic writing word is paired with an informational passage. The informational passage is designed to provide them with strategies for using the academic word in a writing assignment.
- Ask students to choral-read the passage with you and then with their partners.

Note: To reinforce the use of the academic word and informational passage, give students an opportunity to use the word in content-area assignments.

I. Framed Paragraph and Sentence Stems *(Optional, to be used in conjunction with items J and K, following.)*

- Use for various levels of scaffolding, depending on the needs of your students.
- Ask students to point to the subheading paragraph frame. Tell them that a framed paragraph is a tool to assist them in writing a paragraph. The paragraph frame provides a sample topic sentence, transitions, and conclusion. Sentence stems are sentence starters that need to be completed.
- Read the topic sentence and each transitional sentence stem out loud with students.
- Stop after each transitional sentence stem, and assist students in selecting academic word examples that would make sense in the context of the framed paragraph.
- Ask students to chorally read the topic sentence and transitional sentences of the framed paragraph.
- Read the conclusion sentence out loud with students.
- Once the paragraph frame is completed, direct students to reread the entire paragraph to their partners.

J. Paragraph Starters

- For each academic writing word, three related paragraph topics and a suggested topic sentence are provided. Students can use these for independent practice, with a partner, or as a homework activity.

K. Paragraph Topics

- Additional writing topics, which are broad in scope and require little specialized background knowledge, are included for each academic word.

Note: Because Unit 5 (optional) is designed to help struggling students better understand academic writing terms (vs. academic words), it has a Writing Terms Table instead of a Vocabulary Words Table and Word Forms Table, and does not include sections, I, J, or K.

Unit Posttest

Objective	To determine students' acquired knowledge of academic words or writing terms that were taught in the unit
Materials needed	For each student, one copy of the unit's Posttest and two sheets of blank paper
Time allotment	35 minutes (Part A, 10 minutes; Part B, 10 minutes; Part C, 15 minutes)

Instructional Procedure

Step 1   Explain to students that the reason for taking the Posttest is to find out how well they have learned the unit's academic words or terms.

- One part of the Posttest (Units 2–4 only) will include academic words that were covered in previous units.
- Another part of the Posttest will require students to make a graphic organizer, which they will use to form a written response.
- Remind students that only Posttest scores will be recorded as part of their grade.

Step 2   Review the directions in the Posttest.

Step 3   Administer the Posttest.

Unit Generative Assessment *(optional)*

Teachers may choose to use each unit's optional Generative Assessment as the sole assessment measure for the unit (i.e., omit the unit Pretest and Posttest).

Objective	To ensure that students are able to correctly apply the unit academic words or writing terms within a general or personal context
Materials needed	For each student, one copy of the unit's Generative Assessment and two sheets of blank paper
Time allotment	One class period

Instructional Procedure

Step 1 Explain to students that the Generative Assessment is designed to find out how well they understand and are able to apply the unit academic words or writing terms to general knowledge or personal experiences. Students will create their own graphic organizers to prepare written responses, which should include the academic word in the direction.

Step 2 Review the directions in the Generative Assessment.

Step 3 Review the grading criteria (following).

Step 4 Administer the Generative Assessment.

Grading Criteria

To grade a Generative Assessment, we suggest allocating a maximum of 15 points *per assessment item* as follows:

- Up to 5 points for use of a graphic organizer
- Up to 5 points for conventions (correct paragraphing; use of topic, transitional, and conclusion sentences; correct punctuation; correct spelling)
- Up to 5 points for content

chapter 3

Program Introduction to Students

Introduce *Words for Academic Writing* by telling students that they are beginning a program designed to increase their academic word vocabulary (i.e., words and writing terms that are used in school, textbooks, tests, class discussions, and many assignments). Explain that this program will help them to become better writers and improve the quality of all their written school assignments. Say:

- "You are beginning a program that is designed to help you increase your academic word vocabulary. Academic words and writing terms are those that are used in school. These words and terms are commonly found on tests, in textbooks, during class discussions, and in many class assignments. Learning academic vocabulary can help you be more successful in school because academic words are used in all kinds of classes."

- "You will take a Pretest at the beginning of each unit and a Posttest at the end of each unit. The Pretest will be used to determine your prior knowledge of the academic words or writing terms. The Posttest will measure how well you have learned the words or writing terms after we have completed each unit. Only the Posttest scores will be recorded as part of your grade."

Notes:

1. *If you choose to administer the optional Generative Assessment after the unit Posttest, explain to students that this assessment will require them to demonstrate their understanding of the academic words or writing terms by using them appropriately in short written responses.*

2. *You may choose to use each unit's optional Generative Assessment as the sole assessment measure for the unit (i.e., omit the unit Pretest and Posttest).*

Unit 1 Pretest

Objective	To determine students' prior knowledge of academic words that will be taught in Unit 1
Materials needed	For each student, one copy of the Unit 1 Pretest (refer to the accompanying CD-ROM)
Time allotment	20 minutes (Part A, 10 minutes; Part B, 10 minutes)

Instructional Procedure

Step 1   Distribute Unit 1 Pretest to students. Say:
- "Write your name and today's date on the lines at the top of the Pretest."

Step 2   Review the directions for Unit 1 Pretest, then administer the pretest. Say:
- "Look at Part A. Let's read the directions together."
  (Read the directions out loud with students.)
- "Place your finger on each word as I read it: **contrast**, **compare**, **summarize**, **explain**, **analyze**, **discuss**."
- "Now, place your finger on each lowercase letter next to the explanations in the right-hand column. Listen as I read the explanation for each letter."
  - **a.** To give a reason for something; to make something easy to understand
  - **b.** To study something carefully
  - **c.** To tell or show how two or more people, ideas, or things are alike and not alike
  - **d.** To talk about something; to consider different points of view
  - **e.** To show or state the difference(s) between two people, ideas, or things
  - **f.** To write or say a short statement about main points of information
- "Match each word with the explanation that you think is correct. Write the letter of the explanation in the middle column, next to the word."
- "You will have 10 minutes to complete Part A. Ready? Begin."
  (After 10 minutes, proceed to Part B.)
- "Now, look at Part B. It is important to know how to use academic words within the context of print."
- "Read each of the six sentences. Then, refer back to the table in Part A. Use the words in the first column to fill in the blanks of the sentences."
- "You will have 10 minutes to complete Part B. Any questions? Begin."
- After 10 minutes, say, "Please return your tests to me."

> Refer to *Appendix D* for Unit 1 Pretest Answer Key

contrast

Students will:

1. Correctly pronounce the word **contrast**.
2. Define the word **contrast** in an academic context.
3. Identify examples and non-examples of the word **contrast**.
4. Use the word **contrast** and its word forms in an academic context as evidenced by completion of a cloze exercise.
5. Write a paragraph that appropriately **contrasts** two items.

A Introduction and Pronunciation
(*Student Book* page 1)

- Tell students the word: "This word is **contrast**."
- Say the word in parts.
- Ask students to repeat the word in parts and then the whole word.

B Explanation
(*Student Book* page 1)

- Say: "**Contrast** means *to show the difference(s) between two people, ideas, or things.*"
- Ask the class to repeat the explanation.
- Direct Partner 1s to say the explanation to Partner 2s.
- Direct Partner 2s to tell Partner 1s if their explanation was correct.

Unit 1 Lesson 1 contrast

A. **Introduction and Pronunciation**
- This word is **contrast**.
- Say the word in parts and then the whole word.

B. **Explanation**
- **Contrast** means to show the difference(s) between two people, ideas, or things.

C. **Example Sentences**
1. The literature selection **contrasts** good characters with evil ones.
2. In **contrast** to addition and multiplication, subtraction and division are operations in which a number is reduced.

D. **Checking for Understanding**
1. The politician told the audience how his position on raising taxes was different from that of his opponent.
   Question: Did the politician **contrast** his position with another point of view? Yes or No? Why or why not?

2. The weather in Palm Springs, California, has much in common with the weather in Phoenix, Arizona.
   Question: Can we **contrast** the weather in Palm Springs with the weather in Phoenix? Yes or No? Why or why not?

3. Describe the **contrast** between a healthy person and an ill person.

C Example Sentences
(*Student Book* page 1)

> ◆ Students chorally read example sentences with the teacher.
> ◆ Student partners answer scripted questions with provided sentence stems.

- Ask the class to chorally read the first sentence with you:
  1. The literature selection **contrasts** good characters with evil ones.
- Ask: "When we tell how good characters are different from evil characters, what are we doing?"
- Direct students to use the word **contrasting** in their answer with this sentence stem:
  We are **contrasting** _____ [good and evil characters].
- Have students answer to their partners.
- Ask the class to chorally read the second sentence with you:
  2. In **contrast** to addition and multiplication, subtraction and division are operations in which a number is reduced.

- Ask: "When we tell how addition and multiplication are different from subtraction and division, what are we doing?"
- Direct students to use the word **contrasting** in their answer with this sentence stem:

    We are **contrasting** _____ [addition and multiplication with subtraction and division].

- Have students answer to their partners.

D Checking for Understanding
(*Student Book* pages 1 and 2)

> ◆ Students chorally read example sentences with the teacher.
> ◆ Student partners answer scripted "Yes or No" questions with oral or written responses.

- Tell students that it is important to understand the meaning of an academic word when it is used in different forms.
- Explain to students that they will think, say, or write a response to sentences and explain the responses to their partners (e.g., say, "Partner 2s, read and respond to the first sentence. Partner 1s, tell your partner if you agree or disagree").
- Ask the class to chorally read the first sentence with you:
    1. The politician told the audience how his position on raising taxes was different from that of his opponent.
- Ask: "Did the politician **contrast** his position with another point of view?" (Answer: Yes)
- Direct students to respond to their partners by saying "yes" or "no" and explaining the reasons for their response.

    Note: While students are responding, monitor their exchanges. Ask two or three students to share their responses with the class.

- Ask the class to chorally read the second sentence with you:
    2. The weather in Palm Springs, California, has much in common with the weather in Phoenix, Arizona.
- Ask: "Can we **contrast** the weather in Palm Springs with the weather in Phoenix?" (Answer: No)
- Direct students to respond to partners by saying "yes" or "no" and explaining the reasons for their response.

    Note: While students are responding, monitor their exchanges. Ask two or three students to share their responses with the class.

- Ask the class to chorally read the third sentence with you:
    3. Describe the **contrast** between a healthy person and an ill person.
- Direct partners to think, write, and share their answers with the class. (A suggested sentence stem: A healthy person is _____ while in **contrast** an ill person is _____.)
- Ask the class to chorally read the fourth sentence with you:
    4. Describe a situation you have been in when doing what you were supposed to do **contrasted** with what you wanted to do.

- Direct partners to think, write, and share their answers with the class. (A suggested sentence stem: When I wanted _____, it **contrasted** with _____.)

E Vocabulary Words Table
(*Student Book* page 2)

> ◆ Students add the academic word, an explanation of the word, and a usage example to the unit Vocabulary Words Table.

- Direct students to the *Unit 1 Vocabulary Words Table* on page 25 in the *Student Book*.
- Tell students to copy the explanation of the word **contrast** from this lesson or to write their own explanation of **contrast** in the second column.
- Then, direct students to write their own sentence, write another explanation, or draw a picture to represent the word **contrast** in the last column.

Sample Answers

Word	Explanation	Sentence/Explanation/Picture
contrast	To show or state the difference(s) between two people, ideas, or things	In **contrast** to a soft pillow, a rock is quite hard.

F Word Forms Table
(*Student Book* page 2)

> ◆ Students add forms of the academic word to the unit Word Forms Table.

- Tell students that once a word is known, it is easy to learn other forms of the word. Adding a prefix or a suffix to a word makes a new but related word. Word forms have similar spellings, pronunciations, and meanings. They are often different parts of speech.
- Say: "It is important to understand the parts of speech: *nouns, verbs, adjectives,* and *adverbs*. We all know that a noun is a word that represents a person, place, thing, or idea. In school assignments, *nouns* are words that tell you <u>what you are asked to make</u> for an assignment or a test. A verb is a word that represents an action, an experience, or a state. In school assignments and tests, *verbs* are words that tell you <u>what you are to do</u> for the assignment. An adjective is a word that describes a noun or a pronoun. In school assignments, *adjectives* usually <u>give other information</u> about the assignment. An adverb is a word that adds meaning to a verb, an adjective, another adverb, or a sentence. In school assignments, *adverbs* tell you <u>how you should do</u> the assignment."

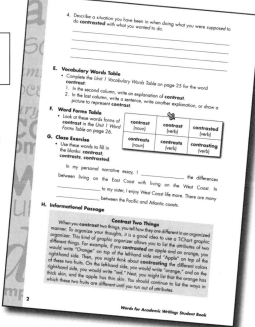

- Direct students to look at the word forms for **contrast** in the *Unit 1 Word Forms Table* on page 26 in the *Student Book*: **contrast** (n), **contrasts** (n), **contrast** (v), **contrasts** (v), **contrasted** (v), **contrasting** (v).
- Instruct students to analyze the format because they will be expected to complete the chart with the remaining words in this unit.

Answer Key

NOUNS What you make or create	VERBS What you have to do for the assignment	ADJECTIVES Specific details about what you must do	ADVERBS Important information about how to do the assignment
contrast	contrast		
contrasts	contrasts		
	contrasted		
	contrasting		

G Cloze Exercise
(*Student Book* page 2)

> ◆ Students use word forms to complete a cloze exercise.

- Direct students to use the words **contrast**, **contrasts**, and **contrasted** to complete the cloze exercise with their partners. Provide sufficient time for them to do so.
- Then, ask students to follow along as you read to determine if their answers to the cloze exercise are correct:

> In my personal narrative essay, I **contrasted** the differences between living on the East Coast with living on the West Coast. In **contrast** to my sister, I enjoy West Coast life more. There are many **contrasts** between the Pacific and Atlantic coasts.

H Informational Passage
(*Student Book* pages 2 and 3)

> ◆ Students chorally read the informational passage with the teacher.
> ◆ Students then read the passage with their partners.

- Say: "This informational passage is designed to provide you with strategies for using the word **contrast** in writing assignments."
- Ask students to read this passage chorally with you and then with their partners.

Note: You may want to make copies of the T-Chart graphic organizer (Graph A-3 on the accompanying CD-ROM) for students to refer to.

Contrast Two Things

When you **contrast** two things, you tell how they are different in an organized manner. To organize your thoughts, it is a good idea to use a T-Chart graphic organizer. This kind of graphic organizer allows you to list the attributes of two different things. For example, if you **contrasted** an apple and an orange, you would write "Orange" on top of the left-hand side and "Apple" on top of the right-hand side. Then, you might think about **contrasting** the different colors of these two fruits. On the left-hand side, you would write "orange," and on the right-hand side, you would write "red." Next, you might list that the orange has thick skin, and the apple list that the orange has thick skin, and the apple has thin skin. You should continue to list the ways in which these two fruits are different until you run out of attributes.

After you complete your T-Chart organizer, you need to place the attributes in logical categories. For example, if you **contrasted** the apple and the orange, you might use three categories to describe the fruits: the skin (color and texture), the center (crisp vs. juicy), and the taste (mild vs. tangy). When you place information into categories, you are ready to write.

First, you need to begin with an introduction that tells the reader what you are going to **contrast**. Next, using your T-Chart organizer as a guide, write about the differences between the two things. Finally, you need to remind the reader what you **contrasted** by restating the introduction with different words.

---

❶ Framed Paragraph and Sentence Stems
(*Student Book* page 3)

(Optional, to be used in conjunction with items J and K, following.)

Note: This section may be used to support struggling students. A framed paragraph is a tool to assist students in writing a paragraph. The paragraph frame provides a sample topic sentence, transitional sentence stems, and a conclusion sentence.

- Tell students that a framed paragraph is a tool to assist them in writing a paragraph.
- Read the topic sentence and the first transitional sentence stem with students.
- Stop reading after the first transitional sentence stem and assist students in completing the sentence in the context of the framed paragraph.

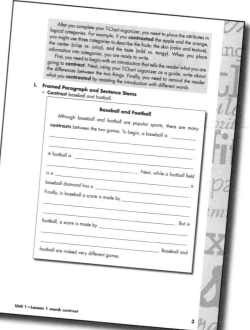

- Continue reading each sentence stem, stopping after each one to assist students in completing the stems.
- Once the paragraph frame is completed, direct students to read the entire paragraph to their partners.

Baseball and Football

Although baseball and football are popular sports, there are many **contrasts** between the two games. To begin, a baseball is <u>white, hard, and round</u>. A football is <u>usually brown and pointed at both ends</u>. Next, while a football field is a <u>large rectangle about 120 yards long</u>, a baseball diamond has a <u>square infield</u>. Finally, in baseball a score is made by <u>a player who touches each base safely and returns to home base without being tagged out</u>. But in football, a score is made by <u>a player who carries the ball or kicks the ball across the opponent's goal line</u>. Baseball and football are indeed very different games.

Topic sentence:	Although baseball and football are popular sports, there are many **contrasts** between the two games.
First transitional sentence stem:	To begin, a baseball is _____.
Second transitional sentence stem:	A football is _____.
Third transitional sentence stem:	Next, while a football field is a _____, a baseball diamond has a _____.
Fourth transitional sentence stem:	Finally, in baseball a score is made by _____.
Fifth transitional sentence stem:	But in football, a score is made by _____.
Conclusion sentence:	Baseball and football are indeed very different games.

J Paragraph Starters

(*Student Book* page 4)

- To reinforce understanding of the word **contrast**, we suggest three related paragraph topics and topic sentences. You can assign these activities as independent practice, partner practice, or homework.

  1. **Paragraph topic: Contrast** hiking and biking.
     Topic sentence: Although hiking and biking are both favorite outdoor pastimes, they are different from one another in many ways.
     - Ask students to think about their hiking and biking trips.

2. **Paragraph topic: Contrast** cake and ice cream.

   Topic sentence: Cake and ice cream are both great desserts; however, there are many differences between the two.

   - Ask students to think about the major differences between ice cream and cake.

3. **Paragraph topic: Contrast** Canada and Mexico.

   Topic sentence: Three important differences exist between these two countries that border the United States.

   - Ask students to write about three differences (e.g., location, weather, language) between Mexico and Canada.

Ⓚ Paragraph Topics

(*Student Book* page 4)

- We suggest additional writing topics of general knowledge that appeal to a diverse student population. Assign these topics for additional practice in applying the academic word **contrast** to students' writing.

  ❏ milk / water

  ❏ computers / typewriters

  ❏ trains / airplanes

  ❏ evergreen trees / leaf-bearing trees

  ❏ French fries / onion rings

  ❏ plants / animals

  ❏ hamburgers / tacos

  ❏ rock music / rap music

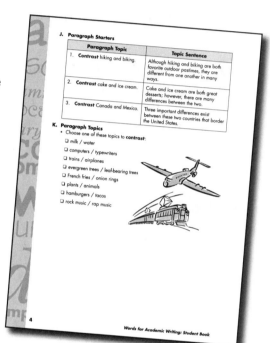

compare

OBJECTIVES

Students will:

1. Correctly pronounce the word **compare**.
2. Define the word **compare** in an academic context.
3. Identify examples and non-examples of the word **compare**.
4. Use the word **compare** and its word forms in an academic context as evidenced by completion of a cloze exercise.
5. Write a paragraph that appropriately **compares** two or more items.

A Introduction and Pronunciation
(*Student Book* page 5)

- Tell students the word: "This word is **compare**."
- Say the word in parts.
- Ask students to repeat the word in parts and then the whole word.

B Explanation
(*Student Book* page 5)

- Say: "**Compare** means *to tell or show how two or more people, ideas, or things are alike and not alike.*"
- Ask the class to repeat the explanation.
- Direct Partner 1s to give the explanation to Partner 2s.
- Direct Partner 2s to tell Partner 1s if their explanation was correct.

C Example Sentences
(*Student Book* page 5)

◆ Students chorally read example sentences with the teacher.
◆ Student partners answer scripted questions with provided sentence stems.

- Ask the class to chorally read the first sentence with you:
  1. We can **compare** dinosaurs to animals that live today in order to learn more about prehistoric animals.
- Ask: "When we tell how dinosaurs are the same and different from animals of today, what are we doing?"
- Direct students to use the word **comparing** in their answer with this sentence stem:

  We are **comparing** _____ [dinosaurs to animals of today].

- Have students answer to their partners.

- Ask the class to chorally read the second sentence with you:
  2. The results of the French exploration of North America can be **compared** to that of the English and Spanish explorations.
- Ask: "When we tell how the French, English, and Spanish explorations were the same and different, what are we doing?"
- Direct students to use the word **comparing** in their answer with this sentence stem:

  We are **comparing** _____ [explorations of the French, English and Spanish].
- Have students answer to their partners.

D Checking for Understanding
(*Student Book* pages 5 and 6)

> ◆ Students chorally read example sentences with the teacher.
> ◆ Student partners answer scripted "Yes or No" questions with oral or written responses.

- Tell students that it is important to understand the meaning of an academic word when it is used in different forms.
- Explain to students that they will think, say, or write a response to sentences and explain the responses to their partners (e.g., say, "Partner 2s, read and respond to the first sentence. Partner 1s, tell your partner if you agree or disagree").
- Ask the class to chorally read the first sentence with you:
  1. The article described what four Native American tribes had in common.
- Ask: "Did the article **compare** four Native American tribes?" (Answer: Yes)
- Direct students to respond to their partners by saying "yes" or "no" and explaining the reasons for their response.

Note: While students are responding, monitor their exchanges. Ask two or three students to share their responses with the class.

- Ask the class to chorally read the second sentence with you:
  2. The college counselor advised students that they could attend a community college and then transfer to a four-year college.
- Ask: "Did the counselor **compare** the two types of colleges?" (Answer: No)
- Direct students to respond to their partners by saying "yes" or "no" and explaining the reasons for their response.

Note: While students are responding, monitor their exchanges. Ask two or three students to share their responses with the class.

- Ask the class to chorally read the third sentence with you:
  3. How does a book **compare** to a movie?
- Direct partners to think, write, and share their answers with the class. (A suggested sentence stem: A book and a movie can be **compared** because they both _____. However, they are also different because _____.)
- Ask the class to chorally read the fourth sentence with you:
  4. Tell about a time when you **compared** the qualities of good friends.

- Direct partners to think, write, and share their answers with the class. (A suggested sentence stem: When I **compare** my friends _____, _____, and _____, they have many of the same qualities such as _____. However, they also have different qualities such as _____.)

E Vocabulary Words Table
(*Student Book* page 6)

> ◆ Students add the academic word, an explanation of the word, and a usage example to the unit Vocabulary Words Table.

- Direct students to the *Unit 1 Vocabulary Words Table* on page 25 in the *Student Book*.
- Tell students to copy the explanation of the word **compare** from this lesson or to write their own explanation of **compare** in the second column.
- Then, direct students to write their own sentence, write another explanation, or draw a picture to represent the word **compare** in the last column.

Sample Answers

Word	Explanation	Sentence/Explanation/Picture
compare	To tell or show how two or more people, ideas, or things are alike and not alike	We can **compare** a book to a movie.

F Word Forms Table
(*Student Book* page 6)

> ◆ Students add forms of the academic word to the unit Word Forms Table.

- Tell students that once a word is known, it is easy to learn other forms of the word. Adding a prefix or a suffix to a word makes a new but related word. Word forms have similar spellings, pronunciations, and meanings. They are often different parts of speech.
- Say: "It is important to understand the parts of speech: *nouns*, *verbs*, *adjectives*, and *adverbs*. We all know that a noun is a word that represents a person, place, thing, or idea. In school assignments, *nouns* are words that tell you <u>what you are asked to make</u> for an assignment or a test. A verb is a word that represents an action, an experience, or a state. In school assignments and tests, *verbs* are words that tell you <u>what you are to do</u> for the assignment. An adjective is a word that describes a noun or a pronoun. In school assignments, *adjectives* usually <u>give other information</u> about the assignment. An adverb

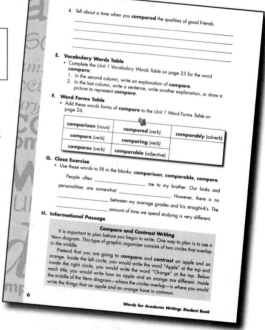

is a word that adds meaning to a verb, an adjective, another adverb, or a sentence. In school assignments, *adverbs* tell you <u>how you should do</u> the assignment."

- Direct students to the *Unit 1 Word Forms Table* on page 26 in the *Student Book*.
- Instruct students to add these word forms of **compare** to the table: **comparison** (n), **compare** (v), **compares** (v), **compared** (v), **comparing** (v), **comparable** (adj), **comparably** (adv).

Answer Key

NOUNS What you make or create	VERBS What you have to do for the assignment	ADJECTIVES Specific details about what you must do	ADVERBS Important information about how to do the assignment
comparison	**compare**	**comparable**	**comparably**
	compares		
	compared		
	comparing		

G Cloze Exercise
(*Student Book* page 6)

> ◆ Students use word forms to complete a cloze exercise.

- Direct students to use the words **comparison**, **comparable**, and **compare** to complete this cloze exercise with their partners. Provide sufficient time for them to do so.
- Then, ask students to follow along as you read to determine if their answers to the cloze exercise are correct.

> People often **compare** me to my brother. Our looks and personalities are somewhat **comparable**. However, there is no **comparison** between my average grades and his straight-A's. The **comparable** amount of time we spend studying is very different.

H Informational Passage
(*Student Book* pages 6 and 7)

> ◆ Students chorally read the informational passage with the teacher.
> ◆ Students then read the passage with their partners.

- Say: "This informational passage is designed to provide you with strategies for using the word **compare** in writing assignments."
- Ask students to read this passage chorally with you and then with their partners.

Note: You may want to make copies of the Venn diagram graphic organizer (Graph A-2 on the accompanying CD-ROM) for students to refer to.

Compare and Contrast Writing

It is important to plan before you begin to write. One way to plan is to use a Venn diagram. This type of graphic organizer consists of two circles that overlap in the middle.

Pretend that you are going to **compare** and **contrast** an apple and an orange. Inside the left circle, you would write the word "Apple" at the top and inside the right circle, you would write the word "Orange" at the top. Below each title, you would write how an apple and an orange are different. Inside the middle of the Venn diagram—where the circles overlap—is where you would write the things that an apple and an orange have in common.

When you **compare** and **contrast**, you need to write several paragraphs. The first paragraph should be the introduction, where you let the reader know **what** you are going to **compare** and **contrast**. In a **comparison** paragraph, you will tell **how the two things are the same**. You will need to use words such as *similar*, *alike*, *still*, and *likewise*, and phrases such as *in the same manner* and *at the same time*. In a **contrasting** paragraph, you will tell **how the two things are different**. Some signal words to use when you make a **contrast** are *however*, *although*, *nevertheless*, *but*, and *yet*, and signal phrases such as *on the other hand*, *on the contrary*, and *in contrast*. Make sure that the similarities and differences are very clear in each paragraph. Finally, you will write a concluding paragraph, in which you restate and review how the two things **compare** and **contrast**. (The concluding paragraph is a summary of your main points.)

❶ Framed Paragraph and Sentence Stems

(Student Book page 7)

(Optional, to be used in conjunction with items J and K, following.)

Note: This section may be used to support struggling students. A framed paragraph is a tool to assist students in writing a paragraph. The paragraph frame provides a sample topic sentence, transitional sentence stems, and a conclusion sentence.

- Tell students that a framed paragraph is a tool to assist them in writing a paragraph.
- Read the topic sentence and the first transitional sentence stem with students.
- Stop reading after the first transitional sentence stem and assist students in completing the stem and adding additional informational sentences within the context of the framed paragraph.

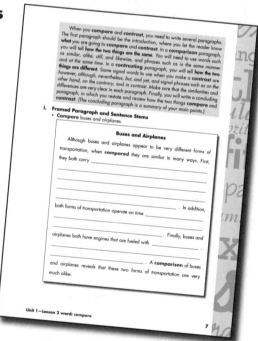

- Continue reading each sentence stem, stopping after each one to assist students in completing the stem and adding additional informational sentences.
- Once the paragraph frame is completed, direct students to read the entire paragraph to their partners.

Sample Completed Framed Paragraph

Buses and Airplanes

Although buses and airplanes appear to be very different forms of transportation, when **compared** they are similar in many ways. First, they both carry <u>passengers and luggage</u>. <u>Many people can sit in rows of seats.</u> <u>Luggage and other items are usually stored in a special compartment inside.</u> In addition, both forms of transportation operate on time <u>schedules</u>. <u>The schedules are posted at bus stations and airports. People use the schedules to find out when buses or airplanes will depart and when they will arrive at destinations.</u> Finally, buses and airplanes both have engines that are fueled with <u>gas</u>. <u>Their gas tanks are refueled before they begin a new trip.</u> A **comparison** of buses and airplanes reveals that these two forms of transportation are very much alike.

Topic sentence:	Although buses and airplanes appear to be very different forms of transportation, when **compared** they are similar in many ways.
First transitional sentence stem:	First, they both carry _____. *Examples of sentence expansion:* Many people can sit in rows of seats. Luggage and other items are usually stored in a special compartment inside.
Second transitional sentence stem:	In addition, both forms of transportation operate on time _____. *Examples of sentence expansion:* The schedules are posted at bus stations and airports. People use the schedules to find out when buses or airplanes will depart and when they will arrive at destinations.
Third transitional sentence stem:	Finally, buses and airplanes both have engines that are fueled with _____ . *Example of sentence expansion:* Their gas tanks are refueled before they begin a new trip.
Conclusion sentence:	A **comparison** of buses and airplanes reveals that these two forms of transportation are very much alike.

J Paragraph Starters

(*Student Book* page 8)

- To reinforce understanding of the word **compare**, we suggest three related paragraph topics and topic sentences. You can assign these activities as independent practice, partner practice, or homework.

  1. **Paragraph topic: Compare** wood and metal.

     Topic sentence: Even though wood and metal are different building materials, they are often used to obtain the same results.

     - Ask students to think about structures and products that are made of wood and metal.

  2. **Paragraph topic: Compare** pizza, hamburgers, and tacos.

     Topic sentence: Fast foods like pizza, hamburgers, and tacos seem to be favorites among people of all ages.

     - Ask students to think about the ingredients, tastes, and common methods of eating these foods.

  3. **Paragraph topic: Compare** dogs, cats, parrots, and tropical fish.

     Topic sentence: Dogs, cats, parrots, or tropical fish all make good pets.

     - Ask students to think about the many reasons that people like to have dogs, cats, parrots, or goldfish as pets.

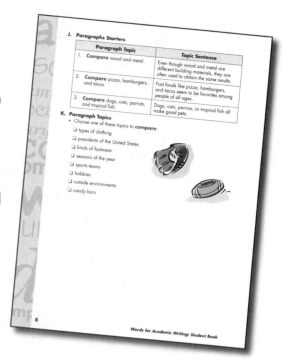

K Paragraph Topics

(*Student Book* page 8)

- We suggest additional writing topics of general knowledge that appeal to a diverse student population. Assign these topics for additional practice in applying the academic word **compare** to students' writing.

  ❏ types of clothing

  ❏ presidents of the United States

  ❏ kinds of footwear

  ❏ seasons of the year

  ❏ sports teams

  ❏ hobbies

  ❏ outside environments

  ❏ candy bars

OBJECTIVES

Students will:

1. Correctly pronounce the word **summarize**.
2. Define the word **summarize** in an academic context.
3. Identify examples and non-examples of the word **summarize**.
4. Use the word **summarize** and its word forms in an academic context as evidenced by completion of a cloze exercise.
5. Write a paragraph that appropriately **summarizes** a written piece or an event.

A Introduction and Pronunciation
(*Student Book* page 9)

- Tell students the word: "This word is **summarize**."
- Say the word in parts.
- Ask students to repeat the word in parts and then the whole word.

B Explanation
(*Student Book* page 9)

- Say: "**Summarize** means *to write or say a short statement about main points of information.*"
- Ask the class to repeat the explanation.
- Direct Partner 1s to say the explanation to Partner 2s.
- Direct Partner 2s to tell Partner 1s if the response was correct.

Unit 1 Lesson 3 **summarize**

A. Introduction and Pronunciation
- This word is **summarize**.
- Say the word in parts and then the whole word.

B. Explanation
- **Summarize** means to write or say a short statement about main points of information.

C. Example Sentences
1. At the end of each chapter in the history book, a **summary** paragraph includes the main points in the chapter.
2. Articulate speakers **summarize** the ideas they wish to convey to their audience.

D. Checking for Understanding
1. After watching the movie, Julie called her best friend to tell her every detail of the movie's plot.
   Question: Did Julie give a **summary** of the movie? Yes or No? Why or why not?

2. The day before the test, the teacher reviewed the main points of the chapter.
   Question: Did the teacher **summarize** the chapter? Yes or No? Why or why not?

3. What source could you use to find a **summary** of a novel you are interested in reading?

9

C Example Sentences
(*Student Book* page 9)

> ◆ Students chorally read example sentences with the teacher.
> ◆ Student partners answer scripted questions with provided sentence stems.

- Ask the class to chorally read the first sentence with you:
  1. At the end of each chapter in the history book, a **summary** paragraph includes the main points in the chapter.
- Ask: "What kind of a short paragraph retells the main points of the chapters?"
- Direct students to use the word **summary** in their answer with this sentence stem:
  A **summary** paragraph _____ [retells the main points of the chapters].

- Have students answer to their partners.
- Ask the class to chorally read the second sentence with you:
  2. Articulate speakers **summarize** the ideas they wish to convey to their audience.
- Ask: "When speakers make their main ideas short and to the point, what are they doing for their audience?"
- Direct students to use the word **summarizing** in their answer with this sentence stem:

  Speakers are **summarizing** _____ [their main ideas].
- Have students answer to their partners.

D Checking for Understanding
(*Student Book* pages 9 and 10)

> ◆ Students chorally read example sentences with the teacher.
> ◆ Student partners answer scripted "Yes or No" questions with oral or written responses.

- Tell students that it is important to understand the meaning of an academic word when it is used in different forms.
- Explain to students that they will think, say, or write a response to sentences and explain the responses to their partners (e.g., say, "Partner 2s, read and respond to the first sentence. Partner 1s, tell your partner if you agree or disagree").
- Ask the class to chorally read the first sentence with you:
  1. After watching the movie, Julie called her best friend to tell her every detail of the movie's plot.
- Ask: "Did Julie give a **summary** of the movie?" (Answer: No)
- Direct students to respond to their partners by saying "yes" or "no" and explaining the reasons for their response.

  Note: While students are responding, monitor their exchanges. Ask two or three students to share their responses with the class.
- Ask the class to chorally read the second sentence with you:
  2. The day before the test, the teacher reviewed the main points of the chapter.
- Ask: "Did the teacher **summarize** the chapter?" (Answer: Yes)
- Direct students to respond to their partners by saying "yes" or "no" and explaining the reasons for their answer.

  Note: While students are responding, monitor their exchanges. Ask two or three students to share their responses with the class.
- Ask the class to chorally read the third sentence with you:
  3. What source could you use to find a **summary** of a novel you are interested in reading?
- Direct partners to think, write, and share their answers with the class. (A suggested sentence stem: If I wanted to find a **summary** of a novel, I might look _____.)
- Ask the class to chorally read the fourth sentence with you:
  4. **Summarize** the events of your last birthday celebration.

- Direct partners to think, write, and share their answers with the class. (A suggested sentence stem: In **summary**, I celebrated my last birthday by _____.)

E Vocabulary Words Table
(*Student Book* page 10)

> ◆ Students add the academic word, an explanation of the word, and a usage example to the unit Vocabulary Words Table.

- Direct students to the *Unit 1 Vocabulary Words Table* on page 25 in the *Student Book*.
- Tell students to copy the explanation of the word **summarize** from this lesson or to write their own explanation of **summarize** in the second column.
- Then, direct students to write their own sentence, write another explanation, or draw a picture to represent the word **summarize** in the last column.

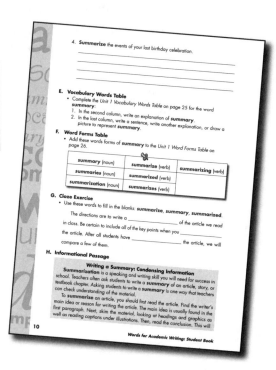

Sample Answers

Word	Explanation	Sentence/Explanation/Picture
summarize	To write or say a short statement about main points of information	The last paragraph **summarized** the content of the chapter.

F Word Forms Table
(*Student Book* page 10)

> ◆ Students add forms of the academic word to the unit Word Forms Table.

- Tell students that once a word is known, it is easy to learn other forms of the word. Adding a prefix or a suffix to a word makes a new but related word. Word forms have similar spellings, pronunciations, and meanings. They are often different parts of speech.
- Say: "It is important to understand the parts of speech: *nouns, verbs, adjectives,* and *adverbs.* We all know that a noun is a word that represents a person, place, thing, or idea. In school assignments, nouns are words that tell you what you are asked to make for an assignment or a test. A verb is a word that represents an action, an experience, or a state. In school assignments and tests, *verbs* are words that tell you what you are to do for the assignment. An adjective is a word that describes a noun or a pronoun. In school assignments, *adjectives* usually give other information about the assignment. An adverb is a word that adds meaning to a verb, an adjective, another adverb, or

a sentence. In school assignments, *adverbs* tell you <u>how you should do</u> the assignment."

- Direct students to the *Unit 1 Word Forms Table* on page 26 in the *Student Book*.
- Instruct students to add these word forms of **summarize** to the table: **summary** (n), **summaries** (n), **summarization** (n), **summarize** (v), **summarized** (v), **summarizes** (v), **summarizing** (v).

Answer Key

NOUNS What you make or create	VERBS What you have to do for the assignment	ADJECTIVES Specific details about what you must do	ADVERBS Important information about how to do the assignment
summary	summarize		
summaries	summarized		
summarization	summarizes		
	summarizing		

G Cloze Exercise
(*Student Book* page 10)

> ◆ Students use word forms to complete a cloze exercise.

- Direct students to use the words **summarize**, **summary**, and **summarized** to complete this cloze exercise with their partners. Provide sufficient time for them to do so.
- Then, ask students to follow along as you read to determine if their answers to the cloze exercise are correct.

> The directions are to write a **summary** of the article we read in class. Be certain to include all of the key points when you **summarize** the article. After all students have **summarized** the article, we will compare a few of them.

H Informational Passage
(*Student Book* pages 10 and 11)

> ◆ Students chorally read the informational passage with the teacher.
> ◆ Students then read the passage with their partners.

- Say: "This informational passage is designed to provide you with strategies for using different forms of the word **summarize** in writing assignments."
- Ask students to read the passage chorally with you and then with their partners.

Note: You may want to make copies of the Web graphic organizer (Graph A-1 on the accompanying CD-ROM) for students to refer to.

Writing a Summary: Condensing Information

Summarization is a speaking and writing skill you will need for success in school. Teachers often ask students to write a **summary** of an article, story, or textbook chapter. Asking students to write a **summary** is one way that teachers can check understanding of the material.

To **summarize** an article, you should first read the article. Find the writer's main idea or reason for writing the article. The main idea is usually found in the first paragraph. Next, skim the material, looking at headings and graphics as well as reading captions under illustrations. Then, read the conclusion. This will give you an overview of the material. Ask yourself, "Why did the author write this piece?"

Next, go back and read the article very carefully. Use a Web graphic organizer to take notes on the main points. Leave out background information, descriptions, and explanations. Now, outline the main points by organizing them in a logical order.

Write your **summary** from your notes, not from the article. This will help to ensure that you are using your own words. To begin the **summary**, state the name of the author, the title of the article, and a general statement about the main idea of the article in the first sentence. The rest of the sentences in your **summary** should focus on how the author supports or defends the main idea. This can be done by using your outline to write a sentence about each main point you found in the article. If you must quote, use quotation marks around quote statement to show that these are not your own words. Never give your opinion in a **summary**. To complete your **summary**, write a conclusion restating the author's main idea.

❶ Framed Paragraph and Sentence Stems

(*Student Book* page 11)

(Optional, to be used in conjunction with items J and K, following.)

Note: This section may be used to support struggling students. A framed paragraph is a tool to assist students in writing a paragraph. The paragraph frame provides a sample topic sentence, transitional sentence stems, and a conclusion sentence.

- Tell students that this framed paragraph will be based on a fictional article about polar bears.
- Read the topic sentence and the first transitional sentence stem with students.

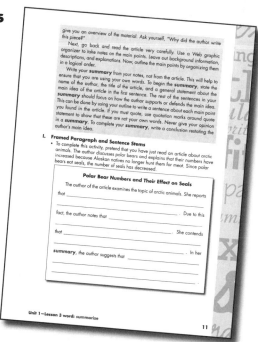

- Stop reading after the first transitional sentence stem and assist students in completing the stem and adding additional informational sentences within the context of the framed paragraph.
- Continue reading each sentence stem, stopping after each one to assist students in completing the stem and adding additional informational sentences.
- Once the paragraph frame is completed, direct students to read the entire paragraph to their partners.
- Say: "To complete this activity, pretend that you have just read an article about arctic animals. The author discusses polar bears and explains that their numbers have increased because Alaskan natives no longer hunt them for meat. Since polar bears eat seals, the number of seals has decreased."

Sample Completed Framed Paragraph

Polar Bear Numbers and Their Effect on Seals

The author of the article examines the topic of arctic animals. She reports that <u>Alaskan natives no longer hunt polar bears as a main source of meat</u>. Due to this fact, the author notes that <u>the polar bear population has increased</u>. She contends that <u>since there are greater numbers of polar bears eating seals, the number of seals has decreased</u>. In her **summary**, the author suggests that <u>if the trend continues, seals could be added to the endangered species list</u>.

Topic sentence:	The author of the article examines the topic of arctic animals.
First transitional sentence stem:	She reports that _____.
Second transitional sentence stem:	Due to this fact, the author notes that _____.
Third transitional sentence stem:	She contends that _____.
Conclusion sentence:	In her summary, the author suggests that _____.

J Paragraph Starters
(*Student Book* page 12)

- To reinforce understanding of the word **summarize**, we suggest three related paragraph topics and topic sentences. You can assign these activities as independent practice, partner practice, or homework.
    1. **Paragraph topic: Summarize** a television documentary.
       Topic sentence: The television documentary explored the topic of _____.
       - Ask students to write about the last television documentary they saw.

2. **Paragraph topic:** Write a **summary** about the last book you read.
   Topic sentence: The last book I read was ___(title of book)___ by ___(name of author)___. The author discusses _____.
   - Ask students to recall the main points of the last book they read.
3. **Paragraph topic: Summarize** the last chapter of your history book.
   Topic sentence: The last chapter in my history book focuses on _____.
   - Ask students to try to remember what the last chapter of their history book is about.

Ⓚ Paragraph Topics
(*Student Book* page 12)

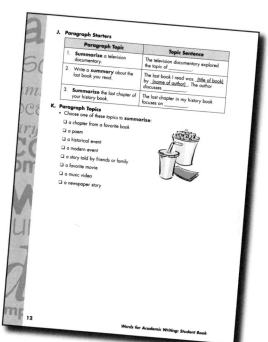

- We suggest additional writing topics of general knowledge that appeal to a diverse student population. Assign these topics for additional practice in applying the academic word **summarize** to students' writing.

  ❏ a chapter from a favorite book

  ❏ a poem

  ❏ a historical event

  ❏ a modern event

  ❏ a story told by friends or family

  ❏ a favorite movie

  ❏ a music video

  ❏ a newspaper story

explain

Students will:
1. Correctly pronounce the word **explain**.
2. Define the word **explain** in an academic context.
3. Identify examples and non-examples of the word **explain**.
4. Use the word **explain** and its word forms in an academic context as evidenced by completion of a cloze exercise.
5. Write a paragraph that appropriately **explains** an event, an action, or a situation.

A Introduction and Pronunciation
(*Student Book* page 13)
- Tell students the word: "This word is **explain**."
- Say the word in parts.
- Ask students to repeat the word in parts and then the whole word.

B Explanation
(*Student Book* page 13)
- Say: "**Explain** means *to give a reason for something; to make something easy to understand.*"
- Ask the class to repeat the explanation.
- Direct Partner 1s to give the explanation to Partner 2s.
- Direct Partner 2s to tell Partner 1s if their explanation was correct.

C Example Sentences
(*Student Book* page 13)

> ◆ Students chorally read example sentences with the teacher.
> ◆ Student partners answer scripted questions with provided sentence stems.

- Ask the class to chorally read the first sentence with you:
  1. Tomas was asked to **explain** the reason for his late arrival at school.
- Ask: "When Tomas gave the reason for his late arrival at school, what was he doing?"
- Direct students to use the word **explaining** in their answer with this sentence stem:
  Tomas was **explaining** _____ [the reason for his late arrival].
- Have students answer to their partners.

- Ask the class to chorally read the second sentence with you:
  2. Our science teacher was careful to **explain** the difference between evaporation and condensation.
- Ask: "When the teacher talked about the difference between evaporation and condensation, what did he do?"
- Direct students to use the word **explained** in their answer with this sentence stem:

  The teacher **explained** _____ [the difference].
- Have students answer to their partners.

D Checking for Understanding
(*Student Book* pages 13 and 14)

- ◆ Students chorally read example sentences with the teacher.
- ◆ Student partners answer scripted "Yes or No" questions with oral or written responses.

- Tell students that it is important to understand the meaning of an academic word when it is used in different forms.
- Explain to students that they will think, say, or write a response to sentences and explain the responses to their partners (e.g., say, "Partner 2s, read and respond to the first sentence. Partner 1s, tell your partner if you agree or disagree").
- Ask the class to chorally read the first sentence with you:
  1. The teacher clearly showed how to reduce fractions to their lowest common denominators.
- Ask: "Did the teacher **explain** how to reduce fractions?" (Answer: Yes)
- Direct students to respond to their partners by saying "yes" or "no" and explaining the reasons for their answer.

  Note: While students are responding, monitor their exchanges. Ask two or three students to share their responses with the class.
- Ask the class to chorally read the second sentence with you:
  2. After reading the many dictionary definitions for the word, Sarah was more confused than ever.
- Ask: "Did the dictionary give a clear **explanation** of the word?" (Answer: No)
- Direct students to respond to their partners by saying "yes" or "no" and explaining the reasons for their answer.

  Note: While students are responding, monitor their exchanges. Ask two or three students to share their responses with the class.
- Ask the class to chorally read the third sentence with you:
  3. **Explain** the easiest way to get to school from your home.
- Direct partners to think, write, and share their answers with the class. (A suggested sentence stem: To **explain** the easiest way _____ .)
- Ask the class to chorally read the fourth sentence with you:
  4. Tell about a time that you were able to **explain** your actions well enough to avoid being punished by your mom or dad.

- Direct partners to think, write, and share their answers with the class. (A suggested sentence stem: Although my (mom/dad) was mad, I **explained** that _____.)

E Vocabulary Words Table
(*Student Book* page 14)

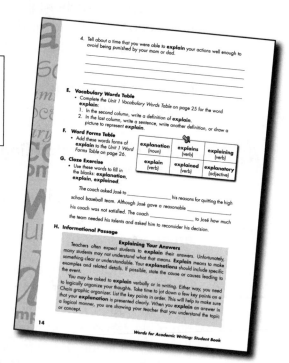

> ◆ Students add the academic word, an explanation of the word, and a usage example to the unit Vocabulary Words Table.

- Direct students to the *Unit 1 Vocabulary Words Table* on page 25 in the *Student Book*.
- Tell students to copy the definition of the word **explain** from this lesson or to write their own definition of **explain** in the second column.
- Then, direct students to write their own sentence, write another definition, or draw a picture to represent the word **explain** in the last column.

Sample Answers

Word	Explanation	Sentence/Explanation/Picture
explain	To give a reason for something; to make something easy to understand	He **explained** why he selected that answer.

F Word Forms Table
(*Student Book* page 14)

> ◆ Students add forms of the academic word to the unit Word Forms Table.

- Tell students that once a word is known, it is easy to learn other forms of the word. Adding a prefix or a suffix to a word makes a new but related word. Word forms have similar spellings, pronunciations, and meanings. They are often different parts of speech.
- Say: "It is important to understand the parts of speech: *nouns, verbs, adjectives,* and *adverbs*. We all know that a noun is a word that represents a person, place, thing, or idea. In school assignments, *nouns* are words that tell you <u>what you are asked to make</u> for an assignment or a test. A verb is a word that represents an action, an experience, or a state. In school assignments and tests, *verbs* are words that tell you <u>what you are to do</u> for the assignment. An adjective is a word that describes a noun or a pronoun. In school assignments, *adjectives* usually <u>give other information</u> about the assignment. An adverb is a word that adds meaning to a verb, an adjective, another adverb, or

a sentence. In school assignments, *adverbs* tell you <u>how you should do</u> the assignment."

- Direct students to the *Unit 1 Word Forms Table* on page 26 in the *Student Book*.
- Instruct students to add these word forms of **explain** to the table: **explanation** (n), **explain** (v), **explains** (v), **explained** (v), **explaining** (v), **explanatory** (adj).

Answer Key

NOUNS What you make or create	VERBS What you have to do for the assignment	ADJECTIVES Specific details about what you must do	ADVERBS Important information about how to do the assignment
explanation	explain	explanatory	
	explains		
	explained		
	explaining		

G Cloze Exercise
(*Student Book* page 14)

> ◆ Students use word forms to complete a cloze exercise.

- Direct students to use the words **explained**, **explain**, and **explanation** to complete this cloze exercise with their partners. Provide sufficient time for them to do so.
- Then, ask students to follow along as you read to determine if their answers to the cloze exercise are correct.

> The coach asked José to __**explain**__ his reasons for quitting the high school baseball team. Although José gave a reasonable __**explanation**__, his coach was not satisfied. The coach __**explained**__ to José how much the team needed his talents and asked him to reconsider his decision.

H Informational Passage
(*Student Book* page 14)

> ◆ Students chorally read the informational passage with the teacher.
> ◆ Students then read the passage with their partners.

- Say: "This informational passage is designed to provide you with strategies for using different forms of the word **explain** in writing assignments."
- Ask students to read the passage chorally with you and then with their partners.

Note: You may want to make copies of the Chain graphic organizer (Graph A-5 on the accompanying CD-ROM) for students to refer to.

Explaining Your Answers

Teachers often expect students to **explain** their answers. Unfortunately, many students may not understand what that means. **Explain** means to make something clear or understandable. Your **explanations** should include specific examples and related details. If possible, state the cause or causes leading to the event.

You may be asked to **explain** verbally or in writing. Either way, you need to logically organize your thoughts. Take time to jot down a few key points on a Chain graphic organizer. List the key points in order. This will help to make sure that your **explanation** is presented clearly. When you **explain** an answer in a logical manner, you are showing your teacher that you understand the topic or concept.

ⓘ Framed Paragraph and Sentence Stems

(*Student Book* page 15)

(Optional, to be used in conjunction with items J and K, following.)

Note: This section may be used to support struggling students. A framed paragraph is a tool to assist students in writing a paragraph. The paragraph frame provides a sample topic sentence, transitional sentence stems, and a conclusion sentence.

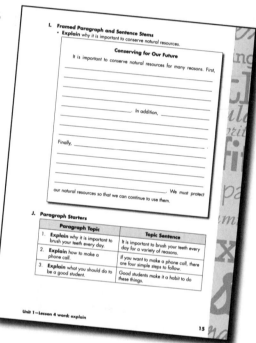

- Tell students that a framed paragraph is a tool to assist them in writing a paragraph.
- Read the topic sentence and the first transitional sentence stem with students.
- Stop reading after the first transitional sentence stem and assist students in completing the stem and adding additional informational sentences within the context of the framed paragraph.
- Continue reading each sentence stem, stopping after each one to assist students in completing the stem and adding additional informational sentences.
- Once the paragraph frame is completed, direct students to read the entire paragraph to their partners.

Sample Completed Framed Paragraph

Conserving for Our Future

It is important to conserve natural resources for many reasons. First, <u>many natural resources like oil and coal are not renewable</u>. In addition, <u>it is important to keep a natural habitat for many animals and plants to survive</u>. Finally, <u>some resources such as fresh water are used for crops, livestock, and as drinking water</u>. We must protect our natural resources so that we can continue to use them.

Topic sentence:	It is important to conserve natural resources for many reasons.
First transitional sentence stem:	First, _____.
Second transitional sentence stem:	In addition, _____.
Third transitional sentence stem:	Finally, _____.
Conclusion sentence:	We must protect our natural resources so that we can continue to use them.

J Paragraph Starters

(*Student Book* page 15)

- To reinforce understanding of the word **explain**, we suggest three related paragraph topics and topic sentences. You can assign these activities as independent practice, partner practice, or homework.

  1. **Paragraph topic: Explain** why it is important to brush your teeth every day.
  Topic sentence: It is important to brush your teeth every day for a variety of reasons.
     - Ask students to document what they know about dental health.

  2. **Paragraph topic: Explain** how to make a phone call.
  Topic sentence: If you want to make a phone call, there are four simple steps to follow.
     - Ask students to list the sequential steps in making a phone call.

  3. **Paragraph topic: Explain** what you should do to be a good student.
  Topic sentence: Good students make it a habit to do these things.
     - Ask students to think about what they have learned about study skills.

K Paragraph Topics

(*Student Book* page 16)

- We suggest additional writing topics of general knowledge that appeal to a diverse student population. Assign these topics for additional practice in applying the academic word **explain** to students' writing.

  ❑ how to use a software program

  ❑ how to study for a test

  ❑ why playground rules are necessary

  ❑ what to do if you smell smoke

  ❑ how to wash dishes

  ❑ how to make your favorite sandwich

  ❑ why it is important to wear seat belts

  ❑ how to buy a ticket for a concert

analyze

Unit 1 Lesson 5 **analyze**

A. Introduction and Pronunciation
• This word is **analyze**.
• Say the word in parts and then the whole word.

B. Explanation
• **Analyze** means to study something carefully.

C. Example Sentences
1. In our history class, students **analyzed** the three branches of government.
2. The doctor will **analyze** the patient's blood sample for signs of disease.

D. Checking for Understanding
1. Tran took a quick look at his notes.
   Question: Did Tran **analyze** his notes? Yes or No? Why or why not?

2. The botanist carefully studied the different parts of the plant.
   Question: Did the botanist **analyze** the plant? Yes or No? Why or why not?

3. How might someone **analyze** his or her own behavior?

17

OBJECTIVES

Students will:
1. Correctly pronounce the word **analyze**.
2. Define the word **analyze** in an academic context.
3. Identify examples and non-examples of the word **analyze**.
4. Use the word **analyze** and its word forms in an academic context as evidenced by completion of a cloze exercise.
5. Write a paragraph that appropriately **analyzes** an event or a situation.

A Introduction and Pronunciation
(*Student Book* page 17)

• Tell students the word: "This word is **analyze**."
• Say the word in parts.
• Ask students to repeat the word in parts and then the whole word.

B Explanation
(*Student Book* page 17)

• Say: "**Analyze** means *to study something carefully.*"
• Ask students to repeat the explanation.
• Direct Partner 1s to give the explanation to Partner 2s.
• Direct Partner 2s to tell Partner 1s if their explanation was correct.

C Example Sentences
(*Student Book* page 17)

> ◆ Students chorally read example sentences with the teacher.
> ◆ Student partners answer scripted questions with provided sentence stems.

• Ask the class to chorally read the first sentence with you:
  1. In our history class, students **analyzed** the three branches of government.
• Ask: "What did the students do?"
• Direct students to use the word **analyzed** in their answer with this sentence stem:
  The students **analyzed** _____ [the three branches of government].
• Have students answer to their partners.
• Ask the class to chorally read the second sentence with you:
  2. The doctor will **analyze** the patient's blood sample for signs of disease.
• Ask: "What will the doctor do with the patient's blood sample?"

- Direct students to use the word **analyze** in their answer with this sentence stem:

  The doctor will **analyze** the blood _____ [to check for signs of disease].
- Have students answer to their partners.

Ⓓ Checking for Understanding
(*Student Book pages 17 and 18*)

> ◆ Students chorally read example sentences with the teacher.
> ◆ Student partners answer scripted "Yes or No" questions with oral or written responses.

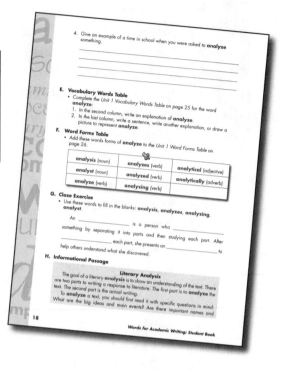

- Tell students that it is important to understand the meaning of an academic word when it is used in different forms.
- Explain to students that they will think, say, or write a response to sentences and explain the responses to their partners (e.g., say, "Partner 2s, read and respond to the first sentence. Partner 1s, tell your partner if you agree or disagree").
- Ask the class to chorally read the first sentence with you:

  1. Tran took a quick look at his notes.
- Ask: "Did Tran **analyze** his notes?" (Answer: No)
- Direct students to respond to their partners by saying "yes" or "no" and explaining the reasons for their answer.

  Note: While students are responding, monitor their exchanges. Ask two or three students to share their responses with the class.
- Ask the class to chorally read the second sentence with you:

  2. The botanist carefully studied the different parts of the plant.
- Ask: "Did the botanist **analyze** the plant?" (Answer: Yes)
- Direct students to respond to their partners by saying "yes" or "no" and explaining the reasons for their answer.

  Note: While students are responding, monitor their exchanges. Ask two or three students to share their responses with the class.
- Ask the class to chorally read the third sentence with you:

  3. How might someone **analyze** his or her own behavior?
- Direct partners to think, write, and share their answers with the class. (A suggested sentence stem: I might **analyze** my own behavior by _____.)
- Ask the class to chorally read the fourth sentence with you:

  4. Give an example of a time in school when you were asked to **analyze** something.

- Direct partners to think, write, and share their answers with the class. (A suggested sentence stem: I once was asked to **analyze** _____.)

E Vocabulary Words Table
(*Student Book* page 18)

◆ Students add the academic word, an explanation of the word, and a usage example to the unit Vocabulary Words Table.

- Direct students to the *Unit 1 Vocabulary Words Table* on page 25 in the *Student Book*.
- Tell students to copy the explanation of the word **analyze** from this lesson or to write their own explanation of **analyze** in the second column.
- Then, direct students to write their own sentence, write another explanation, or draw a picture to represent the word **analyze** in the last column.

Sample Answers

Word	Explanation	Sentence/Explanation/Picture
analyze	To study something carefully	The engineer **analyzed** the plans for the water treatment plant.

F Word Forms Table
(*Student Book* page 18)

◆ Students add forms of the academic word to the unit Word Forms Table.

- Tell students that once a word is known, it is easy to learn other forms of the word. Adding a prefix or a suffix to a word makes a new but related word. Word forms have similar spellings, pronunciations, and meanings. They are often different parts of speech.
- Say: "It is important to understand the parts of speech: *nouns, verbs, adjectives,* and *adverbs.* We all know that a noun is a word that represents a person, place, thing, or idea. In school assignments, *nouns* are words that tell you <u>what you are asked to make</u> for an assignment or a test. A verb is a word that represents an action, an experience, or a state. In school assignments and tests, *verbs* are words that tell you <u>what you are to do</u> for the assignment. An adjective is a word that describes a noun or a pronoun. In school assignments, *adjectives* usually <u>give other information</u> about the assignment. An adverb is a word that adds meaning to a verb, an adjective, another adverb, or a sentence. In school assignments, *adverbs* tell you <u>how you should do</u> the assignment."
- Direct students to the *Unit 1 Word Forms Table* on page 26 in the *Student Book*.
- Instruct students to add these word forms of **analyze** to the table: **analysis** (n), **analyst** (n), **analyze** (v), **analyzes** (v), **analyzed** (v), **analyzing** (v), **analytical** (adj), **analytically** (adv)

NOUNS What you make or create	**VERBS** What you have to do for the assignment	**ADJECTIVES** Specific details about what you must do	**ADVERBS** Important information about how to do the assignment
analysis	analyze	analytical	analytically
analyst	analyzes		
	analyzed		
	analyzing		

G Cloze Exercise
(*Student Book* page 18)

> ◆ Students use word forms to complete a cloze exercise.

- Direct students to use the words **analysis**, **analyzes**, **analyzing**, and **analyst** to complete this cloze exercise with their partners. Provide sufficient time for them to do so.
- Then, ask students to follow along as you read to determine if their answers to the cloze exercise are correct.

> An **analyst** is a person who **analyzes** something by separating it into parts and then studying each part. After **analyzing** each part, she presents an **analysis** to help others understand what she discovered.

H Informational Passage
(*Student Book* pages 18 and 19)

> ◆ Students chorally read the informational passage with the teacher.
> ◆ Students then read the passage with their partners.

- Say: "This informational passage is designed to provide you with strategies for using different forms of the word **analyze** in writing assignments."
- Ask students to read the passage chorally with you and then with their partners.

Note: You may want to make copies of the Tree/Map graphic organizer (Graph A-4 on the accompanying CD-ROM) for students to refer to.

Literary Analysis

The goal of a literary **analysis** is to show an understanding of the text. There are two parts to writing a response to literature. The first part is to **analyze** the text. The second part is the actual writing.

To **analyze** a text, you should first read it with specific questions in mind: What are the big ideas and main events? Are there important names and dates? Next, you should use a Tree/Map graphic organizer to record the basic ideas, names, and events in the text. It is also important to think about your own personal experiences and reactions to the literature: Did you enjoy reading it? Does it relate to your life? Select an important main idea from the text to write about. Then go back and reread the text several times. Look for examples or passages that relate to the main idea.

Once you have **analyzed** the text, taken notes, and decided on a main idea, you are ready to write rough draft. As with any written response, you will start with a topic sentence. The topic sentence will state your basic idea about the text or passage. Next, you will tell the reader the context in which the passage is found. The rest of your response will be an **analytical** discussion of the passage. You could **analyze** how the author used imagery or word choice to relate to the main idea. You could use quotations from the text to support your idea. Be certain that all of your examples relate to your topic sentence.

I Framed Paragraph and Sentence Stems

(*Student Book* page 19)

(Optional, to be used in conjunction with items J and K, following.)

Note: This section may be used to support struggling students. A framed paragraph is a tool to assist students in writing a paragraph. The paragraph frame provides a sample topic sentence, transitional sentence stems, and a conclusion sentence.

- Tell students that a framed paragraph is a tool to assist them in writing a paragraph.
- Read the topic sentence and the first transitional sentence stem with students.
- Stop reading after the first transitional sentence stem and assist students in completing the stem and adding additional informational sentences within the context of the framed paragraph.
- Continue reading each sentence stem, stopping after each one to assist students in completing the stem and adding additional informational sentences.
- Once the paragraph frame is completed, direct students to read the entire paragraph to their partners.

How I Show Respect for the American Flag

When saying the Pledge of Allegiance, I am respectful. First, I <u>stand straight and tall</u>. Then, I <u>keep my eyes on the flag</u>. Next, I <u>place my right hand over my heart</u>. Last, I <u>recite the pledge in a serious tone of voice</u>. My actions show that I respect the American flag.

Topic sentence:	When saying the Pledge of Allegiance, I am respectful.
First transitional sentence stem:	First, I _____.
Second transitional sentence stem:	Then, I _____.
Third transitional sentence stem:	Next, I _____.
Fourth transitional sentence stem:	Last, I _____.
Conclusion sentence:	My actions show that I respect the American flag.

J Paragraph Starters
(*Student Book* page 20)

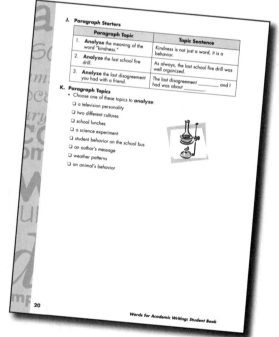

- To reinforce understanding of the word **analyze**, we suggest three related paragraph topics and topic sentences. You can assign these activities as independent practice, partner practice, or homework.

  1. **Paragraph topic: Analyze** the meaning of the word "kindness."
     Topic sentence: Kindness is not just a word, it is a behavior.
     - Ask students to think about a time when someone was kind to them.

  2. **Paragraph topic: Analyze** the last school fire drill.
     Topic sentence: As always, the last school fire drill was well organized.
     - Ask students to remember what happened during the last fire drill.

3. **Paragraph topic: Analyze** the last disagreement you had with a friend.
   Topic sentence: The last disagreement _____ and I had was about
   _____.

   • Ask students to think about both sides of a disagreement they had with a
   friend.

K Paragraph Topics
(*Student Book* page 20)

   • We suggest additional writing topics of general knowledge that appeal to
   a diverse student population. Assign these topics for additional practice in
   applying the academic word **analyze** to students' writing.

   ❑ a television personality

   ❑ two different cultures

   ❑ school lunches

   ❑ a science experiment

   ❑ student behavior on the school bus

   ❑ an author's message

   ❑ weather patterns

   ❑ an animal's behavior

discuss

Students will:

1. Correctly pronounce the word **discuss**.
2. Define the word **discuss** in an academic context.
3. Identify examples and non-examples of the word **discuss**.
4. Use the word **discuss** and its word forms in an academic context as evidenced by completion of a cloze exercise.
5. Write a paragraph that appropriately **discusses** an event or a situation.

A Introduction and Pronunciation
(*Student Book* page 21)

- Tell students the word: "This word is **discuss**."
- Say the word in parts.
- Ask students to repeat the word in parts and then the whole word.

B Explanation
(*Student Book* page 21)

- Say: "**Discuss** means *to talk about something; to consider different points of view.*"
- Ask students to repeat the explanation.
- Direct Partner1s to give the explanation to Partner 2s.
- Direct Partner 2s to tell Partner1s if their explanation was correct.

C Example Sentences
(*Student Book* page 21)

- ◆ Students chorally read example sentences with the teacher.
- ◆ Student partners answer scripted questions with provided sentence stems.

- Ask the class to chorally read the first sentence with you:
  1. The history teacher will **discuss** the many impacts of the Vietnam War.
- Ask: "What will the history teacher do?"
- Direct students to use the word **discuss** in their answer with this sentence stem: The teacher will **discuss** _____ [the impacts of the Vietnam War].
- Have students answer to their partners.
- Ask the class to chorally read the second sentence with you:
  2. Kayla and her friends **discussed** whether to go shopping at the mall or go to a movie.
- Ask: "What were Kayla and her friends doing?"

- Direct students to use the word **discussing** in their answer with this sentence stem:
  They were **discussing** _____ [whether to go shopping or see a movie].
- Have students answer to their partners.

D Checking for Understanding
(*Student Book* pages 21 and 22)

> ◆ Students chorally read example sentences with the teacher.
> ◆ Student partners answer scripted "Yes or No" questions with oral or written responses.

- Tell students that it is important to understand the meaning of an academic word when it is used in different forms.
- Explain to students that they will think, say, or write a response to sentences and explain the responses to their partners (e.g., say, "Partner 2s, read and respond to the first sentence. Partner 1s, tell your partner if you agree or disagree").
- Ask the class to chorally read the first sentence with you:
  1. Our family talked about whether or not to get a pet. Each person gave his or her opinion.
- Ask: "Did the family **discuss** the possibility of pet ownership?" (Answer: Yes)
- Direct students to respond to their partners by saying "yes" or "no" and explaining the reasons for their answer.

  Note: While students are responding, monitor their exchanges. Ask two or three students to share their responses with the class.

- Ask the class to chorally read the second sentence with you:
  2. Maria's mother refused to listen to Maria's reasons for wanting to have a later curfew.
- Ask: "Did Maria and her mother **discuss** the idea of Maria getting home later?" (Answer: No)
- Direct students to respond to their partners by saying "yes" or "no" and explaining the reasons for their answer.

  Note: While students are responding, monitor their exchanges. Ask two or three students to share their responses with the class.

- Ask the class to chorally read the third sentence with you:
  3. Tell about a time you engaged in a serious **discussion** with a friend or family member.
- Direct partners to think, write, and share their answers with the class. (A suggested sentence stem: My brother/sister and I once **discussed** _____.)
- Ask the class to chorally read the fourth sentence with you:
  4. Give an example of something you might be asked to **discuss** in one of your classes.
- Direct partners to think, write, and share their answers with the class. (A suggested sentence stem: In my _____ class, students might be asked to **discuss** _____.)

E Vocabulary Words Table
(*Student Book* page 22)

> ◆ Students add the academic word, an explanation of the word, and a usage example to the unit Vocabulary Words Table.

- Direct students to the *Unit 1 Vocabulary Words Table* on page 25 in the *Student Book*.
- Tell students to copy the explanation of the word **discuss** from this lesson or to write their own explanation of **discuss** in the second column.
- Then, direct students to write their own sentence, write another explanation, or draw a picture to represent the word **discuss** in the last column.

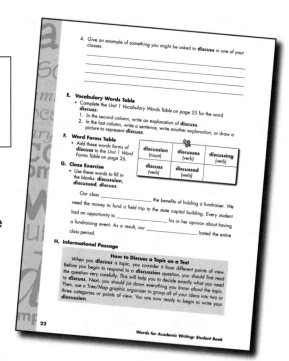

Sample Answers

Word	Explanation	Sentence/Explanation/Picture
discuss	To talk about something; to consider different points of view	The class **discussed** the idea of having a school picnic.

F Word Forms Table
(*Student Book* page 22)

> ◆ Students add forms of the academic word to the unit Word Forms Table.

- Tell students that once a word is known, it is easy to learn other forms of the word. Adding a prefix or a suffix to a word makes a new but related word. Word forms have similar spellings, pronunciations, and meanings. They are often different parts of speech.
- Say: "It is important to understand the parts of speech: *nouns, verbs, adjectives,* and *adverbs.* We all know that a noun is a word that represents a person, place, thing, or idea. In school assignments, *nouns* are words that tell you <u>what you are asked to make</u> for an assignment or a test. A verb is a word that represents an action, an experience, or a state. In school assignments and tests, *verbs* are words that tell you <u>what you are to do</u> for the assignment. An adjective is a word that describes a noun or a pronoun. In school assignments, *adjectives* usually <u>give other information</u> about the assignment. An adverb is a word that adds meaning to a verb, an adjective, another adverb, or a sentence. In school assignments, *adverbs* tell you <u>how you should do</u> the assignment."
- Direct students to the *Unit 1 Word Forms Table* on page 26 in the *Student Book*.

- Instruct students to add these word forms of **discuss** to the table:
discussion (n), **discuss** (v), **discusses** (v), **discussed** (v), **discussing** (v).

Answer Key

NOUNS What you make or create	**VERBS** What you have to do for the assignment	**ADJECTIVES** Specific details about what you must do	**ADVERBS** Important information about how to do the assignment
discussion	discuss		
	discusses		
	discussed		
	discussing		

G Cloze Exercise
(*Student Book* page 22)

- ◆ Students use word forms to complete a cloze exercise.

- Direct students to use the words **discussion**, **discussed**, and **discuss** to complete this cloze exercise with their partners. Provide sufficient time for them to do so.
- Then, ask students to follow along as you read to determine if their answers to the cloze exercise are correct.

> Our class **discussed** the benefits of holding a fundraiser. We need the money to fund a field trip to the state capitol building. Every student had an opportunity to **discuss** his or her opinion about having a fundraising event. As a result, our **discussion** lasted the entire class period.

H Informational Passage
(*Student Book* pages 22 and 23)

- ◆ Students chorally read the informational passage with the teacher.
- ◆ Students then read the passage with their partners.

- Say: "This informational passage is designed to provide you with strategies for using different forms of the word **discuss** in writing assignments."
- Ask students to read the passage chorally with you and then with their partners.

Note: You may want to make copies of the Tree/Map graphic organizer (Graph A-4 on the accompanying CD-ROM) for students to refer to.

How to Discuss a Topic on a Test

When you **discuss** a topic, you consider it from different points of view. Before you begin to respond to a **discussion** question, you should first read the question very carefully. This will help you to decide exactly what you need to **discuss**. Next, you should jot down everything you know about the topic. Then, use a Tree/Map graphic organizer to group all of your ideas into two or three categories or points of view. You are now ready to begin to write your **discussion**.

Start by restating the question. Be sure to use key words and indicate that there are different points of view about the topic. Briefly list all of the different viewpoints. Use transition signal words such as *first*, *second*, *next*, *also*, and *finally*. This will let the reader know that you are moving from one point to another. **Discuss** each point of view using examples, reasons, and supporting information. Avoid using words such as *all*, *none*, *every*, and *no one*. Finally, restate your points of view as they relate to the topic question.

Ⓘ Framed Paragraph and Sentence Stems

(Student Book page 23)

(Optional, to be used in conjunction with items J and K, following.)

Note: This section may be used to support struggling students. A framed paragraph is a tool to assist students in writing a paragraph. The paragraph frame provides a sample topic sentence, transitional sentence stems, and a conclusion sentence.

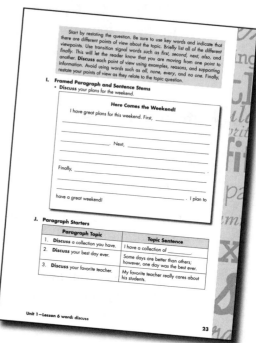

- Tell students that a framed paragraph is a tool to assist them in writing a paragraph.
- Read the topic sentence and the first transitional sentence stem with students.
- Stop reading after the first transitional sentence stem and assist students in completing the stem and adding additional informational sentences within the context of the framed paragraph.
- Continue reading each sentence stem, stopping after each one to assist students in completing the stem and adding additional informational sentences.
- Once the paragraph frame is completed, direct students to read the entire paragraph to their partners.

Here Comes the Weekend!

I have great plans for this weekend. First, <u>I plan to shop for a new pair of</u> <u>shoes</u>. Next, <u>I plan to see a movie</u>. Finally, <u>I plan to relax and hang out with my</u> <u>friends for a few hours</u>. I plan to have a great weekend!

Topic sentence:	I have great plans for this weekend.
First transitional sentence stem:	First, _____.
Second transitional sentence stem:	Next, _____.
Third transitional sentence stem:	Finally, _____.
Conclusion sentence:	I plan to have a great weekend!

J **Paragraph Starters**

(*Student Book* page 23)

- To reinforce understanding of the word **discuss**, we suggest three related paragraph topics and topic sentences. You can assign these activities as independent practice, partner practice, or homework.

  1. **Paragraph topic: Discuss** a collection you have.
     Topic sentence: I have a collection of _____ .
     - Ask students to write about something they collect.

  2. **Paragraph topic: Discuss** your best day ever.
     Topic sentence: Some days are better than others; however, one day was the best ever.
     - Ask students to remember the best day they ever had. What made that day so special?

  3. **Paragraph topic: Discuss** your favorite teacher.
     Topic sentence: My favorite teacher really cares about his students.
     - Ask students to think about the characteristics of their favorite teacher.

K Paragraph Topics
(*Student Book* page 24)

- We suggest additional writing topics of general knowledge that appeal to a diverse student population. Assign these topics for additional practice in applying the academic word **discuss** to students' writing.

  ❏ skateboarding

  ❏ after-school activities

  ❏ cars

  ❏ clothing styles

  ❏ video games

  ❏ vegetarian diet

  ❏ different cultures

  ❏ musical groups

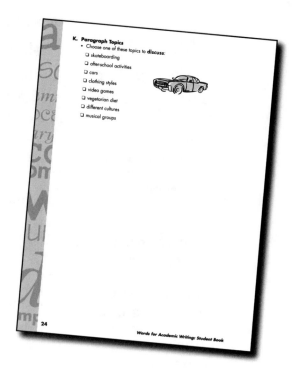

Unit 1 Posttest

Objective	To determine students' understanding of the academic words that were presented in Unit 1
Materials needed	For each student, one copy of the Unit 1 Posttest (refer to the accompanying CD-ROM) and two sheets of blank paper
Time allotment	35 minutes (Part A, 10 minutes; Part B, 10 minutes; Part C, 15 minutes)

Instructional Procedure

Step 1 Distribute Unit 1 Posttest and two sheets of blank paper to each student. Say:
- "Write your name and today's date on the lines at the top of the Posttest and at the top of each sheet of blank paper. I will collect all of them after you have finished the posttest."

Step 2 Review the directions for the Unit 1 Posttest, then administer the posttest. Say:
- "Only this Posttest score will be recorded as part of your grade. So do your very best."
- "Look at Part A. Let's read the directions together."
  (Read directions out loud with students.)
- "Place your finger on each word as I read it: **contrast**, **compare**, **summarize**, **explain**, **analyze**, **discuss**."
- "Now, place your finger on each lowercase letter next to the explanations in the right-hand column. Listen as I read the explanation for each letter."
  - **a.** To give a reason for something; to make something easy to understand
  - **b.** To study something carefully
  - **c.** To tell or show how two or more people, ideas, or things are alike and not alike
  - **d.** To talk about something; to consider different points of view
  - **e.** To show or state the difference(s) between two people, ideas, or things
  - **f.** To write or say a short statement about main points of information
- "Match each word with the explanation that you think is correct. Write the letter of the explanation in the middle column, next to the word."
- "You will have 10 minutes to complete Part A. Ready? Begin."
  (After 10 minutes, proceed to Part B.)
- "Now, look at Part B. It is important to know how to use academic words within the context of print."

- "Read each of the six sentences. Then, refer back to the table in Part A. Use the words in the first column to fill in the blanks of the sentences."
- "You will have 10 minutes to complete Part B. Any questions? Begin." *(After 10 minutes, proceed to Part C.)*
- "Now, read the directions for Part C. Remember to make a graphic organizer on one sheet of paper to plan your answer. Then write a paragraph using a topic sentence, transitional sentences, and a conclusion sentence on the other sheet of paper. You can receive up to 15 points for this section: 5 points for the graphic organizer, 5 points for using a paragraph format, and 5 points for content."
- "You will have 15 minutes to complete Part C. Any questions? Begin." *(After 10 minutes, tell students they have 5 minutes to finish.)*
- After 5 minutes pass, say, "Please turn in your tests and papers to me."

Refer to *Appendix D* for Unit 1 Posttest Answer Key

Unit 1 Generative Assessment *(optional)*

Objective	To ensure that students are able to correctly apply Unit 1 academic words in a generalized setting
Materials needed	For each student, one copy of the Unit 1 Generative Assessment (refer to the accompanying CD-ROM) and two sheets of blank paper
Time allotment	One class period

Instructional Procedure

Step 1 Distribute Unit 1 Generative Assessment and two sheets of blank paper to each student. Say:
- "Write your name and today's date on the lines at the top of the assessment and at the top of each sheet of blank paper. I will collect all of them after you have finished the assessment."

Step 2 Review the directions for the Unit 1 Generative Assessment, then administer the assessment. Say:
- "This assessment is designed to find out how well you are able to apply the Unit 1 academic words to general situations. This assessment will ask you to demonstrate your understanding of the Unit 1 words by providing examples based on your personal knowledge and experiences."
- "Read each direction, and then use the blank paper to create your own graphic organizer to plan your answer."
- "Then, use your graphic organizer to help you write a short paragraph using a topic sentence, transitional sentences, and a conclusion sentence."
- "You can receive up to 15 points for each answer: 5 points for your graphic organizer, 5 points for using a paragraph format, and 5 points for content. You will have the whole class period to complete this assessment."
- "Any questions? When you have finished, please turn in your assessment and graphic organizers to me. Begin."

Grading Criteria

To grade a Generative Assessment, we suggest allocating a maximum of 15 points *per assessment item* as follows:
- Up to 5 points for use of a graphic organizer
- Up to 5 points for conventions (correct paragraphing; use of topic, transitional, and conclusion sentences; correct punctuation; correct spelling)
- Up to 5 points for content

Objective	To determine students' prior knowledge of academic words that will be taught in Unit 2
Materials needed	For each student, one copy of the Unit 2 Pretest (refer to the accompanying CD-ROM)
Time allotment	20 minutes (Part A, 10 minutes; Part B, 10 minutes)

Instructional Procedure

Step 1 Distribute Unit 2 Pretest to students. Say:
* "Write your name and today's date on the lines at the top of the Pretest."

Step 2 Review the directions for Unit 2 Pretest, then administer the pretest. Say:
* "Look at Part A. Let's read the directions together."
  (*Read the directions out loud with students.*)
* "Place your finger on each word as I read it: **define**, **outline**, **justify**, **evaluate**, **illustrate**, **clarify**."
* "Now, place your finger on each lowercase letter next to the explanations in the right-hand column. Listen as I read the explanation for each letter."
   a. To write main points in an order using only headings and subheadings, not details
   b. To give an opinion of worth or value
   c. To make an idea or statement very clear or easy to understand with examples
   d. To show or tell what something is or means
   e. To prove or show why something is right or acceptable
   f. To create a mental picture by clearly explaining or giving examples
* "Match each word with the explanation that you think is correct. Write the letter of the explanation in the middle column, next to the word."
* "You will have 10 minutes to complete Part A. Ready? Begin."
  (*After 10 minutes, proceed to Part B.*)
* "Now, look at Part B. It is important to know how to use academic words within the context of print."
* "Read each of the six sentences. Then, refer back to the table in Part A. Use the words in the first column to fill in the blanks of the sentences."
* "You will have 10 minutes to complete Part B. Any questions? Begin."
* After 10 minutes, say, "Please return your tests to me."

> Refer to *Appendix D* for Unit 2 Pretest Answer Key

define

Students will:

1. Correctly pronounce the word **define**.
2. Define the word **define** in an academic context.
3. Identify examples and non-examples of the word **define**.
4. Use the word **define** and its word forms in an academic context as evidenced by completion of a cloze exercise.
5. Write a paragraph that appropriately **defines** a word, a term, a situation, or an event.

A Introduction and Pronunciation
(*Student Book* page 29)

• Tell students the word: "This word is **define**."
• Say the word in parts.
• Ask students to repeat the word in parts and then the whole word.

B Explanation
(*Student Book* page 29)

• Say: "**Define** means *to show or tell what something is or means*."
• Ask the class to repeat the explanation.
• Direct Partner 1s to say the explanation to Partner 2s.
• Direct Partner 2s to tell Partner 1s if their explanation was correct.

C Example Sentences
(*Student Book* page 29)

┌───┐
 ◆ Students chorally read example sentences with the teacher.
 ◆ Student partners answer scripted questions with provided sentence stems.
└───┘

• Ask the class to chorally read the first sentence with you:
  1. To check students' understanding, teachers often ask them to **define** words or concepts.
• Ask: "What is one way that teachers check for understanding?"
• Direct students to use the word **define** in their answer with this sentence stem: Teachers ask students to **define** _____ [words or concepts].
• Have students answer to their partners.

- Ask the class to chorally read the second sentence with you:

   2. When José was able to **define** the term "photosynthesis," he realized that he understood how plants use sunlight to grow.

- Ask: "When José realized that he understood how plants use sunlight to grow, what was he doing?"

- Direct students to use the word **defining** in their answer with this sentence stem:

   José was **defining** _____ [the term "photosynthesis"].

- Have students answer to their partners.

D Checking for Understanding

(*Student Book* pages 29 and 30)

> ◆ Students chorally read example sentences with the teacher.
> ◆ Student partners answer scripted "Yes or No" questions with oral or written responses.

- Tell students that it is important to understand the meaning of an academic word when it is used in different forms.

- Explain to students that they will think, say, or write a response to sentences and explain the responses to their partners (e.g., say, "Partner 2s, read and respond to the first sentence. Partner 1s, tell your partner if you agree or disagree").

- Ask the class to chorally read the first sentence with you:

   1. On a test, Jerry was asked to **define** the word "revolution."

- Ask: "Should Jerry tell what a revolution is?" (Answer: Yes)

- Direct students to respond to their partners by saying "yes" or "no" and explaining the reasons for their response.
   Note: While students are responding, monitor their exchanges. Ask two or three students to share their responses with the class.

- Ask the class to chorally read the second sentence with you:

   2. Juan told his mother that he wanted to attend San Diego State University, but he didn't know why.

- Ask: "Was Juan able to **define** why he wanted to go to that school?" (Answer: No)

- Direct students to respond to their partners by saying "yes" or "no" and explaining the reasons for their response.
   Note: While students are responding, monitor their exchanges. Ask two or three students to share their responses with the class.

- Ask the class to chorally read the third sentence with you:

   3. Use three words to **define** the word "school."

- Direct partners to think, write, and share their answers with the class. (A suggested sentence stem: Three words that best **define** school are _____.)

- Ask the class to chorally read the fourth sentence with you:

   4. What is your **definition** of friendship?

- Direct partners to think, write, and share their answers with the class. (A suggested sentence stem: To me, friendship is _____.)

E Vocabulary Words Table

(Student Book page 30)

> ◆ Students add the academic word, an explanation of the word, and a usage example to the unit Vocabulary Words Table.

- Direct students to the *Unit 2 Vocabulary Words Table* on page 53 in the *Student Book.*
- Tell students to copy the explanation of the word **define** from this lesson or to write their own explanation of **define** in the second column.
- Then, direct students to write their own sentence, write another explanation, or draw a picture to represent the word **define** in the last column.

Sample Answers

Word	Explanation	Sentence/Explanation/Picture
define	To show or tell what something is or means	Students are able to **define** the word "mutation."

F Word Forms Table

(Student Book page 30)

> ◆ Students add forms of the academic word to the unit Word Forms Table.

- Tell students that once a word is known, it is easy to learn other forms of the word. Adding a prefix or a suffix to a word makes a new but related word. Word forms have similar spellings, pronunciations, and meanings. They are often different parts of speech.
- Say: "It is important to understand the parts of speech: *nouns, verbs, adjectives,* and *adverbs.* We all know that a noun is a word that represents a person, place, thing, or idea. In school assignments, *nouns* are words that tell you <u>what you are asked to make</u> for an assignment or a test. A verb is a word that represents an action, an experience, or a state. In school assignments and tests, *verbs* are words that tell you <u>what you are to do</u> for the assignment. An adjective is a word that describes a noun or a pronoun. In school assignments, *adjectives* usually <u>give other information</u> about the assignment. An adverb is a word that adds meaning to a verb, an adjective, another adverb, or a sentence. In school assignments, *adverbs* tell you <u>how you should do</u> the assignment."
- Direct students to the *Unit 2 Word Forms Table* on page 54 in the *Student Book.*

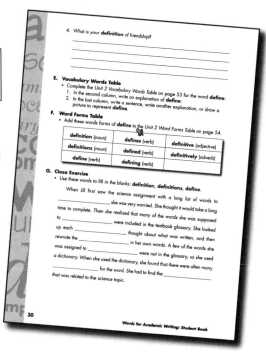

- Instruct students to add these word forms of **define** to the table: **definition** (n), **definitions** (n), **define** (v), **defines** (v), **defined** (v), **defining** (v), **definitive** (adj), **definitively** (adv).

Answer Key

NOUNS What you make or create	VERBS What you have to do for the assignment	ADJECTIVES Specific details about what you must do	ADVERBS Important information about how to do the assignment
definition	define	definitive	definitively
definitions	defines		
	defined		
	defining		

G Cloze Exercise
(*Student Book* page 30)

◆ Students use word forms to complete a cloze exercise.

- Direct students to use the words **definition**, **definitions**, and **define** to complete this cloze exercise with their partners. Provide sufficient time for them to do so.
- Then, ask students to follow along as you read to determine if their answers to the cloze exercise are correct.

> When Jill first saw the science assignment with a long list of words to __**define**__, she was very worried. She thought it would take a long time to complete. Then she realized that many of the words she was supposed to __**define**__ were included in the textbook glossary. She looked up each __**definition**__, thought about what was written, and then rewrote the __**definition**__ in her own words. A few of the words she was assigned to __**define**__ were not in the glossary, so she used a dictionary. When she used the dictionary, she found that there were often many __**definitions**__ for the word. She had to find the __**definition**__ that was related to the science topic.

H Informational Passage
(*Student Book* page 31)

◆ Students chorally read the informational passage with the teacher.
◆ Students then read the passage with their partners.

- Say: "This informational passage is designed to provide you with strategies for using the word **define** in writing assignments."
- Ask students to read this passage chorally with you and then with their partners. *Note: You may want to make copies of the Web graphic organizer (Graph A-1 on the accompanying CD-ROM) for students to refer to.*

Define: Explain the Meaning

Definitions call for concise, clear answers. These answers should be short and to the point. To write a **definition**, you must first organize your thoughts. Make a Web graphic organizer and jot down some key words that show the attributes of the word or concept you are asked to **define**. You should write the **definition** in your own words. Avoid using extreme words such as *all, always, only, none, never, no one, best,* or *worst* because there are often exceptions to any statement. It is better to use words like *may, usually, some, probably, might, frequently, seldom, few, often,* and *many.* These words allow you to **define** a word, yet provide for an exception to a statement.

❶ Framed Paragraph and Sentence Stems
(Student Book page 31)

(Optional, to be used in conjunction with items J and K, following.)

Note: This section may be used to support struggling students. A framed paragraph is a tool to assist students in writing a paragraph. The paragraph frame provides a sample topic sentence, transitional sentence stems, and a conclusion sentence.

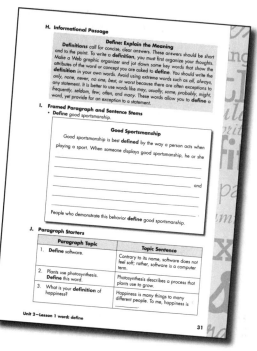

- Tell students that a framed paragraph is a tool to assist them in writing a paragraph.
- Read the topic sentence and the first transitional sentence stem with students.
- Stop reading after the first transitional sentence stem and assist students in completing the sentence in the context of the framed paragraph.
- Continue reading each sentence stem, stopping after each one to assist students in completing the stems.
- Once the paragraph frame is completed, direct students to read the entire paragraph to their partners.

Sample Completed Framed Paragraph

Good Sportsmanship

Good sportsmanship is best **defined** by the way a person acts when playing a sport. When someone displays good sportsmanship, he or she <u>is honest</u>, <u>plays fair</u>, and <u>congratulates other players' accomplishments</u>. People who demonstrate this behavior **define** good sportsmanship

Topic sentence:	Good sportsmanship is best **defined** by the way a person acts when playing a sport.
Transitional sentence stem:	When someone displays good sportsmanship, he or she _____, _____, and _____.
Conclusion sentence:	People who demonstrate this behavior **define** good sportsmanship.

J Paragraph Starters

(*Student Book* page 31)

- To reinforce understanding of the word **define**, we suggest three related paragraph topics and topic sentences. You can assign these activities as independent practice, partner practice, or homework.

  1. **Paragraph topic: Define** software.

     Topic sentence: Contrary to its name, software does not feel soft; rather, software is a computer term.
     - Ask students to think about computer software and how it is used.

  2. **Paragraph topic:** Plants use photosynthesis. **Define** this word.

     Topic sentence: Photosynthesis describes a process that plants use to grow.
     - Ask students to think about what they know about photosynthesis and what it does for plants.

  3. **Paragraph topic:** What is your **definition** of happiness?

     Topic sentence: Happiness is many things to many different people. To me, happiness is _____.
     - Ask students to think about specific times they are happy and what causes them to be happy.

K Paragraph Topics

(Student Book page 32)

- We suggest additional writing topics of general knowledge that appeal to a diverse student population. Assign these topics for additional practice in applying the academic word **define** to students' writing.

  ❑ evaporation/condensation

  ❑ a light-year

  ❑ lightning

  ❑ honesty

  ❑ friendship

  ❑ Westward movement in U.S. history

  ❑ adventure

  ❑ The Industrial Revolution

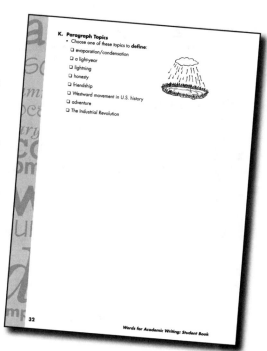

outline

Students will:

1. Correctly pronounce the word **outline**.
2. Define the word **outline** in an academic context.
3. Identify examples and non-examples of the word **outline**.
4. Use the word **outline** and its word forms in an academic context as evidenced by completion of a cloze exercise.
5. Write a paragraph that appropriately **outlines** an event or a task.

A Introduction and Pronunciation
(*Student Book* page 33)

- Tell students the word: "This word is **outline**."
- Say the word in parts.
- Ask students to repeat the word in parts and then the whole word.

B Explanation
(*Student Book* page 33)

- Say: "**Outline** means *to write main points in an order using only headings and subheadings, not details.*"
- Ask students to repeat the explanation.
- Direct Partner 1s to say the explanation to Partner 2s.
- Direct Partner 2s to tell Partner 1s if their explanation was correct.

(Inset image of Student Book page 33)

Unit 2 Lesson 2 **outline**

A. Introduction and Pronunciation
- This word is **outline**.
- Say the word in parts and then the whole word.

B. Explanation
- **Outline** means to write main points in an order using only headings and subheadings, not details.

C. Example Sentences
1. The teacher **outlined** the theory of relativity.
2. Juan made an **outline** of his duties as team manager.

D. Checking for Understanding
1. Jazmine was directed to compare and contrast the state legislature with the federal legislature.
   Question: Did the teacher expect Jazmine to **outline** the answer? Yes or No? Why or why not?

2. Marc wrote a list of the major steps in building a brick wall.
   Question: Did Marc make a type of **outline**? Yes or No? Why or why not?

3. The class advisor told students that there were many things they needed to do to make sure that the school dance would be a success.
   Question: What might be in the **outline** for preparing the school dance?

33

C Example Sentences
(*Student Book* page 33)

> ◆ Students chorally read example sentences with the teacher.
> ◆ Student partners answer scripted questions with provided sentence stems.

- Ask the class to chorally read the first sentence with you:
  1. The teacher **outlined** the theory of relativity.
- Ask: "What was the teacher doing?"
- Direct students to use the word **outlining** in their answer with this sentence stem:
  The teacher was **outlining** _____ [the theory of relativity].
- Have students answer to their partners.
- Ask the class to chorally read the second sentence with you:
  2. Juan made an **outline** of his duties as team manager.

- Ask: "When Juan explained his duties as team manager, what was he doing?"
- Direct students to use the word **outlining** in their answer with this sentence stem:

  Juan was **outlining** _____ [his duties as team manager].
- Have students answer to their partners.

D Checking for Understanding
(*Student Book* pages 33 and 34)

> ◆ Students chorally read example sentences with the teacher.
> ◆ Student partners answer scripted "Yes or No" questions with oral or written responses.

- Tell students that it is important to understand the meaning of an academic word when it is used in different forms.
- Explain to students that they will think, say, or write a response to sentences and explain the responses to their partners (e.g., say, "Partner 2s, read and respond to the first sentence. Partner 1s, tell your partner if you agree or disagree").
- Ask the class to chorally read the first sentence with you:
  1. Jazmine was directed to compare and contrast the state legislature with the federal legislature.
- Ask: "Did the teacher expect Jazmine to **outline** the answer?" (Answer: No)
- Direct students to respond to their partners by saying "yes" or "no" and explaining the reasons for their response.
  Note: While students are responding, monitor their exchanges. Ask two or three students to share their responses with the class.
- Ask the class to chorally read the second sentence with you:
  2. Marc wrote a list of the major steps in building a brick wall.
- Ask: "Did Marc make a type of **outline**?" (Answer: Yes)
- Direct students to respond to their partners by saying "yes" or "no" and explaining the reasons for their response.
  Note: While students are responding, monitor their exchanges. Ask two or three students to share their responses with the class.
- Ask the class to chorally read the third sentence with you:
  3. The class advisor told students that there were many things they needed to do to make sure that the school dance would be a success.
- Ask: "What might be in the **outline** for preparing the school dance?"
- Direct partners to think, write and share their answers with the class. (A suggested sentence stem: An **outline** of the school dance might include _____.)
- Ask the class to chorally read the fourth sentence with you:
  4. List some areas in your life where an **outline** of duties or responsibilities would be helpful.
- Direct partners to think, write and share their answers with the class. (A suggested sentence stem: Some areas of my life where an **outline** would be helpful are _____.)

E Vocabulary Words Table

(Student Book page 34)

◆ Students add the academic word, an explanation of the word, and a usage example to the unit Vocabulary Words Table.

- Direct students to the *Unit 2 Vocabulary Words Table* on page 53 in the *Student Book*.
- Tell students to copy the explanation of the word **outline** from this lesson or to write their own explanation of **outline** in the second column.
- Then, direct students to write their own sentence, write another explanation, or draw a picture to represent the word **outline** in the last column.

Sample Answers

Word	Explanation	Sentence/Explanation/Picture
outline	To write main points in an order that uses only headings and subheadings, not details	Juan made an **outline** of his duties as team manager.

F Word Forms Table

(Student Book page 34)

◆ Students add forms of the academic word to the unit Word Forms Table.

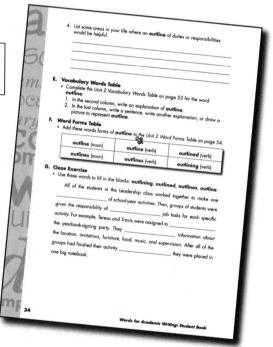

- Tell students that once a word is known, it is easy to learn other forms of the word. Adding a prefix or a suffix to a word makes a new but related word. Word forms have similar spellings, pronunciations, and meanings. They are often different parts of speech.

- Say: "It is important to understand the parts of speech: *nouns, verbs, adjectives,* and *adverbs*. We all know that a noun is a word that represents a person, place, thing, or idea. In school assignments, *nouns* are words that tell you <u>what you are asked to make</u> for an assignment or a test. A verb is a word that represents an action, an experience, or a state. In school assignments and tests, *verbs* are words that tell you <u>what you are to do</u> for the assignment. An adjective is a word that describes a noun or a pronoun. In school assignments, *adjectives* usually <u>give other information</u> about the assignment. An adverb is a word that adds meaning to a verb, an adjective, another adverb, or a sentence. In school assignments, *adverbs* tell you <u>how you should do</u> the assignment."

- Direct students to the *Unit 2 Word Forms Table* on page 54 in the *Student Book*.

- Instruct students to add these word forms of **outline** to the table: **outline** (n), **outlines** (n), **outline** (v), **outlines** (v), **outlined** (v), **outlining** (v).

Answer Key

NOUNS What you make or create	VERBS What you have to do for the assignment	ADJECTIVES Specific details about what you must do	ADVERBS Important information about how to do the assignment
outline	outline		
outlines	outlines		
	outlined		
	outlining		

G Cloze Exercise
(*Student Book* page 34)

◆ Students use word forms to complete a cloze exercise.

- Direct students to use the words **outlining**, **outlined**, **outlines**, and **outline** to complete this cloze exercise with their partners. Provide sufficient time for them to do so.
- Then, ask students to follow along as you read to determine if their answers to the cloze exercise are correct.

All of the students in the Leadership class worked together to make one __outline__ of school-year activities. Then, groups of students were given the responsibility of __outlining__ job tasks for each specific activity. For example, Teresa and Travis were assigned to __outline__ the yearbook-signing party. They __outlined__ information about the location, invitations, furniture, food, music, and supervision. After all of the groups had finished their activity __outlines__, they were placed in one big notebook.

H Informational Passage
(*Student Book* page 35)

◆ Students chorally read the informational passage with the teacher.
◆ Students then read the passage with their partners.

- Say: "This informational passage is designed to provide you with strategies for using the word **outline** in writing assignments."
- Ask students to read this passage chorally with you and then with their partners. *Note: You may want to make copies of the Outline graphic organizer (Graph A-6 on the accompanying CD-ROM) for students to refer to.*

Outline: A Step-by-Step Process

An **outline** should be clear and concise. When your teacher asks for an **outline**, he or she expects you to provide information in a logical, organized manner. Take time to jot down a brief **outline** on an Outline graphic organizer. Make sure you have all of your information in order, listing only the main points and essential supporting information. Omit minor details.

You need to be organized when you write an **outline**. You must be prepared to list information in a logical, step-by-step process. It is important to find out exactly how a teacher expects you to write an **outline** for a test answer or an assignment. For example, a teacher may expect you to use Roman numerals before the main points followed by capital letters before essential information points. Other times, a teacher might want a brief listing of steps in a logical order.

❶ Framed Outline

(*Student Book* page 35)

(Optional, to be used in conjunction with items J and K, following.)

Note: This section may be used to support struggling students. A framed outline is a tool to assist students in writing an outline. The outline frame provides a sample topic and sequential main headings and subheadings.

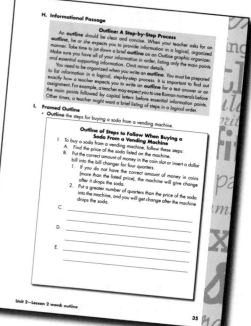

- Tell students that a framed outline is a tool to assist them in writing an outline.
- Read the direction in the *Student Book* with students.
- Then, read the main heading entry (Roman numeral I) to students, pointing out that this line is a main heading.
- Continue reading each subheading (lines A, B, 1, and 2), stopping after each one to point out that these lines are subheadings.
- Direct students to complete subheading entries for lines C, D, and E of the outline.
- When students complete their outline, direct them to read it to their partners.

Outline of Steps to Follow When Buying a Soda From a Vending Machine

I. To buy a soda from a vending machine, follow these steps:
    A. Find the price of the soda listed on the machine.
    B. Put the correct amount of money in the coin slot or insert a dollar bill into the bill changer for four quarters.
        1. If you do not have the correct amount of money in coins (more than the listed price), the machine will give change after it drops the soda.
        2. Put a greater number of quarters than the price of the soda into the machine, and you will get change after the machine drops the soda.
    C. <u>Push the button for the soda you want.</u>
    D. <u>Pick up the soda from the dispenser at the bottom of the machine.</u>
    E. <u>If you put in more money than the price of the soda, get your change from the slot near the bottom of the machine.</u>

J Paragraph Starters

(*Student Book* page 36)

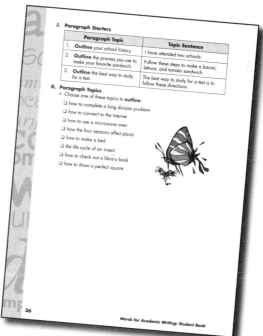

- To reinforce understanding of the word **outline**, we suggest three related paragraph topics and topic sentences. You can assign these activities as independent practice, partner practice, or homework.

  1. **Paragraph topic: Outline** your school history.

      Topic sentence: I have attended two schools.

      - Ask students to think about the schools they have attended.

  2. **Paragraph topic: Outline** the process you use to make your favorite sandwich.

      Topic sentence: Follow these steps to make a bacon, lettuce, and tomato sandwich.

      - Ask students to think about their favorite sandwich and how they would tell someone else to make it.

  3. **Paragraph topic: Outline** the best way to study for a test.

      Topic sentence: The best way to study for a test is to follow these directions.

      - Ask students to think about what they know about studying for a test and then to put that information in a logical order.

K Paragraph Topics
(*Student Book* page 36)

- We suggest additional writing topics of general knowledge that appeal to a diverse student population. Assign these topics for additional practice in applying the academic word **outline** to students' writing.

  ❑ how to complete a long division problem

  ❑ how to connect to the Internet

  ❑ how to use a microwave oven

  ❑ how the four seasons affect plants

  ❑ how to make a bed

  ❑ the life cycle of an insect

  ❑ how to check out a library book

  ❑ how to draw a perfect square

justify

Students will:

1. Correctly pronounce the word **justify**.
2. Define the word **justify** in an academic context.
3. Identify examples and non-examples of the word **justify**.
4. Use the word **justify** and its word forms in an academic context as evidenced by completion of a cloze exercise.
5. Write a paragraph that appropriately **justifies** a point of view, a situation, or an event.

A Introduction and Pronunciation
(*Student Book* page 37)

- Tell students the word: "This word is **justify**."
- Say the word in parts.
- Ask students to repeat the word in parts and then the whole word.

B Explanation
(*Student Book* page 37)

- Say: "**Justify** means *to prove or show why something is right or acceptable.*"
- Ask students to repeat the explanation.
- Direct Partner 1s to say the explanation to Partner 2s.
- Direct Partner 2s to tell Partner 1s if their explanation was correct.

Unit 2 Lesson 3

justify

A. Introduction and Pronunciation
- This word is **justify**.
- Say the word in parts and then the whole word.

B. Explanation
- **Justify** means to prove or show why something is right or acceptable.

C. Example Sentences
1. **Justify** the entry of the United States of America into World War II.
2. Predict what you think will happen to the Colorado River in the next 50 years, and **justify** your answer.

D. Checking for Understanding
1. Laranzo explained why he thought his team lost the game.
   Question: Did Laranzo try to **justify** *his team's loss?*
   Yes or No? Why or why not?

2. Mrs. Alverez told the class to open their books to page 53 and start reading.
   Question: Did Mrs. Alverez **justify** *her directions?*
   Yes or No? Why or why not?

3. Give three reasons to **justify** being tardy to school.

37

C Example Sentences
(*Student Book* page 37)

> ◆ Students chorally read example sentences with the teacher.
> ◆ Student partners answer scripted questions with provided sentence stems.

- Ask the class to chorally read the first sentence with you:
  1. **Justify** the entry of the United States of America into World War II.
- Ask: "When someone gives reasons to explain why the American entry into World War II was appropriate, what is that person doing?"
- Direct students to use the word **justifying** in their answer with this sentence stem:
  The person is **justifying** _____ [the American entry into World War II].
- Have students answer to their partners.
- Ask the class to chorally read the second sentence with you:

2. Predict what you think will happen to the Colorado River in the next 50 years, and **justify** your answer.

- Ask: "When people predict what will happen to the Colorado River in the next 50 years and they back up their predictions with reasons that explain why, what are they doing?"
- Direct students to use the word **justifying** in their answer with this sentence stem:

  People are **justifying** _____ [their predictions].
- Have students answer to their partners.

D Checking for Understanding
(*Student Book* pages 37 and 38)

> ◆ Students chorally read example sentences with the teacher.
> ◆ Student partners answer scripted "Yes or No" questions with oral or written responses.

- Tell students that it is important to understand the meaning of an academic word when it is used in different forms.
- Explain to students that they will think, say, or write a response to sentences and explain the responses to their partners (e.g., say, "Partner 2s, read and respond to the first sentence. Partner 1s, tell your partner if you agree or disagree").
- Ask the class to chorally read the first sentence with you:

  1. Laranzo explained why he thought his team lost the game.
- Ask: "Did Laranzo try to **justify** his team's loss?" (Answer: Yes)
- Direct students to respond to their partners by saying "yes" or "no" and explaining the reasons for their response.
  Note: While students are responding, monitor their exchanges. Ask two or three students to share their responses with the class.
- Ask the class to chorally read the second sentence with you:

  2. Mrs. Alverez told the class to open their books to page 53 and start reading.
- Ask: "Did Mrs. Alverez **justify** her directions?" (Answer: No)
- Direct students to respond to their partners by saying "yes" or "no" and explaining the reasons for their response.
  Note: While students are responding, monitor their exchanges. Ask two or three students to share their responses with the class.
- Ask the class to chorally read the third sentence with you:

  3. Give three reasons to **justify** being tardy to school.
- Direct partners to think, write, and share their answers with the class. (A suggested sentence stem: Three reasons I could use to **justify** being tardy are _____.)
- Ask the class to chorally read the fourth sentence with you:

  4. When was the last time you **justified** your behavior to your parents?
- Direct partners to think, write, and share their answers with the class. (A suggested sentence stem: The last time I **justified** my behavior to my parents was _____.)

Words for Academic Writing: Teacher Guide

E Vocabulary Words Table

(*Student Book* page 38)

> ◆ Students add the academic word, an explanation of the word, and a usage example to the unit Vocabulary Words Table.

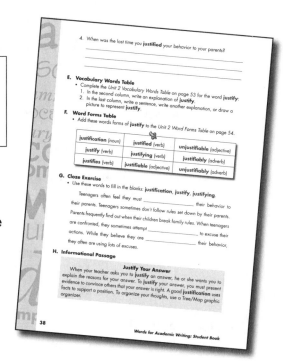

- Direct students to the *Unit 2 Vocabulary Words Table* on page 53 in the *Student Book*.

- Tell students to copy the explanation of the word **justify** from this lesson or to write their own explanation of **justify** in the second column.

- Then, direct students to write their own sentence, write another explanation, or draw a picture to represent the word **justify** in the last column.

Sample Answers

Word	Explanation	Sentence/Explanation/Picture
justify	To prove or show why something is right or acceptable	John was able to **justify** why he did not attend the show.

F Word Forms Table

(*Student Book* page 38)

> ◆ Students add forms of the academic word to the unit Word Forms Table.

- Tell students that once a word is known, it is easy to learn other forms of the word. Adding a prefix or a suffix to a word makes a new but related word. Word forms have similar spellings, pronunciations, and meanings. They are often different parts of speech.

- Say: "It is important to understand the parts of speech: *nouns*, *verbs*, *adjectives*, and *adverbs*. We all know that a noun is a word that represents a person, place, thing, or idea. In school assignments, *nouns* are words that tell you <u>what you are asked to make</u> for an assignment or a test. A verb is a word that represents an action, an experience, or a state. In school assignments and tests, *verbs* are words that tell you <u>what you are to do</u> for the assignment. An adjective is a word that describes a noun or a pronoun. In school assignments, *adjectives* usually <u>give other information</u> about the assignment. An adverb is a word that adds meaning to a verb, an adjective, another adverb, or a sentence. In school assignments, *adverbs* tell you <u>how you should do</u> the assignment."

- Direct students to the *Unit 2 Word Forms Table* on page 54 in the *Student Book*.

- Instruct students to add these word forms of **justify** to the chart: **justification** (n), **justify** (v), **justifies** (v), **justified**, (v), **justifying**, (verb), **justifiable** (adj), **unjustifiable** (adj), **justifiably** (adv), **unjustifiably** (adv).

Answer Key

NOUNS What you make or create	VERBS What you have to do for the assignment	ADJECTIVES Specific details about what you must do	ADVERBS Important information about how to do the assignment
justification	justify	justifiable	justifiably
	justifies	unjustifiable	unjustifiably
	justified		
	justifying		

G Cloze Exercise
(*Student Book* page 38)

◆ Students use word forms to complete a cloze exercise.

- Direct students to use the words **justification**, **justify**, and **justifying** to complete this cloze exercise with their partners. Provide sufficient time for them to do so.
- Then, ask students to follow along as you read to determine if their answers to the cloze exercise are correct.

> Teenagers often feel they must __justify__ their behavior to their parents. Teenagers sometimes don't follow rules set down by their parents. Parents frequently find out when their children break family rules. When teenagers are confronted, they sometimes attempt __justification__ to excuse their actions. While they believe they are __justifying__ their behavior, they often are using lots of excuses.

H Informational Passage
(*Student Book* pages 38 and 39)

◆ Students chorally read the informational passage with the teacher.
◆ Students then read the passage with their partners.

- Say: "This informational passage is designed to provide you with strategies for using different forms of the word **justify** in writing assignments."
- Ask students to read the passage chorally with you and then with their partners.

Note: You may want to make copies of the Tree/Map graphic organizer (Graph A-4 on the accompanying CD-ROM) for students to refer to.

Justify Your Answer

When your teacher asks you to **justify** an answer, he or she wants you to explain the reasons for your answer. To **justify** your answer, you must present evidence to convince others that your answer is right. A good **justification** uses facts to support a position. To organize your thoughts, use a Tree/Map graphic organizer.

To begin a **justification**, you should restate the question. Next, you should state the main point. Then you must **justify** why something is true or right with facts. Be logical in your reasoning. Provide examples to support your points. When possible, use subject-matter terms. Be clear and concise. Do not use extreme words such as *always, only, none, never, no one, best, worst,* or *everyone*. Avoid using double negatives such as *not uncommon* or *not illegal*. These word combinations make the statement positive.

When you **justify**, use signal words to show the connection between your examples and the main point. To do this, you should use words such as *because, since, while,* and *although* as well as phrases like *in view of the fact that*. Keep your **justification** brief.

❶ Framed Paragraph and Sentence Stems

(*Student Book* page 39)

(Optional, to be used in conjunction with items J and K, following.)

Note: This section may be used to support struggling students. A framed paragraph is a tool to assist students in writing a paragraph. The paragraph frame provides a sample topic sentence, transitional sentence stems, and a conclusion sentence.

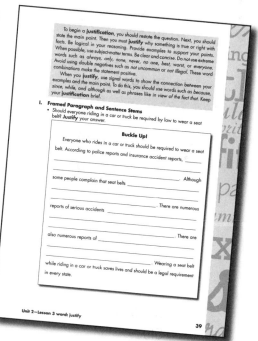

- Tell students that a framed paragraph is a tool to assist them in writing a paragraph.
- Read the topic sentence and the first transitional sentence stem with students.
- Stop reading after the first transitional sentence stem and assist students in completing the sentence in the context of the framed paragraph.
- Continue reading each sentence stem, stopping after each one to assist students in completing the stems.
- Once the paragraph frame is completed, direct students to read the entire paragraph to their partners.

Buckle Up!

Everyone who rides in a car or truck should be required to wear a seat belt. According to police reports and insurance accident reports, <u>people who wear seat belts are less likely to die or be seriously injured in accidents than people who do not wear seat belts</u>. Although some people complain that seat belts <u>are uncomfortable or restrain movement, seat belts provide protection from being thrown through the windshield or out of the vehicle</u>. There are numerous reports of serious accidents <u>in which a vehicle is demolished and the person who was wearing a seat belt walked away with minor injuries—or no injuries at all</u>. There are also numerous reports of <u>people being killed or seriously injured in minor accidents because they were not wearing seat belts</u>. Wearing a seat belt while riding in a car or truck saves lives and should be a legal requirement in every state.

Topic sentence/ restatement of the question:	Everyone who rides in a car or truck should be required to wear a seat belt.
First transitional sentence stem:	According to police reports and insurance accident reports, _____.
Second transitional sentence stem:	Although some people complain that seat belts _____.
Third transitional sentence stem:	There are numerous reports of serious accidents _____.
Fourth transitional sentence stem:	There are also numerous reports of _____.
Conclusion sentence:	Wearing a seat belt while riding in a car or truck saves lives and should be a legal requirement in every state.

J Paragraph Starters

(Student Book page 40)

- To reinforce understanding of the word **justify**, we suggest three related paragraph topics and topic sentences. You can assign these activities as independent practice, partner practice, or homework.

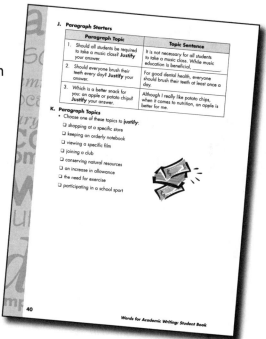

  1. **Paragraph topic:** Should all students be required to take a music class? **Justify** your answer.

     Topic sentence: It is not necessary for all students to take a music class. While music education is beneficial, _____.

     - Ask students to think about their experiences with learning music either in or out of school.

  2. **Paragraph topic:** Should everyone brush their teeth every day? **Justify** your answer.

     Topic sentence: For good dental health, everyone should brush their teeth at least once a day.

     - Ask students to think about dental health and the reasons why people brush their teeth.

  3. **Paragraph topic:** Which is a better snack for you: an apple or potato chips? **Justify** your answer.

     Topic sentence: Although I really like potato chips, when it comes to nutrition, an apple is better for me.

     - Ask students to think about the nutritional values of both foods and then develop their justification of choice.

K Paragraph Topics

(Student Book page 40)

- We suggest additional writing topics of general knowledge that appeal to a diverse student population. Assign these topics for additional practice in applying the academic word **justify** to students' writing.

  ❏ shopping at a specific store

  ❏ keeping an orderly notebook

  ❏ viewing a specific film

  ❏ joining a club

  ❏ conserving natural resources

  ❏ an increase in allowance

  ❏ the need for exercise

  ❏ participating in a school sport

evaluate

OBJECTIVES

Students will:

1. Correctly pronounce the word **evaluate**.
2. Define the word **evaluate** in an academic context.
3. Identify examples and non-examples of the word **evaluate**.
4. Use the word **evaluate** and its word forms in an academic context as evidenced by completion of a cloze exercise.
5. Write a paragraph that appropriately **evaluates** a piece of writing, an event, or an idea.

A Introduction and Pronunciation
(*Student Book* page 41)

- Tell students the word: "This word is **evaluate**."
- Say the word in parts.
- Ask students to repeat the word in parts and then the whole word.

B Explanation
(*Student Book* page 41)

- Say: "**Evaluate** means *to give an opinion of worth or value.*"
- Ask the class to repeat the explanation.
- Direct Partner 1s to give the explanation to Partner 2s.
- Direct Partner 2s to tell Partner 1s if their explanation was correct.

C Example Sentences
(*Student Book* page 41)

> ◆ Students chorally read example sentences with the teacher.
> ◆ Student partners answer scripted questions with provided sentence stems.

- Ask the class to chorally read the first sentence with you:

  1. To **evaluate** student work, the teacher reads each paper carefully.

- Ask: "What is the teacher doing when she reads each paper carefully?"
- Direct students to use the word **evaluating** in their answer with this sentence stem:

  The teacher is **evaluating** _____ [student work].

- Have students answer to their partners.
- Ask the class to chorally read the second sentence with you:

  2. The principal **evaluates** the use of classroom computers.

Sidebar (Student Book page 41 reproduction):

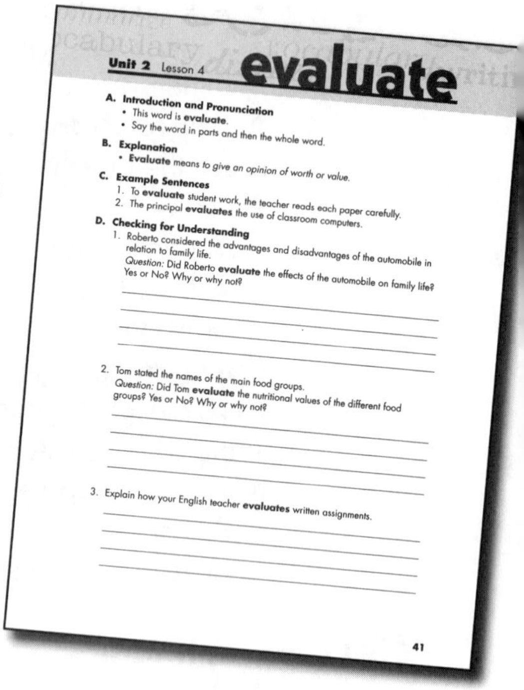

Unit 2 Lesson 4   **evaluate**

A. Introduction and Pronunciation
- This word is **evaluate**.
- Say the word in parts and then the whole word.

B. Explanation
- **Evaluate** means *to give an opinion of worth or value.*

C. Example Sentences
1. To **evaluate** student work, the teacher reads each paper carefully.
2. The principal **evaluates** the use of classroom computers.

D. Checking for Understanding
1. Roberto considered the advantages and disadvantages of the automobile in relation to family life.
   Question: Did Roberto **evaluate** the effects of the automobile on family life? Yes or No? Why or why not?

2. Tom stated the names of the main food groups.
   Question: Did Tom **evaluate** the nutritional values of the different food groups? Yes or No? Why or why not?

3. Explain how your English teacher **evaluates** written assignments.

41

- Ask: "What does the principal do about the computers?"
- Direct students to use the word **evaluates** in their answer with this sentence stem:

  The principal **evaluates** _____ [the use of classroom computers].
- Have students answer to their partners.

D Checking for Understanding
(*Student Book* pages 41 and 42)

◆ Students chorally read example sentences with the teacher.
◆ Student partners answer scripted "Yes or No" questions with oral or written responses.

- Tell students that it is important to understand the meaning of an academic word when it is used in different forms.
- Explain to students that they will think, say, or write a response to sentences and explain the responses to their partners (e.g., say, "Partner 2s, read and respond to the first sentence. Partner 1s, tell your partner if you agree or disagree").
- Ask the class to chorally read the first sentence with you:
  1. Roberto considered the advantages and disadvantages of the automobile in relation to family life.
- Ask: "Did Roberto **evaluate** the effects of the automobile on family life?" (Answer: Yes)
- Direct students to respond to their partners by saying "yes" or "no" and explaining the reasons for their response.
  Note: While students are responding, monitor their exchanges. Ask two or three students to share their responses with the class.
- Ask the class to chorally read the second sentence with you:
  2. Tom stated the names of the main food groups.
- Ask: "Did Tom **evaluate** the nutritional values of the different food groups?" (Answer: No)
- Direct students to respond to their partners by saying "yes" or "no" and explaining the reasons for their response.
  Note: While students are responding, monitor their exchanges. Ask two or three students to share their responses with the class.
- Ask the class to chorally read the third sentence with you:
  3. Explain how your English teacher **evaluates** written assignments.
- Direct partners to think, write, and share their answers with the class. (A suggested sentence stem: My English teacher **evaluates** _____.)
- Ask the class to chorally read the fourth sentence with you:
  4. What is your **evaluation** of the last television program you watched?
- Direct partners to think, write, and share their answers with the class. (A suggested sentence stem: My **evaluation** of the last television show I watched _____.)

E) Vocabulary Words Table

(*Student Book* page 42)

> ◆ Students add the academic word, an explanation of the word, and a usage example to the unit Vocabulary Words Table.

- Direct students to the *Unit 2 Vocabulary Words Table* on page 53 in the *Student Book*.
- Tell students to copy the explanation of the word **evaluate** from this lesson or to write their own explanation of **evaluate** in the second column.
- Then, direct students to write their own sentence, write another explanation, or draw a picture to represent the word **evaluate** in the last column.

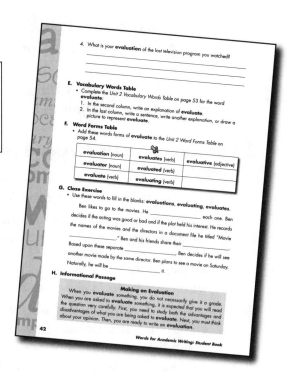

Sample Answers

Word	Explanation	Sentence/Explanation/Picture
evaluate	To give an opinion of worth or value	The teacher will **evaluate** Juana's essay.

F) Word Forms Table

(*Student Book* page 42)

> ◆ Students add forms of the academic word to the unit Word Forms Table.

- Tell students that once a word is known, it is easy to learn other forms of the word. Adding a prefix or a suffix to a word makes a new but related word. Word forms have similar spellings, pronunciations, and meanings. They are often different parts of speech.
- Say: "It is important to understand the parts of speech: *nouns*, *verbs*, *adjectives*, and *adverbs*. We all know that a noun is a word that represents a person, place, thing, or idea. In school assignments, *nouns* are words that tell you what you are asked to make for an assignment or a test. A verb is a word that represents an action, an experience, or a state. In school assignments and tests, *verbs* are words that tell you what you are to do for the assignment. An adjective is a word that describes a noun or a pronoun. In school assignments, *adjectives* usually give other information about the assignment. An adverb is a word that adds meaning to a verb, an adjective, another adverb, or a sentence. In school assignments, *adverbs* tell you how you should do the assignment."
- Direct students to the *Unit 2 Word Forms Table* on page 54 in the *Student Book*.

- Instruct students to add these word forms of **evaluate** to the table: **evaluation** (n), **evaluator** (n), **evaluate** (v), **evaluates** (v), **evaluated** (v), **evaluating** (v), **evaluative** (adj).

Answer Key

NOUNS What you make or create	VERBS What you have to do for the assignment	ADJECTIVES Specific details about what you must do	ADVERBS Important information about how to do the assignment
evaluation	evaluate	evaluative	
evaluator	evaluates		
	evaluated		
	evaluating		

G Cloze Exercise
(*Student Book* page 42)

◆ Students use word forms to complete a cloze exercise.

- Direct students to use the words **evaluations**, **evaluating**, and **evaluates** to complete this cloze exercise with their partners. Provide sufficient time for them to do so.
- Then, ask students to follow along as you read to determine if their answers to the cloze exercise are correct.

Ben likes to go to the movies. He **evaluates** each one. Ben decides if the acting was good or bad and if the plot held his interest. He records the names of the movies and the directors in a document file he titled "Movie **Evaluations**." Ben and his friends share their **evaluations**. Based upon these separate **evaluations**, Ben decides if he will see another movie made by the same director. Ben plans to see a movie on Saturday. Naturally, he will be **evaluating** it.

H Informational Passage
(*Student Book* pages 42 and 43)

◆ Students chorally read the informational passage with the teacher.
◆ Students then read the passage with their partners.

- Say: "This informational passage is designed to provide you with strategies for using the word **justify** in writing assignments."
- Ask students to read this passage chorally with you and then with their partners.

Note: You may want to make copies of the Venn diagram graphic organizer (Graph A-2) and the T-Chart graphic organizer (Graph A-3) on the accompanying CD-ROM for students to refer to.

Making an Evaluation

When you **evaluate** something, you do not necessarily give it a grade. When you are asked to **evaluate** something, it is expected that you will read the question very carefully. First, you need to study both the advantages and disadvantages of what you are being asked to **evaluate**. Next, you must think about your opinion. Then, you are ready to write an **evaluation**.

Before you begin to write your **evaluation**, read the question again. Underline the words in the question that indicate what you are expected to **evaluate**. Then use a T-Chart graphic organizer to list the topic's pluses and minuses. You may also want to use a Venn diagram graphic organizer to compare your subject to something else.

Begin your **evaluation** by rephrasing the question. A long introduction is not required. Get to the point quickly, and include the key point of the question in your first sentence. This will define your **evaluation** and help to keep you on the topic. Then, use your lists to write well-organized paragraphs. Be specific. Write in complete sentences. Finally, complete your **evaluation** with a brief summary statement.

Ⓘ Framed Paragraph and Sentence Stems

(*Student Book* page 43)

(Optional, to be used in conjunction with items J and K, following.)

Note: This section may be used to support struggling students. A framed paragraph is a tool to assist students in writing a paragraph. The paragraph frame provides a sample topic sentence, transitional sentence stems, and a conclusion sentence.

- Tell students that a framed paragraph is a tool to assist them in writing a paragraph.
- Read the topic sentence and the first transitional sentence stem with students.
- Stop reading after the first transitional sentence stem and assist students in completing the sentence in the context of the framed paragraph.
- Continue reading each sentence stem, stopping after each one to assist students in completing the stems.
- Once the paragraph frame is completed, direct students to read the entire paragraph to their partners.

Sample Completed Framed Paragraph

Easy Does It

Fast-food hamburgers and French fries make up a very popular meal that can be **evaluated**. Although fast-food hamburgers <u>are made of meat and served on a warm bun, they are packed with calories</u>. Also, French fries <u>may be delicious, but they are fried in trans fat oil</u>. <u>This kind of oil contains bad cholesterol, which can cause heart problems</u>. In addition, <u>many people have more than one hamburger and sometimes eat a couple of orders of fries</u>! In conclusion, while fast-food hamburgers and French fries are popular, they probably are not the best foods to eat every day.

Topic sentence:	Fast-food hamburgers and French fries make up a very popular meal that can be **evaluated**.
First transitional sentence stem:	Although fast-food hamburgers _____.
Second transitional sentence stem:	Also, French fries _____.
Third transitional sentence stem:	In addition, _____,
Conclusion sentence:	In conclusion, while fast-food hamburgers and French fries are popular, they probably are not the best foods to eat every day.

J Paragraph Starters

(*Student Book* page 44)

- To reinforce understanding of the word **evaluate**, we suggest three related paragraph topics and topic sentences. You can assign these activities as independent practice, partner practice, or homework.

  1. **Paragraph topic: Evaluate** student behavior on the school bus.
     Topic sentence: An **evaluation** of student behavior on the school bus reveals that while most students follow the rules, others _____.
     - Ask students to think about both appropriate and inappropriate student behavior on school buses.

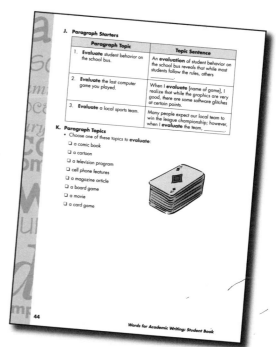

2. **Paragraph topic: Evaluate** the last computer game you played.
   Topic sentence: When I **evaluate** [name of game], I realize that while the graphics are very good, there are some software glitches at certain points.
   - Ask students to think about what they like best and least about the last computer game they played.
3. **Paragraph topic: Evaluate** a local sports team.
   Topic sentence: Many people expect our local team to win the league championship; however, when I **evaluate** the team, _____.
   - Ask students to think about their favorite sports team. Why do they like this sport? Why do they like this team? What could make the team better?

K Paragraph Topics
(*Student Book* page 44)

- We suggest additional writing topics of general knowledge that appeal to a diverse student population. Assign these topics for additional practice in applying the academic word **evaluate** to students' writing.

  ❏ a comic book

  ❏ a cartoon

  ❏ a television program

  ❏ cell phone features

  ❏ a magazine article

  ❏ a board game

  ❏ a movie

  ❏ a card game

illustrate

Students will:

1. Correctly pronounce the word **illustrate**.
2. Define the word **illustrate** in an academic context.
3. Identify examples and non-examples of the word **illustrate**.
4. Use the word **illustrate** and its word forms in an academic context as evidenced by completion of a cloze exercise.
5. Write a paragraph that appropriately **illustrates** an event or a situation.

A Introduction and Pronunciation
(*Student Book* page 45)

• Tell students the word: "This word is **illustrate**."
• Say the word in parts.
• Ask students to repeat the word in parts and then the whole word.

B Explanation
(*Student Book* page 45)

• Say: "**Illustrate** means *to create a mental picture by clearly explaining or giving examples.*"
• Ask students to repeat the explanation.
• Direct Partner 1s to give the explanation to Partner 2s.
• Direct Partner 2s to tell Partner 1s if their explanation was correct.

C Example Sentences
(*Student Book* page 45)

◆ Students chorally read example sentences with the teacher.
◆ Student partners answer scripted questions with provided sentence stems.

• Ask the class to chorally read the first sentence with you:
   1. In his report, Miguel will **illustrate** how germs travel.
• Ask: "What will Miguel do in his report?"
• Direct students to use the word **illustrate** in their answer with this sentence stem:
   Miguel will **illustrate** _____ [how germs travel].
• Have students answer to their partners.
• Ask the class to chorally read the second sentence with you:
   2. The book **illustrates** the use of ship cannons in the Revolutionary War.

- Ask: "What does the book do?"
- Direct students to use the word **illustrates** in their answer with this sentence stem:

  The book **illustrates** _____ [the use of ship cannons in the Revolutionary War].
- Have students answer to their partners.

D Checking for Understanding
(*Student Book* pages 45 and 46)

> ◆ Students chorally read example sentences with the teacher.
> ◆ Student partners answer scripted "Yes or No" questions with oral or written responses.

- Tell students that it is important to understand the meaning of an academic word when it is used in different forms.
- Explain to students that they will think, say, or write a response to sentences and explain the responses to their partners (e.g., say, "Partner 2s, read and respond to the first sentence. Partner 1s, tell your partner if you agree or disagree").
- Ask the class to chorally read the first sentence with you:
  1. The vice principal talked about the dress code and described examples of clothing that would be considered acceptable.
- Ask: "Did the vice principal **illustrate** the dress code?" (Answer: Yes)
- Direct students to respond to their partners by saying "yes" or "no" and explaining the reasons for their response.
  Note: While students are responding, monitor their exchanges. Ask two or three students to share their responses with the class.
- Ask the class to chorally read the second sentence with you:
  2. Chris talked about the time it took to drive from Johnson City to Dallas.
- Ask: "Did Chris **illustrate** road conditions?" (Answer: No)
- Direct students to respond to their partners by saying "yes" or "no" and explaining the reasons for their response.
  Note: While students are responding, monitor their exchanges. Ask two or three students to share their responses with the class.
- Ask the class to chorally read the third sentence with you:
  3. Tell me a story that will **illustrate** the importance of being honest.
- Direct partners to think, write, and share their answers with the class. (A suggested sentence stem: I could **illustrate** the importance of being honest with a story about _____.)
- Ask the class to chorally read the fourth sentence with you:
  4. Use words to **illustrate** what you ate for dinner last night.
- Direct partners to think, write, and share their answers with the class. (A suggested sentence stem: I had the best [worst] dinner last night. The food was _____.)

E Vocabulary Words Table

(*Student Book* page 46)

> ◆ Students add the academic word, an explanation of the word, and a usage example to the unit Vocabulary Words Table.

- Direct students to the *Unit 2 Vocabulary Words Table* on page 53 in the *Student Book*.
- Tell students to copy the explanation of the word **illustrate** from this lesson or to write their own explanation of **illustrate** in the second column.
- Then, direct students to write their own sentence, write another explanation, or draw a picture to represent the word **illustrate** in the last column.

Sample Answers

Word	Explanation	Sentence/Explanation/Picture
illustrate	To create a mental picture by clearly explaining or giving examples	Using only words, Karen was able to **illustrate** the importance of landscape care.

F Word Forms Table

(*Student Book* page 46)

> ◆ Students add forms of the academic word to the unit Word Forms Table.

- Tell students that once a word is known, it is easy to learn other forms of the word. Adding a prefix or a suffix to a word makes a new but related word. Word forms have similar spellings, pronunciations, and meanings. They are often different parts of speech.
- Say: "It is important to understand the parts of speech: *nouns, verbs, adjectives,* and *adverbs.* We all know that a noun is a word that represents a person, place, thing, or idea. In school assignments, *nouns* are words that tell you <u>what you are asked to make</u> for an assignment or a test. A verb is a word that represents an action, an experience, or a state. In school assignments and tests, *verbs* are words that tell you <u>what you are to do</u> for the assignment. An adjective is a word that describes a noun or a pronoun. In school assignments, *adjectives* usually give <u>other information</u> about the assignment. An adverb is a word that adds meaning to a verb, an adjective, another adverb, or a sentence. In school assignments, *adverbs* tell you <u>how you should do</u> the assignment."
- Direct students to the *Unit 2 Word Forms Table* on page 54 in the *Student Book*.

- Instruct students to add these word forms of **illustrate** to the table:
  illustration (n), **illustrate** (v), **illustrates** (v), **illustrated** (v),
  illustrating (v), **illustrative** (adj).

Answer Key

NOUNS What you make or create	VERBS What you have to do for the assignment	ADJECTIVES Specific details about what you must do	ADVERBS Important information about how to do the assignment
illustration	illustrate	illustrative	
	illustrates		
	illustrated		
	illustrating		

G Cloze Exercise
(*Student Book* page 46)

> ◆ Students use word forms to complete a cloze exercise.

- Direct students to use the words **illustrate**, **illustrates**, and **illustrations** to complete this cloze exercise with their partners. Provide sufficient time for them to do so.
- Then, ask students to follow along as you read to determine if their answers to the cloze exercise are correct.

> Mr. Mansfield is a good history teacher because he **illustrates** points that he wants to make clear. He describes many details about people and events. Because Mr. Mansfield chooses to **illustrate** historical events, students are able to make mental pictures. Students say that his **illustrations** help to clarify historical times and events. Some students say that when Mr. Mansfield makes **illustrations**, they feel like they have been carried back in time. Mr. Mansfield uses words and details to **illustrate** historical events.

H Informational Passage
(*Student Book* pages 46 and 47)

> ◆ Students chorally read the informational passage with the teacher.
> ◆ Students then read the passage with their partners.

- Say: "This informational passage is designed to provide you with strategies for using the word **illustrate** in writing assignments."
- Ask students to read this passage chorally with you and then with their partners.

Note: You may want to make copies of the Chain graphic organizer (Graph A-5 on the accompanying CD-ROM) for students to refer to.

Illustrate: Use Words to Create a Picture

An assignment direction or essay question may include the word **illustrate**. Students sometimes wonder if teachers want them to simply draw a picture. Sometimes, this is true. However, teachers usually want students to use very descriptive words in their answer. Teachers usually ask students to **illustrate** in order to check understanding of a term or concept. In an assignment direction, the word **illustrate** means to present the main points with clear examples. Some teachers may also want a simple diagram or a chart; however, this is usually only one part of the assignment.

If you find the word **illustrate** in a question, you should reread the question and/or directions very carefully. Pay close attention to the key words. You may find it helpful to circle or underline those words. This will help you to clarify your thinking. Decide exactly what the teacher wants you to **illustrate**. Take a few minutes to make a Chain graphic organizer and briefly jot down everything you know about the topic. Organize the facts that you will **illustrate** in a logical order. Begin the first sentence by rephrasing the question. It is important to repeat many of the words found in the assignment direction.

I **Framed Paragraph and Sentence Stems**

(*Student Book* page 47)

(Optional, to be used in conjunction with items J and K, following.)

Note: This section may be used to support struggling students. A framed paragraph is a tool to assist students in writing a paragraph. The paragraph frame provides a sample topic sentence, transitional sentence stems, and a conclusion sentence.

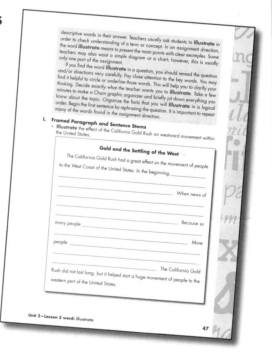

- Tell students that a framed paragraph is a tool to assist them in writing a paragraph.
- Read the topic sentence and the first transitional sentence stem with students.
- Stop reading after the first transitional sentence stem and assist students in completing the sentence in the context of the framed paragraph.
- Continue reading each sentence stem, stopping after each one to assist students in completing the stems.
- Once the paragraph frame is completed, direct students to read the entire paragraph to their partners.

Gold and the Settling of the West

The California Gold Rush had a great effect on the movement of people to the West Coast of the United States. In the beginning, <u>men came to California to search for gold</u>. When news of <u>a warm climate and good soil reached those in the East, many families decided to pack everything into covered wagons and move west</u>. Because so many people <u>wanted to go west, railroads were built to make travel easier</u>. More people <u>decided to travel by train for vacations, but when they saw the opportunities and good weather, they also decided to move west</u>. The California Gold Rush did not last long, but it helped start a huge movement of people to the western part of the United States.

Topic sentence:	The California Gold Rush had a great effect on the movement of people to the West Coast of the United States.
First transitional sentence stem:	In the beginning, _____.
Second transitional sentence stem:	When news of _____.
Third transitional sentence stem:	Because so many people _____.
Fourth transitional sentence stem:	More people _____.
Conclusion sentence:	The California Gold Rush did not last long, but it helped start a huge movement of people to the western part of the United States.

J Paragraph Starters

(*Student Book* page 48)

- To reinforce understanding of the word **illustrate**, we suggest three related paragraph topics and topic sentences. You can assign these activities as independent practice, partner practice, or homework.

  1. **Paragraph topic: Illustrate** the life cycle of a butterfly.
     Topic sentence: The life cycle of a butterfly can be best **illustrated** by describing the insect's four major life stages.
     - Ask students to think about the life cycle of a butterfly and how they could best illustrate it using descriptive words.

  2. **Paragraph topic: Illustrate** the safest way to cross a busy street.
     Topic sentence: There are several precautions you must take in order to safely cross a busy street.
     - Ask students to think about how to describe safely crossing a busy street.

3. **Paragraph topic: Illustrate** how light and darkness are the result of Earth's rotation.

   Topic sentence: To **illustrate** how light and darkness occur, imagine that Earth is a large ball.

   - Ask students to describe what they know about Earth's rotation and its relation to light and darkness.

K **Paragraph Topics**

(*Student Book* page 48)

- We suggest additional writing topics of general knowledge that appeal to a diverse student population. Assign these topics for additional practice in applying the academic word **illustrate** to students' writing.

  ❏ how to complete a two-place multiplication problem

  ❏ the rain cycle

  ❏ the growth of a flower

  ❏ how to use a microwave oven

  ❏ how to wash dishes

  ❏ how to turn off a computer

  ❏ how to prepare breakfast

  ❏ how to brush your teeth

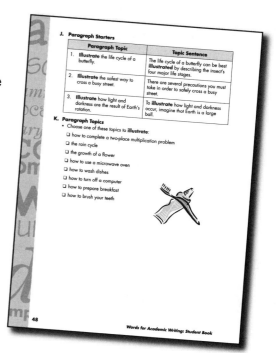

clarify

Students will:

1. Correctly pronounce the word **clarify**.
2. Define the word **clarify** in an academic context.
3. Identify examples and non-examples of the word **clarify**.
4. Use the word **clarify** and its word forms in an academic context as evidenced by completion of a cloze exercise.
5. Write a paragraph that appropriately **clarifies** a point of view, a situation, or an event.

A Introduction and Pronunciation
(*Student Book* page 49)

- Tell students the word: "This word is **clarify**."
- Say the word in parts.
- Ask students to repeat the word in parts and then the whole word.

B Explanation
(*Student Book* page 49)

- Say: "**Clarify** means *to make an idea or statement very clear or easy to understand with examples*."
- Ask the class to repeat the explanation.
- Direct Partner 1s to give the explanation to Partner 2s.
- Direct Partner 2s to tell Partner 1s if their explanation was correct.

C Example Sentences
(*Student Book* page 49)

- ◆ Students chorally read example sentences with the teacher.
- ◆ Student partners answer scripted questions with provided sentence stems.

- Ask the class to chorally read the first sentence with you:
  1. Our teacher will **clarify** the directions for each phase of the lab experiment.
- Ask: "What will your teacher do?"
- Direct students to use the word **clarify** in their answer with this sentence stem: Our teacher will **clarify** _____ [the directions for each phase of the lab experiment].
- Have students answer to their partners.

- Ask the class to chorally read the second sentence with you:
  2. Sarita **clarified** the meaning of friendship by helping Ann when no one else wanted to.
- Ask: "What did Sarita do?"
- Direct students to use the word **clarified** in their answer with this sentence stem:
  Sarita **clarified** _____ [the meaning of friendship].
- Have students answer to their partners.

D Checking for Understanding
(*Student Book* pages 49 and 50)

> ◆ Students chorally read example sentences with the teacher.
> ◆ Student partners answer scripted "Yes or No" questions with oral or written responses.

- Tell students that it is important to understand the meaning of an academic word when it is used in different forms.
- Explain to students that they will think, say, or write a response to sentences and explain the responses to their partners (e.g., say, "Partner 2s, read and respond to the first sentence. Partner 1s, tell your partner if you agree or disagree").
- Ask the class to chorally read the first sentence with you:
  1. Miguel listed and provided specific details about hurricanes, tornados, and earthquakes.
- Ask: "Did Miguel **clarify** the types of natural disasters that often occur in North America?" (Answer: Yes)
- Direct students to respond to their partners by saying "yes" or "no" and explaining the reasons for their response.
  Note: While students are responding, monitor their exchanges. Ask two or three students to share their responses with the class.
- Ask the class to chorally read the second sentence with you:
  2. The computer teacher told Clarissa the names of different types of software.
- Ask: "Did the computer teacher **clarify** safety procedures?" (Answer: No)
- Direct students to respond to their partners by saying "yes" or "no" and explaining the reasons for their response.
  Note: While students are responding, monitor their exchanges. Ask two or three students to share their responses with the class.
- Ask the class to chorally read the third sentence with you:
  3. How does our school **clarify** fire drill procedures?
- Direct partners to think, write, and share their answers with the class. (A suggested sentence stem: At our school, _____.)
- Ask the class to chorally read the fourth sentence with you:
  4. Provide a weather report for tomorrow. **Clarify** your response.
- Direct partners to think, write, and share their answers with the class. (A suggested sentence stem: Tomorrow, the weather _____.)

E Vocabulary Words Table

(Student Book page 50)

> ◆ Students add the academic word, an explanation of the word, and a usage example to the unit Vocabulary Words Table.

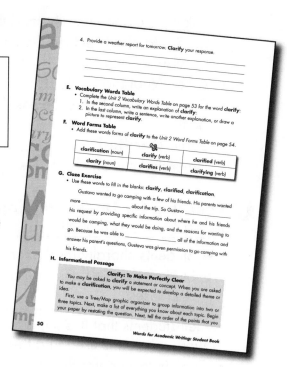

- Direct students to the *Unit 2 Vocabulary Words Table* on page 53 in the *Student Book*.
- Tell students to copy the explanation of the word **clarify** from this lesson or to write their own explanation of **clarify** in the second column.
- Then, direct students to write their own sentence, write another explanation, or draw a picture to represent the word **clarify** in the last column.

Sample Answers

Word	Explanation	Sentence/Explanation/Picture
clarify	To make an idea or statement very clear or easy to understand with examples	Steven will **clarify** his goals for this school year.

F Word Forms Table

(Student Book page 50)

> ◆ Students add forms of the academic word to the unit Word Forms Table.

- Tell students that once a word is known, it is easy to learn other forms of the word. Adding a prefix or a suffix to a word makes a new but related word. Word forms have similar spellings, pronunciations, and meanings. They are often different parts of speech.
- Say: "It is important to understand the parts of speech: *nouns, verbs, adjectives,* and *adverbs*. We all know that a noun is a word that represents a person, place, thing, or idea. In school assignments, *nouns* are words that tell you <u>what you are asked to make</u> for an assignment or a test. A verb is a word that represents an action, an experience, or a state. In school assignments and tests, *verbs* are words that tell you <u>what you are to do</u> for the assignment. An adjective is a word that describes a noun or a pronoun. In school assignments, *adjectives* usually <u>give other information</u> about the assignment. An adverb is a word that adds meaning to a verb, an adjective, another adverb, or a sentence. In school assignments, *adverbs* tell you <u>how you should do</u> the assignment."
- Direct students to the *Unit 2 Word Forms Table* on page 54 in the *Student Book*.

- Instruct students to add these word forms of **clarify** to the table: **clarification** (n), **clarity** (n), **clarify** (v), **clarifies** (v), **clarified** (v), **clarifying** (v).

Answer Key

NOUNS What you make or create	VERBS What you have to do for the assignment	ADJECTIVES Specific details about what you must do	ADVERBS Important information about how to do the assignment
clarification	clarify		
clarity	clarifies		
	clarified		
	clarifying		

G Cloze Exercise
(*Student Book* page 50)

◆ Students use word forms to complete a cloze exercise.

- Direct students to use the words **clarify**, **clarified**, and **clarification** to complete this cloze exercise with their partners. Provide sufficient time for them to do so.
- Then, ask students to follow along as you read to determine if their answers to the cloze exercise are correct.

> Gustavo wanted to go camping with a few of his friends. His parents wanted more __**clarification**__ about the trip. So Gustavo __**clarified**__ his request by providing specific information about where he and his friends would be camping, what they would be doing, and the reasons for wanting to go. Because he was able to __**clarify**__ all of the information and answer his parent's questions, Gustavo was given permission to go camping with his friends.

H Informational Passage
(*Student Book* pages 50 and 51)

◆ Students chorally read the informational passage with the teacher.
◆ Students then read the passage with their partners.

- Say: "This informational passage is designed to provide you with strategies for using the word **clarify** in writing assignments."
- Ask students to read this passage chorally with you and then with their partners.

Note: You may want to make copies of the Tree/Map graphic organizer (Graph A-4) on the accompanying CD-ROM for students to refer to.

Clarify: To Make Perfectly Clear

You may be asked to **clarify** a statement or concept. When you are asked to make a **clarification**, you will be expected to develop a detailed theme or idea.

First, use a Tree/Map graphic organizer to group information into two or three topics. Next, make a list of everything you know about each topic. Begin your paper by restating the question. Next, tell the order of the points that you will **clarify**. Then, use your graphic organizer notes to **clarify** each point. Use examples and facts to support your statements. Take care to tell when or how something happened, or why it is true. Finish your paper by writing a summary.

Remember: when you are asked to make a **clarification**, your teacher expects you to make a statement or concept perfectly clear and understandable by providing supportive details.

1 Framed Paragraph and Sentence Stems

(*Student Book* page 51)

(Optional, to be used in conjunction with items J and K, following.)

Note: This section may be used to support struggling students. A framed paragraph is a tool to assist students in writing a paragraph. The paragraph frame provides a sample topic sentence, transitional sentence stems, and a conclusion sentence.

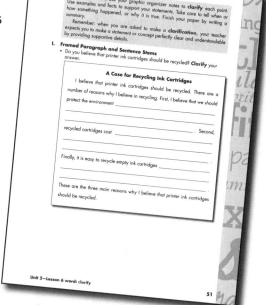

- Tell students that a framed paragraph is a tool to assist them in writing a paragraph.
- Read the topic sentence and the first transitional sentence stem with students.
- Stop reading after the first transitional sentence stem and assist students in completing the sentence in the context of the framed paragraph.
- Continue reading each sentence stem, stopping after each one to assist students in completing the stems.
- Once the paragraph frame is completed, direct students to read the entire paragraph to their partners.

Sample Completed Framed Paragraph

A Case for Recycling Ink Cartridges

I believe that printer ink cartridges should be recycled. There are a number of reasons why I believe in recycling. First, I believe that we should protect the environment <u>from the pollution of toxic elements that are inside ink cartridges</u>. Second, recycled cartridges cost <u>less money than new ones, and they work just as well</u>. Finally, it is easy to recycle empty ink cartridges <u>by taking them back to the store for a partial credit on the cost of a full cartridge</u>. These are the three main reasons why I believe that printer ink cartridges should be recycled.

J Paragraph Starters

(*Student Book* page 52)

- To reinforce understanding of the word **clarify**, we suggest three related paragraph topics and topic sentences. You can assign these activities as independent practice, partner practice, or homework.

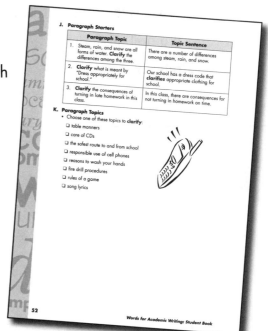

1. **Paragraph topic:** Steam, rain, and snow are all forms of water. **Clarify** the differences among the three.

   Topic sentence: There are a number of differences among steam, rain, and snow.

   - Ask students to think about what controls these different forms of water (e.g., atmospheric temperature, shape of individual water particles, clouds).

2. **Paragraph topic: Clarify** what is meant by "Dress appropriately for school."

   Topic sentence: Our school has a dress code that **clarifies** appropriate clothing for school.

   - Ask students to think about the school dress code and what it means in terms of deciding what clothes to wear to school.

3. **Paragraph topic: Clarify** the consequences of turning in late homework in this class.

   Topic sentence: In this class, there are consequences for not turning in homework on time.

   - Ask students to think about what happens if they are late with turning in homework assignments.

K Paragraph Topics

(*Student Book* page 52)

- We suggest additional writing topics of general knowledge that appeal to a diverse student population. Assign these topics for additional practice in applying the academic word **clarify** to students' writing.

  ❏ table manners

  ❏ care of CDs

  ❏ the safest route to and from school

  ❏ responsible use of cell phones

  ❏ reasons to wash your hands

  ❏ fire drill procedures

  ❏ rules of a game

  ❏ song lyrics

Unit 2 Posttest

Objective	To determine students' understanding of the academic words that were presented in Unit 2
Materials needed	For each student, one copy of the Unit 2 Posttest (refer to the accompanying CD-ROM) and two sheets of blank paper
Time allotment	35 minutes (Part A, 10 minutes; Part B, 10 minutes; Part C, 15 minutes)

Instructional Procedure

Step 1 Distribute Unit 2 Posttest and two sheets of blank paper to each student. Say:
- "Write your name and today's date on the lines at the top of the Posttest and at the top of each sheet of blank paper. I will collect all of them after you have finished the posttest."

Step 2 Review the directions for the Unit 2 Posttest, then administer the posttest. Say:
- "Only this Posttest score will be recorded as part of your grade. So do your very best."
- "Look at Part A. Let's read the directions together." *(Read directions out loud with students.)*
- "Place your finger on each word as I read it: **define**, **outline**, **justify**, **evaluate**, **illustrate**, **clarify**."
- "Now, place your finger on each lowercase letter next to the explanations in the right-hand column. Listen as I read the explanation for each letter."
    - **a.** To write main points in an order using only headings and subheadings, not details
    - **b.** To give an opinion of worth or value
    - **c.** To make an idea or statement very clear or easy to understand with examples
    - **d.** To show or tell what something is or means
    - **e.** To prove or show why something is right or acceptable
    - **f.** To create a mental picture by clearly explaining or giving examples
- "Match each word with the explanation that you think is correct. Write the letter of the explanation in the middle column, next to the word."
- "You will have 10 minutes to complete Part A. Ready? Begin." *(After 10 minutes, proceed to Part B.)*
- "Now, look at Part B. It is important to know how to use academic words within the context of print."
- "Read each sentence and fill in the blank with one of the words listed in the directions."

- "You will have 10 minutes to complete Part B. Any questions? Begin." *(After 10 minutes, proceed to Part C.)*
- "Now, read the directions for Part C. Remember to make a graphic organizer on one sheet of paper to plan your answer. Then write a paragraph using a topic sentence, transitional sentences, and a conclusion sentence on the other sheet of paper. You can receive up to 15 points for this section: 5 points for the graphic organizer, 5 points for using a paragraph format, and 5 points for content."
- "You will have 15 minutes to complete Part C. Any questions? Begin." *(After 10 minutes, tell students they have 5 minutes to finish.)*
- After 5 minutes pass, say, "Please turn in your tests and papers to me."

Refer to *Appendix D* for Unit 2 Posttest Answer Key

Unit 2 Generative Assessment (optional)

Objective	To ensure that students are able to correctly apply Unit 2 academic words in a generalized setting
Materials needed	For each student, one copy of the Unit 2 Generative Assessment (refer to the accompanying CD-ROM) and two sheets of blank paper
Time allotment	One class period

Instructional Procedure

Step 1   Distribute Unit 2 Generative Assessment and two sheets of blank paper to each student. Say:
- "Write your name and today's date on the lines at the top of the assessment and at the top of each sheet of blank paper. I will collect all of them after you have finished the assessment."

Step 2   Review the directions for the Unit 2 Generative Assessment, then administer the assessment. Say:
- "This assessment is designed to find out how well you are able to apply the Unit 2 academic words to general situations. This assessment will ask you to demonstrate your understanding of the Unit 2 words by providing examples based on your personal knowledge and experiences."
- "Read each direction, and then use the blank paper to create your own graphic organizer to plan your answer."
- "Then, use your graphic organizer to help you write a short paragraph using a topic sentence, transitional sentences, and a conclusion sentence."
- "You can receive up to 15 points for each answer: 5 points for your graphic organizer, 5 points for using a paragraph format, and 5 points for content. You will have the whole class period to complete this assessment."
- "Any questions? When you have finished, please turn in your assessment and graphic organizers to me. Begin."

Grading Criteria

To grade a Generative Assessment, we suggest allocating a maximum of 15 points *per assessment item* as follows:
- Up to 5 points for use of a graphic organizer
- Up to 5 points for conventions (correct paragraphing; use of topic, transitional, and conclusion sentences; correct punctuation; correct spelling)
- Up to 5 points for content

Objective	To determine students' prior knowledge of academic words that will be taught in Unit 3
Materials needed	For each student, one copy of the Unit 3 Pretest (refer to the accompanying CD-ROM)
Time allotment	20 minutes (Part A, 10 minutes; Part B, 10 minutes)

Instructional Procedure

Step 1   Distribute Unit 3 Pretest to students. Say:
- "Write your name and today's date on the lines at the top of the Pretest."

Step 2   Review the directions for Unit 3 Pretest, then administer the pretest. Say:
- "Look at Part A. Let's read the directions together."
  (Read the directions out loud with students.)
- "Place your finger on each word as I read it: **review**, **differentiate**, **interpret**, **trace**, **list**, **prove**."
- "Now, place your finger on each lowercase letter next to the explanations in the right-hand column. Listen as I read the explanation for each letter."
  - **a.** To follow something back to its beginning
  - **b.** To write a set of information, one item per line
  - **c.** To personally decide the meaning of something
  - **d.** To show or state the difference(s) between two or more people, ideas, or things
  - **e.** To carefully examine and judge the main parts of something
  - **f.** To show that something is true
- "Match each word with the explanation that you think is correct. Write the letter of the explanation in the middle column, next to the word."
- "You will have 10 minutes to complete Part A. Ready? Begin."
  (After 10 minutes, proceed to Part B.)
- "Now, look at Part B. It is important to know how to use academic words within the context of print."
- "Read each of the six sentences. Then, refer back to the table in Part A. Use the words in the first column to fill in the blanks of the sentences."
- "You will have 10 minutes to complete Part B. Any questions? Begin."
- After 10 minutes, say, "Please return your tests to me."

> Refer to *Appendix D* for Unit 3 Pretest Answer Key

review

Students will:

1. Correctly pronounce the word **review**.
2. Define the word **review** in an academic context.
3. Identify examples and non-examples of the word **review**.
4. Use the word **review** and its word forms in an academic context as evidenced by completion of a cloze exercise.
5. Write a paragraph that appropriately **reviews** an event, a product, or a situation.

A Introduction and Pronunciation
(*Student Book* page 57)

- Tell students the word: "This word is **review**."
- Say the word in parts.
- Ask students to repeat the word in parts and then the whole word.

B Explanation
(*Student Book* page 57)

- Say: "**Review** means *to carefully examine and judge the main parts of something.*"
- Ask students to repeat the explanation.
- Direct Partner 1s to give the explanation to Partner 2s.
- Direct Partner 2s to tell Partner 1s if their explanation was correct.

Unit 3 Lesson 1 **review**

A. **Introduction and Pronunciation**
  • This word is **review**.
  • Say the word in parts and then the whole word

B. **Explanation**
  • **Review** means *to carefully examine and judge the main parts of something.*

C. **Example Sentences**
  1. Before the fire drill, we will **review** safety procedures.
  2. Our assignment is to read a historical novel and then write a **review** of it.

D. **Checking for Understanding**
  1. The study group examined and made a judgment about the events that led to the Boston Tea Party.
     Question: Did the group **review** the events that brought about the Boston Tea Party? Yes or No? Why or why not?

  2. Tom was asked to list all of the planets in Earth's solar system.
     Question: Was Tom expected to complete a **review** of Earth's planets? Yes or No? Why or why not?

  3. **Review** the advantages and disadvantages of attending summer school.

57

C Example Sentences
(*Student Book* page 57)

> ◆ Students chorally read example sentences with the teacher.
> ◆ Student partners answer scripted questions with provided sentence stems.

- Ask the class to chorally read the first sentence with you:
  1. Before the fire drill, we will **review** safety procedures.
- Ask: "When we examine and judge safety procedures for a fire drill, what are we doing?"
- Direct students to use the word **reviewing** in their answer with this sentence stem:
  We are **reviewing** _____ [safety procedures].
- Have students answer to their partners.

- Ask the class to chorally read the second sentence with you:

  2. Our assignment is to read a historical novel and then write a **review** of it.
- Ask: "When students examine a historical novel and then make judgments about it, what are they doing?"
- Direct students to use the word **reviewing** in their answer with this sentence stem:

  Students are **reviewing** _____ [the historical novel].
- Have students answer to their partners.

D Checking for Understanding
(*Student Book* pages 57 and 58)

> ◆ Students chorally read example sentences with the teacher.
> ◆ Student partners answer scripted "Yes or No" questions with oral or written responses.

- Tell students that it is important to understand the meaning of an academic word when it is used in different forms.
- Explain to students that they will think, say, or write a response to sentences and explain the responses to their partners (e.g., say, "Partner 2s, read and respond to the first sentence. Partner 1s, tell your partner if you agree or disagree").
- Ask the class to chorally read the first sentence with you:

  1. The study group examined and made a judgment about the events that led to the Boston Tea Party.
- Ask: "Did the group **review** the events that brought about the Boston Tea Party?" (Answer: Yes)
- Direct students to respond to their partners by saying "yes" or "no" and explaining the reasons for their response.
  Note: While students are responding, monitor their exchanges. Ask two or three students to share their responses with the class.
- Ask the class to chorally read the second sentence with you:

  2. Tom was asked to list all of the planets in Earth's solar system.
- Ask: "Was Tom expected to complete a **review** of Earth's planets?" (Answer: No)
- Direct students to respond to their partners by saying "yes" or "no" and explaining the reasons for their response.
  Note: While students are responding, monitor their exchanges. Ask two or three students to share their responses with the class.
- Ask the class to chorally read the third sentence with you:

  3. Review the advantages and disadvantages of attending summer school.
- Direct partners to think, write, and share their answers with the class. (A suggested sentence stem: When I **review** the advantages and disadvantages of attending summer school, I think _____.)
- Ask the class to chorally read the fourth sentence with you:

  4. Tell about a book you **reviewed** for a class.
- Direct partners to think, write, and share their answers with the class. (A suggested sentence stem: I once **reviewed** [book title] _____.)

E Vocabulary Words Table

(*Student Book* page 58)

◆ Students add the academic word, an explanation of the word, and a usage example to the unit Vocabulary Words Table.

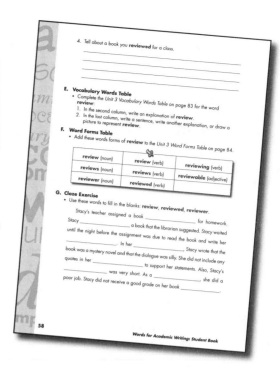

- Direct students to the *Unit 3 Vocabulary Words Table* on page 83 in the *Student Book*.

- Tell students to copy the explanation of the word **review** from this lesson or to write their own explanation of **review** in the second column.

- Then, direct students to write their own sentence, write another explanation, or draw a picture to represent the word **review** in the last column.

Sample Answers

Word	Explanation	Sentence/Explanation/Picture
review	To carefully examine and judge the main parts of something	Brent will read a short story and then write a **review** of it.

F Word Forms Table

(*Student Book* page 58)

◆ Students add forms of the academic word to the unit Word Forms Table.

- Tell students that once a word is known, it is easy to learn other forms of the word. Adding a prefix or a suffix to a word makes a new but related word. Word forms have similar spellings, pronunciations, and meanings. They are often different parts of speech.

- Say: "It is important to understand the parts of speech: *nouns, verbs, adjectives,* and *adverbs*. We all know that a noun is a word that represents a person, place, thing, or idea. In school assignments, *nouns* are words that tell you <u>what you are asked to make</u> for an assignment or a test. A verb is a word that represents an action, an experience, or a state. In school assignments and tests, *verbs* are words that tell you <u>what you are to do</u> for the assignment. An adjective is a word that describes a noun or a pronoun. In school assignments, *adjectives* usually <u>give other information</u> about the assignment. An adverb is a word that adds meaning to a verb, an adjective, another adverb, or a sentence. In school assignments, *adverbs* tell you <u>how you should do</u> the assignment."

- Direct students to the *Unit 3 Word Forms Table* on page 84 in the *Student Book*.

- Direct students to add these word forms of **review** to the table: **review** (n), **reviews** (n), **reviewer** (n), **review** (v), **reviews** (v), **reviewed** (v), **reviewing** (v), **reviewable** (adj).

Answer Key

NOUNS What you make or create	VERBS What you have to do for the assignment	ADJECTIVES Specific details about what you must do	ADVERBS Important information about how to do the assignment
review	review	reviewable	
reviews	reviews		
reviewer	reviewed		
	reviewing		

G Cloze Exercise
(*Student Book* page 58)

> ◆ Students use word forms to complete a cloze exercise.

- Direct students to use the words **review**, **reviewed**, and **reviewer** to complete this cloze exercise with their partners. Provide sufficient time for them to do so.
- Then, ask students to follow along as you read to determine if their answers to the cloze exercise are correct.

> Stacy's teacher assigned a book **review** for homework. Stacy **reviewed** a book that the librarian suggested. Stacy waited until the night before the assignment was due to read the book and write her **review**. In her **review**, Stacy wrote that the book was a mystery novel and that the dialogue was silly. She did not include any quotes in her **review** to support her statements. Also, Stacy's **review** was very short. As a **reviewer**, she did a poor job. Stacy did not receive a good grade on her book **review**.

H Informational Passage
(*Student Book* page 59)

> ◆ Students chorally read the informational passage with the teacher.
> ◆ Students then read the passage with their partners.

- Say: "This informational passage is designed to provide you with strategies for using the word **review** in writing assignments."
- Ask students to read the passage chorally with you and then with their partners. *Note: You may want to make copies of the Outline graphic organizer (Graph A-6 on the accompanying CD-ROM) for students to refer to.*

Words for Academic Writing: Teacher Guide

A Book Review

A book **review** describes the contents of a book and presents an opinion about how the book was written. A book **review** is usually about two or three pages long. Book **reviews** are often organized in a particular format. Use an Outline graphic organizer to record your notes.

First, present bibliographical information. This kind of information consists of the name of the author, the title of the book, and publishing information. Second, write a general summary that explains what the book is about. Third, state why you think the author wrote the book. Ask yourself questions like "What point is the author trying to make?" and "What information does the author present to make the point?" Fourth, identify at least two of the book's strengths and/or weaknesses. You may want to focus on the style of writing, the arguments that the author presents, or the sources of information the author uses. Also, use book quotations to support your points.

At the end of the book **review**, explain how you believe the author could fix the book's weaknesses or improve the book. Finally, indicate who you think would benefit from reading the book.

I. Framed Paragraph and Sentence Stems
(*Student Book* pages 59 and 60)

(Optional, to be used in conjunction with items J and K, following.)

Note: This section may be used to support struggling students. A framed paragraph is a tool to assist students in writing a paragraph. The paragraph frame provides a sample topic sentence, transitional sentence stems, and a conclusion sentence.

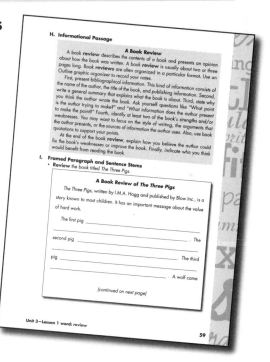

- Tell students that a framed paragraph is a tool to assist them in writing a paragraph.
- Read the topic sentences and the first transitional sentence stem with students.
- Stop reading after the first transitional sentence stem and assist students in completing the sentence in the context of the framed paragraph.
- Continue reading each sentence stem, stopping after each one to assist students in completing the stems.
- Once the paragraph frame is completed, direct students to read all paragraphs to their partners.

A Book Review of *The Three Pigs*

The Three Pigs, written by I.M.A. Hogg and published by Blow Inc., is a story known to most children. It has an important message about the value of hard work.

The first pig <u>built a house made with hay</u>. The second pig <u>built a house using sticks</u>. The third pig <u>worked hard and spent a lot of time building a house with bricks</u>. A wolf came along and <u>blew down the house made of hay and the house made of sticks. But the wolf could not blow down the brick house</u>.

Mr. Hogg wrote the book to illustrate the benefits of hard work. However, I see a problem with the writing. Some people do not understand <u>the message in the story</u>. The author could fix this problem by <u>more clearly pointing out that the first two pigs selected the easiest and fastest way to build their houses, while the third pig did not. He worked very hard using stronger and heavier building materials. If children could easily understand the message of the story, they would benefit from reading this book</u>.

The story of *The Three Pigs* is not only a favorite children's story but also has a good message about the rewards that hard work can bring.

Topic sentences:	*The Three Pigs*, written by I.M.A. Hogg and published by Blow Inc., is a story known to most children. It has an important message about the value of hard work.
First transitional sentence stem:	The first pig _____.
Second transitional sentence stem:	The second pig _____.
Third transitional sentence stem:	The third pig _____.
Fourth transitional sentence stem:	A wolf came along and _____.
Fifth transitional sentence stem:	Mr. Hogg wrote the book to illustrate the benefits of hard work. However, I see a problem with the writing. Some people do not understand _____.
Sixth transitional sentence stem:	The author could fix this problem by _____.
Conclusion sentence:	The story of *The Three Pigs* is not only a favorite children's story but also has a good message about the rewards that hard work can bring.

J Paragraph Starters

(*Student Book* page 60)

* To reinforce understanding of the word **review**, we suggest three related paragraph topics and topic sentences. You can assign these activities as independent practice, partner practice, or homework.

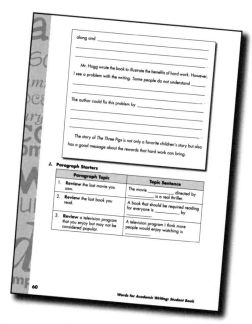

1. **Paragraph topic: Review** the last movie you saw.

   Topic sentence: The movie _____, directed by _____, is a real thriller.

   * Ask students to think about what they liked most and least about the last movie they saw. How could it have been better?

2. **Paragraph topic: Review** the last book you read.

   Topic sentence: A book that should be required reading for everyone is _____ by _____.

   * Ask students to reflect on the last book they read. What was the author's message or purpose for writing the book?

3. **Paragraph topic: Review** a television program that you enjoy but may not be considered popular.

   Topic sentence: A television program I think more people would enjoy watching is _____.

   * Ask students to think about a television program they enjoy but is not considered popular. What do they think is interesting about the series? What is it about the show that other people would enjoy if they only watched it, too?

K. Paragraph Topics

(*Student Book* page 61)

* We suggest additional writing topics of general knowledge that appeal to a diverse student population. Assign these topics for additional practice in applying the academic word **review** to students' writing.

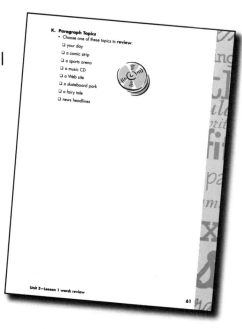

* ❏ your day
* ❏ a comic strip
* ❏ a sports arena
* ❏ a music CD
* ❏ a Web site
* ❏ a skateboard park
* ❏ a fairy tale
* ❏ news headlines

Students will:

1. Correctly pronounce the word **differentiate**.
2. Define the word **differentiate** in an academic context.
3. Identify examples and non-examples of the word **differentiate**.
4. Use the word **differentiate** and its word forms in an academic context as evidenced by completion of a cloze exercise.
5. Write a paragraph that appropriately **differentiates** people, items, events, or situations.

A Introduction and Pronunciation

(*Student Book* page 62)

- Tell students the word: "This word is **differentiate**."
- Say the word in parts.
- Ask students to repeat the word in parts and then the whole word.

B Explanation

(*Student Book* page 62)

- Say: "**Differentiate** means *to show or state the difference(s) between two or more people, ideas, or things.*"
- Ask the class to repeat the explanation.
- Direct Partner 1s to say the explanation to Partner 2s.
- Direct Partner 2s to tell Partner 1s if their explanation was correct.

C Example Sentences

(*Student Book* page 62)

> ◆ Students chorally read example sentences with the teacher.
> ◆ Student partners answer scripted questions with provided sentence stems.

- Ask the class to chorally read the first sentence with you:

  1. To **differentiate**, our history teacher often explains how two or more similar events are not alike.

- Ask: "When your history teacher explains how two or more similar events are not alike, what is she doing?"
- Direct students to use the word **differentiating** in their answer with this sentence stem:

  The teacher is **differentiating** _____ [between the events].

- Have students answer to their partners.
- Ask the class to chorally read the second sentence with you:
  2. Some people can **differentiate** between Coke and Pepsi.
- Ask: "When people can taste the difference between Coke and Pepsi, what can they do?"
- Direct students to use the word **differentiate** in their answer with this sentence stem:

  People can **differentiate** between _____ [Coke and Pepsi].
- Have students answer to their partners.

D Checking for Understanding
(*Student Book* pages 62 and 63)

> ◆ Students chorally read example sentences with the teacher.
> ◆ Student partners answer scripted "Yes or No" questions with oral or written responses.

- Tell students that it is important to understand the meaning of an academic word when it is used in different forms.
- Explain to students that they will think, say, or write a response to sentences and explain the responses to their partners (e.g., say, "Partner 2s, read and respond to the first sentence. Partner 1s, tell your partner if you agree or disagree").
- Ask the class to chorally read the first sentence with you:
  1. Mel was assigned to **differentiate** between plants, animals, and minerals. He wrote about how plants need water, air, and food to live.
- Ask: "Did Mel **differentiate** between plants, animals, and minerals?" (Answer: No)
- Direct students to respond to their partners by saying "yes" or "no" and explaining the reasons for their response.
  Note: While students are responding, monitor their exchanges. Ask two or three students to share their responses with the class.
- Ask the class to chorally read the second sentence with you:
  2. Regina explained how fruits and vegetables are not the same.
- Ask: "Did Regina **differentiate** between fruits and vegetables?" (Answer: Yes)
- Direct students to respond to their partners by saying "yes" or "no" and explaining the reasons for their response.
  Note: While students are responding, monitor their exchanges. Ask two or three students to share their responses with the class.
- Ask the class to chorally read the third sentence with you:
  3. How does our school **differentiate** between girls' and boys' sports?
- Direct partners to think, write, and share their answers with the class. (A suggested sentence stem: Our school **differentiates** between girls' and boys' sports by _____.)
- Ask the class to chorally read the fourth sentence with you:
  4. Differentiate between the kind of music you like to listen to and the kind you do not.

- Direct partners to think, write, and share their answers with the class. (A suggested sentence stem: I can easily **differentiate** between _____ and _____ by _____.)

E Vocabulary Words Table
(*Student Book* page 63)

> ◆ Students add the academic word, an explanation of the word, and a usage example to the unit Vocabulary Words Table.

- Direct students to the *Unit 3 Vocabulary Words Table* on page 83 in the *Student Book*.
- Tell students to copy the explanation of the word **differentiate** from this lesson or to write their own explanation of **differentiate** in the second column.
- Then, direct students to write their own sentence, write another explanation, or draw a picture to represent the word **differentiate** in the last column.

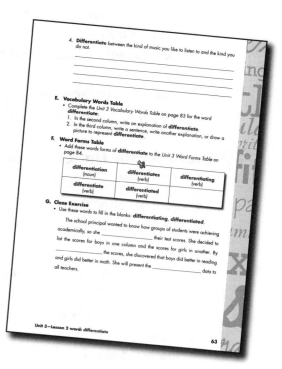

Sample Answers

Word	Explanation	Sentence/Explanation/Picture
differentiate	To show or state the difference(s) between two or more people, ideas, or things	My little sister can **differentiate** between snow and rain.

F Word Forms Table
(*Student Book* page 63)

> ◆ Students add forms of the academic word to the unit Word Forms Table.

- Tell students that once a word is known, it is easy to learn other forms of the word. Adding a prefix or a suffix to a word makes a new but related word. Word forms have similar spellings, pronunciations, and meanings. They are often different parts of speech.
- Say: "It is important to understand the parts of speech: *nouns, verbs, adjectives,* and *adverbs.* We all know that a noun is a word that represents a person, place, thing, or idea. In school assignments, *nouns* are words that tell you <u>what you are asked to make</u> for an assignment or a test. A verb is a word that represents an action, an experience, or a state. In school assignments and tests, *verbs* are words that tell you <u>what you are to do</u> for the assignment. An adjective is a word that describes a noun or a pronoun. In school assignments, *adjectives* usually <u>give other information</u> about the assignment. An adverb is a word that adds meaning to a verb, an adjective, another adverb, or

a sentence. In school assignments, *adverbs* tell you <u>how you should do</u> the assignment."

- Direct students to the *Unit 3 Word Forms Table* on page 84 in the *Student Book*.
- Instruct students to add these word forms of **differentiate** to the table: **differentiation** (n), **differentiate** (v), **differentiates** (v), **differentiated** (v), **differentiating** (v).

Answer Key

NOUNS What you make or create	VERBS What you have to do for the assignment	ADJECTIVES Specific details about what you must do	ADVERBS Important information about how to do the assignment
differentiation	differentiate		
	differentiates		
	differentiated		
	differentiating		

G Cloze Exercise

(*Student Book* page 63)

◆ Students use word forms to complete a cloze exercise.

- Direct students to use the words **differentiating** and **differentiated** to complete this cloze exercise with their partners. Provide sufficient time for them to do so.
- Then, ask students to follow along as you read to determine if their answers to the cloze exercise are correct.

The school principal wanted to know how groups of students were achieving academically, so she **differentiated** their test scores. She decided to list the scores for boys in one column and the scores for girls in another. By **differentiating** the scores, she discovered that boys did better in reading and girls did better in math. She will present the **differentiated** data to all teachers.

H Informational Passage

(*Student Book* page 64)

◆ Students chorally read the informational passage with the teacher.
◆ Students then read the passage with their partners.

- Say: "This informational passage is designed to provide you with strategies for using the word **differentiate** in writing assignments."
- Ask students to read the passage chorally with you and then with their partners. *Note: You may want to make copies of the Venn diagram graphic organizer (Graph A-2) on the accompanying CD-ROM for students to refer to.*

Differentiate: Things That Are Not Alike

When you are asked to **differentiate**, you are expected to write about the differences between two or more people, ideas, or things. You will find it easy to **differentiate** if you first organize your ideas. One way to get organized is to use a Venn diagram.

As you recall, a Venn diagram consists of two overlapping circles. Let's say that you have been asked to **differentiate** between fish and birds. On the outside circle sections, you would **differentiate** by listing all the ways that fish and birds are not alike. You might note that one of these animals swims in water and the other usually flies in the air. You could also add that one has scales and the other has feathers. You would list information that is the same about both fish and birds in the middle (overlapping) section.

Because you are being asked to **differentiate**, you will write about how things are different. In this case, you would use the information you have listed in the outside circle sections of the Venn diagram to write your response.

I Framed Paragraph and Sentence Stems

(Student Book page 64)

(Optional, to be used in conjunction with items J and K, following.)

Note: This section may be used to support struggling students. A framed paragraph is a tool to assist students in writing a paragraph. The paragraph frame provides a sample topic sentence, transitional sentence stems, and a conclusion sentence.

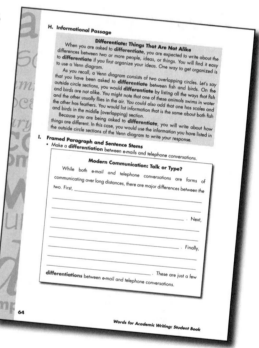

- Tell students that a framed paragraph is a tool to assist them in writing a paragraph.
- Read the topic sentence and the first transitional sentence stem with students.
- Stop reading after the first transitional sentence stem and assist students in completing the sentence in the context of the framed paragraph.
- Continue reading each sentence stem, stopping after each one to assist students in completing the stems.
- Once the paragraph frame is completed, direct students to read the entire paragraph to their partners.

Modern Communication: Talk or Type?

While both e-mail and telephone conversations are forms of communicating over long distances, there are major differences between the two. First, <u>telephone conversations are verbal and e-mails are written</u>. Next, <u>to connect with someone on a telephone, the caller must use a set of numbers. With e-mail, the person who initiates the message must use the Internet and know the e-mail address of the person to be contacted.</u> Finally, <u>telephone conversations take place when two people talk to each other at the same time. But with e-mail, people can take days to have a series of conversations with each other.</u> These are just a few **differentiations** between e-mail and telephone conversations.

Topic sentence:	While both e-mail and telephone conversations are forms of communicating over long distances, there are major differences between the two.
First transitional sentence stem:	First, _____.
Second transitional sentence stem:	Next, _____.
Third transitional sentence stem:	Finally, _____.
Conclusion sentence:	These are just a few of the major differences between e-mail and telephone conversations.

J Paragraph Starters

(*Student Book* page 65)

- To reinforce understanding of the word **differentiate**, we suggest three related paragraph topics and topic sentences. You can assign these activities as independent practice, partner practice, or homework.

  1. **Paragraph topic: Differentiate** between evaporation and condensation.

     Topic sentence: While both evaporation and condensation are parts of the water cycle, they are different in several ways.

     - Direct students to use a Venn diagram to help them **differentiate** between evaporation and condensation.

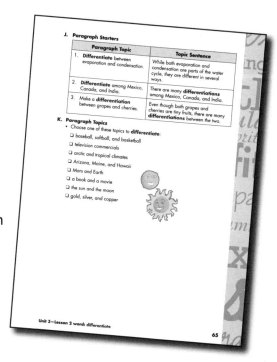

Note: You may want to make copies of the Venn diagram graphic organizer (Graph A-2) on the accompanying CD-ROM for students to refer to.

2. **Paragraph topic: Differentiate** between Mexico, Canada, and India.
   Topic sentence: There are many **differentiations** between Mexico, Canada, and India.
   - Ask students to think about these countries' different geographies, languages, weather, and natural resources.

3. **Paragraph topic:** Make a **differentiation** between grapes and cherries.
   Topic sentence: Even though both grapes and cherries are tiny fruits, there are many **differentiations** between the two.
   - Ask students to write a list of attributes for cherries and a corresponding list for grapes.

Ⓚ Paragraph Topics
(*Student Book* page 65)

- We suggest additional writing topics of general knowledge that appeal to a diverse student population. Assign these topics for additional practice in applying the academic word **differentiate** to students' writing.

  ❏ baseball, softball, and basketball

  ❏ television commercials

  ❏ arctic and tropical climates

  ❏ Arizona, Maine, and Hawaii

  ❏ Mars and Earth

  ❏ a book and a movie

  ❏ the sun and the moon

  ❏ gold, silver, and copper

interpret

Students will:
1. Correctly pronounce the word **interpret**.
2. Define the word **interpret** in an academic context.
3. Identify examples and non-examples of the word **interpret**.
4. Use the word **interpret** and its word forms in an academic context as evidenced by completion of a cloze exercise.
5. Write a paragraph that appropriately **interprets** a subject, a situation, or an event.

A Introduction and Pronunciation
(*Student Book* page 66)

- Tell students the word: "This word is **interpret**."
- Say the word in parts.
- Ask students to repeat the word in parts and then the whole word.

B Explanation
(*Student Book* page 66)

- Say: "**Interpret** means *to personally decide the meaning of something.*"
- Ask students to repeat the explanation.
- Direct Partner 1s to say the explanation to Partner 2s.
- Direct Partner 2s to tell Partner 1s if their explanation was correct.

C Example Sentences
(*Student Book* page 66)

> ◆ Students chorally read example sentences with the teacher.
> ◆ Student partners answer scripted questions with provided sentence stems.

- Ask the class to chorally read the first sentence with you:
  1. Judges often **interpret** the law.
- Ask: "When judges decide the meaning of a law, what are they doing?"
- Direct students to use the word **interpreting** in their answer with this sentence stem:

  Judges are **interpreting** _____ [the law].
- Have students answer to their partners.
- Ask the class to chorally read the second sentence with you:
  2. Sometimes it is difficult to **interpret** modern art.

- Ask: "Sometimes when people look at modern art, they don't understand its meaning. What are they having a difficult time doing?"
- Direct students to use the word **interpreting** in their answer with this sentence stem:

  People are having a difficult time **interpreting** _____ [modern art].
- Have students answer to their partners.

D Checking for Understanding
(*Student Book* pages 66 and 67)

> ◆ Students chorally read example sentences with the teacher.
> ◆ Student partners answer scripted "Yes or No" questions with oral or written responses.

- Tell students that it is important to understand the meaning of an academic word when it is used in different forms.
- Explain to students that they will think, say, or write a response to sentences and explain the responses to their partners (e.g., say, "Partner 2s, read and respond to the first sentence. Partner 1s, tell your partner if you agree or disagree").
- Ask the class to chorally read the first sentence with you:
  1. Our teacher asked us to **interpret** a poem.
- Ask: "Does your teacher expect you to decide the meaning of the poem?" (Answer: Yes)
- Direct students to respond to their partners by saying "yes" or "no" and explaining the reasons for their response.
  Note: While students are responding, monitor their exchanges. Ask two or three students to share their responses with the class.
- Ask the class to chorally read the second sentence with you:
  2. The first row of students was asked to list the names of the last ten U.S. presidents.
- Ask: "Will students be expected to interpret what each president accomplished in his term?" (Answer: No)
- Direct students to respond to their partners by saying "yes" or "no" and explaining the reasons for their response.
  Note: While students are responding, monitor their exchanges. Ask two or three students to share their responses with the class.
- Ask the class to chorally read the third sentence with you:
  3. What would you say if your teacher asked you to **interpret** school procedures for buying lunch in the cafeteria?
- Direct partners to think, write, and share their answers with the class. (A suggested sentence stem: If my teacher asked me to **interpret** school procedures for buying lunch in the cafeteria, _____.)
- Ask the class to chorally read the fourth sentence with you:
  4. When was the last time you were assigned to read a novel and **interpret** the author's meaning?
- Direct partners to think, write, and share their answers with the class. (A suggested sentence stem: The last time I read and **interpreted** a novel, _____.)

E. Vocabulary Words Table

(*Student Book* page 67)

> ◆ Students add the academic word, an explanation of the word, and a usage example to the unit Vocabulary Words Table.

- Direct students to turn to the *Unit 3 Vocabulary Words Table* on page 83 in the *Student Book*.
- Tell students to copy the explanation of the word **interpret** from this lesson or to write their own explanation of **interpret** in the second column.
- Then, direct students to write their own sentence, write another explanation, or draw a picture to represent the word **interpret** in the last column.

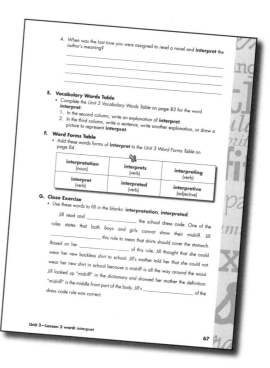

Sample Answers

Word	Explanation	Sentence/Explanation/Picture
interpret	To personally decide the meaning of something	Jill will **interpret** the author's intent for writing the book.

F. Word Forms Table

(*Student Book* page 67)

> ◆ Students add forms of the academic word to the unit Word Forms Table.

- Tell students that once a word is known, it is easy to learn other forms of the word. Adding a prefix or a suffix to a word makes a new but related word. Word forms have similar spellings, pronunciations, and meanings. They are often different parts of speech.
- Say: "It is important to understand the parts of speech: *nouns*, *verbs*, *adjectives*, and *adverbs*. We all know that a noun is a word that represents a person, place, thing, or idea. In school assignments, *nouns* are words that tell you <u>what you are asked to make</u> for an assignment or a test. A verb is a word that represents an action, an experience, or a state. In school assignments and tests, *verbs* are words that tell you <u>what you are to do</u> for the assignment. An adjective is a word that describes a noun or a pronoun. In school assignments, *adjectives* usually <u>give other information</u> about the assignment. An adverb is a word that adds meaning to a verb, an adjective, another adverb, or a sentence. In school assignments, *adverbs* tell you <u>how you should do</u> the assignment."
- Direct students to the *Unit 3 Word Forms Table* on page 84 in the *Student Book*.

- Instruct students to add these word forms of **interpret** to the table: **interpretation** (n), **interpret** (v), **interprets** (v), **interpreted** (v), **interpreting** (v), **interpretive** (adj).

Answer Key

NOUNS What you make or create	VERBS What you have to do for the assignment	ADJECTIVES Specific details about what you must do	ADVERBS Important information about how to do the assignment
interpretation	interpret	interpretive	
	interprets		
	interpreted		
	interpreting		

G Cloze Exercise
(*Student Book* page 67)

> ◆ Students use word forms to complete a cloze exercise.

- Direct students to use the words **interpretation** and **interpreted** to complete this cloze exercise with their partners. Provide sufficient time for them to do so.
- Then, ask students to follow along as you read to determine if their answers to the cloze exercise are correct.

> Jill read and **interpreted** the school dress code. One of the rules states that both boys and girls cannot show their midriff. Jill **interpreted** this rule to mean that shirts should cover the stomach. Based on her **interpretation** of this rule, Jill thought that she could wear her new backless shirt to school. Jill's mother told her that she could not wear her new shirt in school because a midriff is all the way around the waist. Jill looked up "midriff" in the dictionary and showed her mother the definition: "midriff" is the middle front part of the body. Jill's **interpretation** of the dress code rule was correct.

H Informational Passage
(*Student Book* page 68)

> ◆ Students chorally read the informational passage with the teacher.
> ◆ Students then read the passage with their partners.

- Say: "This informational passage is designed to provide you with strategies for using the word **interpret** in writing assignments."
- Ask students to read this passage chorally with you and then with their partners.

Note: You may want to make copies of the Web graphic organizer (Graph A-1 on the accompanying CD-ROM) for students to refer to.

Interpret: Present Your Opinion

When you are asked to **interpret** something, you are expected to decide the meaning of it. To present an **interpretation**, you need to organize your thoughts. Use a Web graphic organizer to jot down everything you know about the subject. You should include facts, ideas, and concepts. Make a short outline of the major points. This will help you to organize your thoughts and present a clear **interpretation** of the subject.

Restate the question when you begin to write. Present your **interpretation** of the subject in a logical order. Back up your statements with facts, names, and dates. Explain why you believe your **interpretation** is reasonable.

I **Framed Paragraph and Sentence Stems**

(*Student Book* page 68)

(Optional, to be used in conjunction with items J and K, following.)

Note: This section may be used to support struggling students. A framed paragraph is a tool to assist students in writing a paragraph. The paragraph frame provides a sample topic sentence, transitional sentence stems, and a conclusion sentence.

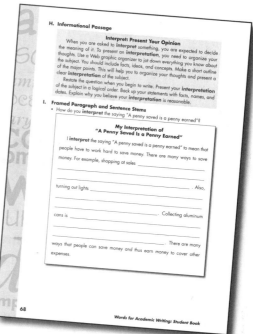

- Tell students that a framed paragraph is a tool to assist them in writing a paragraph.
- Read the topic sentences and the first transitional sentence stem with students.
- Stop reading after the first transitional sentence stem and assist students in completing the sentence in the context of the framed paragraph.
- Continue reading each sentence stem, stopping after each one to assist students in completing the stems.
- Once the paragraph frame is completed, direct students to read the entire paragraph to their partners.

Sample Completed Framed Paragraph

My Interpretation of "A Penny Saved Is a Penny Earned"

I **interpret** the saying "A penny saved is a penny earned" to mean that people have to work hard to save money. There are many ways to save money. For example, shopping at sales <u>is one way. When you buy something for less money than you planned, you can put what you saved into a savings account</u>. Also, turning out lights <u>when you don't need them keeps the electric bill down and prevents unnecessary expense from the family budget</u>. Collecting aluminum cans is <u>another easy way to earn and save money. While every can is worth only a few cents, the cents add up to dollars over time</u>. There are many ways that people can save money and thus earn money to cover other expenses.

Topic sentences:	I **interpret** the saying "A penny saved is a penny earned" to mean that people have to work hard to save money. There are many ways to save money.
First transitional sentence stem:	For example, shopping at sales _____.
Second transitional sentence stem:	Also, turning out lights _____.
Third transitional sentence stem:	Collecting aluminum cans is _____.
Conclusion sentence:	There are many ways that people can save money and thus earn money to cover other expenses.

J Paragraph Starters
(*Student Book* page 69)

- To reinforce understanding of the word **interpret**, we suggest three related paragraph topics and topic sentences. You can assign these activities as independent practice, partner practice, or homework.

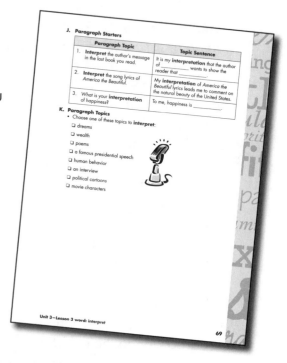

1. **Paragraph topic: Interpret** the author's message in the last book you read.

   Topic sentence: It is my **interpretation** that the author of _____ wants to show the reader that _____.

   - Ask students to think about the last book they read, reasons why the author may have written the book, and what they learned after reading it.

2. **Paragraph topic: Interpret** the song lyrics of *America the Beautiful*.
   Topic sentence: My **interpretation** of *America the Beautiful* lyrics leads me to comment on the natural beauty of the United States.

   - Ask students to think about the beautiful natural sights they have seen anywhere in the United States.

3. **Paragraph topic:** What is your **interpretation** of happiness?
   Topic sentence: To me, happiness is _____.

   - Ask students to think about specific times when they were happy and then think about why those times made them feel that way.

K Paragraph Topics

(Student Book page 69)

- We suggest additional writing topics of general knowledge that appeal to a diverse student population. Assign these topics for additional practice in applying the academic word **interpret** to students' writing.

  - ❏ dreams

  - ❏ wealth

  - ❏ poems

  - ❏ a famous presidential speech

  - ❏ human behavior

  - ❏ an interview

  - ❏ political cartoons

  - ❏ movie characters

trace

Students will:

1. Correctly pronounce the word **trace**.
2. Define the word **trace** in an academic context.
3. Identify examples and non-examples of the word **trace**.
4. Use the word **trace** and its word forms in an academic context as evidenced by completion of a cloze exercise.
5. Write a paragraph that appropriately **traces** a series of events or actions.

A Introduction and Pronunciation
(*Student Book* page 70)

- Tell students the word: "This word is **trace**."
- Say the word.
- Ask students to repeat the word.

B Explanation
(*Student Book* page 70)

- Say: "**Trace** means *to follow something back to its beginning*."
- Ask the class to repeat the explanation.
- Direct Partner 1s to say the explanation to Partner 2s.
- Direct Partner 2s to tell Partner 1s if their explanation was correct.

Unit 3 Lesson 4 — trace

A. Introduction and Pronunciation
- This word is **trace**.
- Repeat the word.

B. Explanation
- **Trace** means *to follow something back to its beginning*.

C. Example Sentences
1. The class will **trace** the events that led to the Civil War.
2. Bob will **trace** his family history in his essay.

D. Checking for Understanding
1. Maria defined the words on the vocabulary list.
   Question: Did Maria **trace** the history of the words?
   Yes or No? Why or why not?

2. Steve wrote a paper that documented the events leading to the election of the current president of Mexico.
   Question: Did Steve **trace** the course of events leading to the election of the current Mexican president?
   Yes or No? Why or why not?

3. Students were given the assignment to **trace** the formation of a hurricane.
   Question: How would you organize this assignment?

70

Words for Academic Writing: Student Book

C Example Sentences
(*Student Book* page 70)

> ◆ Students chorally read example sentences with the teacher.
> ◆ Student partners answer scripted questions with provided sentence stems.

- Ask the class to chorally read the first sentence with you:
  1. The class will **trace** the events that led to the Civil War.
- Ask: "When the class reviews the events leading to the Civil War, what will it be doing?"
- Direct students to use the word **tracing** in their answer with this sentence stem: The class will be **tracing** _____ [the events].
- Have students answer to their partners.
- Ask the class to chorally read the second sentence with you:
  2. Bob will **trace** his family history in his essay.
- Ask: "When Bob follows his family history back to the 1800s, what will he be doing?"

- Direct students to use the word **tracing** in their answer with this sentence stem: Bob will be **tracing** _____ [his family history back to the 1800s].
- Have students answer to their partners.

D Checking for Understanding
(*Student Book* pages 70 and 71)

> ◆ Students chorally read example sentences with the teacher.
> ◆ Student partners answer scripted "Yes or No" questions with oral or written responses.

- Tell students that it is important to understand the meaning of an academic word when it is used in different forms.
- Explain to students that they will think, say, or write a response to sentences and explain the responses to their partners (e.g., say, "Partner 2s, read and respond to the first sentence. Partner 1s, tell your partner if you agree or disagree").
- Ask the class to chorally read the first sentence with you:
  1. Maria defined the words on the vocabulary list.
- Ask: "Did Maria **trace** the history of the words?" (Answer: No)
- Direct students to respond to their partners by saying "yes" or "no" and explaining the reasons for their response.
  Note: While students are responding, monitor their exchanges. Ask two or three students to share their responses with the class.
- Ask the class to chorally read the second sentence with you:
  2. Steve wrote a paper that documented the events leading to the election of the current president of Mexico.
- Ask: "Did Steve **trace** the course of events leading to the election of the current Mexican president?" (Answer: Yes)
- Direct students to respond to their partners by saying "yes" or "no" and explaining the reasons for their response.
  Note: While students are responding, monitor their exchanges. Ask two or three students to share their responses with the class.
- Ask the class to chorally read the third sentence with you:
  3. Students were given the assignment to **trace** the formation of a hurricane.
- Ask: "How would you organize this assignment?"
- Direct partners to think, write, and share their answers with the class. (A suggested sentence stem: To **trace** the formation of a hurricane, _____.)
- Ask the class to chorally read the fourth sentence with you:
  4. **Trace** the major events in your life.
- Direct partners to think, write, and share their answers with the class. (A suggested sentence stem: To **trace** the major events in my life, _____.)

E Vocabulary Words Table

(*Student Book* page 71)

> ◆ Students add the academic word, an explanation of the word, and a usage example to the unit Vocabulary Words Table.

- Direct students to the *Unit 3 Vocabulary Words Table* on page 83 in the *Student Book*.
- Tell students to copy the explanation of the word **trace** from this lesson or to write their own explanation of **trace** in the second column.
- Then, direct students to write their own sentence, write another explanation, or draw a picture to represent the word **trace** in the last column.

Sample Answers

Word	Explanation	Sentence/Explanation/Picture
trace	To follow something back to its beginning	José will **trace** the history of the development of the gasoline engine.

F Word Forms Table

(*Student Book* page 71)

> ◆ Students add forms of the academic word to the unit Word Forms Table.

- Tell students that once a word is known, it is easy to learn other forms of the word. Adding a prefix or a suffix to a word makes a new but related word. Word forms have similar spellings, pronunciations, and meanings. They are often different parts of speech.
- Say: "It is important to understand the parts of speech: *nouns, verbs, adjectives,* and *adverbs*. We all know that a noun is a word that represents a person, place, thing, or idea. In school assignments, *nouns* are words that tell you <u>what you are asked to make</u> for an assignment or a test. A verb is a word that represents an action, an experience, or a state. In school assignments and tests, *verbs* are words that tell you <u>what you are to do</u> for the assignment. An adjective is a word that describes a noun or a pronoun. In school assignments, *adjectives* usually <u>give other information</u> about the assignment. An adverb is a word that adds meaning to a verb, an adjective, another adverb, or a sentence. In school assignments, *adverbs* tell you <u>how you should do</u> the assignment."
- Direct students to the *Unit 3 Word Forms Table* on page 84 in the *Student Book*.
- Instruct students to add these word forms of **trace** to the table: **trace** (v), **traces** (v), **traced** (v), **tracing** (v), **traceable** (adj).

NOUNS What you make or create	VERBS What you have to do for the assignment	ADJECTIVES Specific details about what you must do	ADVERBS Important information about how to do the assignment
	trace	**traceable**	
	traces		
	traced		
	tracing		

G Cloze Exercise
(*Student Book* page 71)

> ◆ Students use word forms to complete a cloze exercise.

- Direct students to use the words **tracing**, **trace**, and **traced** to complete this cloze exercise with their partners. Provide sufficient time for them to do so.
- Then, ask students to follow along as you read to determine if their answers to the cloze exercise are correct.

> To help students realize how much time they actually have to complete homework, Mr. Riddle asked them to __**trace**__ their activities over the course of one week. To complete this assignment, Kyle made a chart to __**trace**__ the use of his time. After he __**traced**__ the sequence of events, he examined the chart. By __**tracing**__ his weekly activities, Kyle could clearly see that he spent a lot of time playing computer games. Kyle now plans to complete his homework before he plays any computer games. Because Mr. Riddle asked students to __**trace**__ their time, Kyle now knows that he has plenty of time to complete his homework.

H Informational Passage
(*Student Book* page 72)

> ◆ Students chorally read the informational passage with the teacher.
> ◆ Students then read the passage with their partners.

- Say: "This informational passage is designed to provide you with strategies for using the word **trace** in writing assignments."
- Ask students to read this passage chorally with you and then with their partners.

Note: You may want to make copies of the Chain graphic organizer (Graph A-5 on the accompanying CD-ROM) for students to refer to.

Tracing Events

One meaning of **trace** is to follow a line or a course. When you were younger, you may have **traced** a picture by connecting the dots. The dots were placed in either numerical or alphabetical order. You started **tracing** at the beginning number or letter and went to the end. When you finished, you usually had a clear picture or outline of an object.

When you are asked by a teacher to **trace** something, the teacher wants you to report the stages of progress or sequence of events, actions, or steps from a beginning point. Once you complete the task, you should have a historical understanding of the concept or event.

When you **trace** a course of events, a Chain graphic organizer will help you organize your thoughts. List the stages or sequences of events from beginning to end. When you write or give an oral report, you will need to use sequence signal words. Sequence signal words will alert readers or listeners to the order in which events occurred. Use words such as *before, first, during, while, after, then, next, when, now,* and *finally* or phrases such as *at the same time* or *at last.*

I Framed Paragraph and Sentence Stems
(*Student Book* page 72)

(Optional, to be used in conjunction with items J and K, following.)

Note: This section may be used to support struggling students. A framed paragraph is a tool to assist students in writing a paragraph. The paragraph frame provides a sample topic sentence, transitional sentence stems, and a conclusion sentence.

- Tell students that a framed paragraph is a tool to assist them in writing a paragraph.
- Read the topic sentence and the first transitional sentence stem with students.
- Stop reading after the first transitional sentence stem and assist students in completing the sentence in the context of the framed paragraph.
- Continue reading each sentence stem, stopping after each one to assist students in completing the stems.
- Once the paragraph frame is completed, direct students to read the entire paragraph to their partners.

Tracing the Four Seasons

There are four seasons in a calendar year. First, <u>there is winter. Winter is the coldest season of the year, and most plants do not grow</u>. Next, <u>spring slowly appears with a warming sun and rain showers. Leaves begin to grow on trees and shrubs. Flowers start to bud and blossom</u>. Then, <u>summer comes, with plenty of heat and hot sun. Plants need a lot of water to survive</u>. Finally, <u>fall comes. The days get shorter, and the weather gets cooler. Many trees lose colorful leaves, and flowers stop blooming to get ready for winter</u>. These are the four seasons that occur in a calendar year.

Topic sentence:	There are four seasons in a calendar year.
First transitional sentence stem:	First, _____.
Second transitional sentence stem:	Next, _____.
Third transitional sentence stem:	Then, _____.
Fourth transitional sentence stem:	Finally, _____.
Conclusion sentence:	These are the four seasons that occur in a calendar year.

J Paragraph Starters

(*Student Book* page 73)

- To reinforce understanding of the word **interpret**, we suggest three related paragraph topics and topic sentences. You can assign these activities as independent practice, partner practice, or homework.

  1. **Paragraph topic: Trace** your school history, beginning with kindergarten.
     Topic sentence: I began kindergarten at _____ school, and _____ was my teacher.
     - Ask students to make a list of the schools and teachers they have had since they started kindergarten.

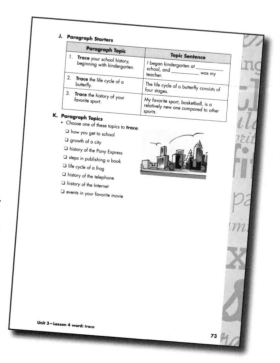

2. **Paragraph topic: Trace** the life cycle of a butterfly.

   Topic sentence: The life cycle of a butterfly consists of four stages.
   - Ask students to think about the stages in the life of a butterfly and to list and describe the stages in sequential order.

3. **Paragraph topic: Trace** the history of your favorite sport.

   Topic sentence: My favorite sport, basketball, is a relatively new one compared to other sports.
   - Ask students to think about their favorite sport. Tell them to jot down what they know about the sport and its history.

K Paragraph Topics
(*Student Book* page 73)

- We suggest additional writing topics of general knowledge that appeal to a diverse student population. Assign these topics for additional practice in applying the academic word **trace** to students' writing.

  ❑ how you get to school

  ❑ growth of a city

  ❑ history of the Pony Express

  ❑ steps in publishing a book

  ❑ life cycle of a frog

  ❑ history of the telephone

  ❑ history of the Internet

  ❑ events in your favorite movie

list

OBJECTIVES

Students will:
1. Correctly pronounce the word **list**.
2. Define the word **list** in an academic context.
3. Identify examples and non-examples of the word **list**.
4. Use the word **list** and its word forms in an academic context as evidenced by completion of a cloze exercise.
5. Write a **list** of things, people, places, or events.

A Introduction and Pronunciation
(*Student Book* page 74)

- Tell students the word: "This word is **list**."
- Say the word.
- Ask students to repeat the word.

B Explanation
(*Student Book* page 74)

- Say: "**List** means *to write a set of information, one item per line.*"
- Ask students to repeat the explanation.
- Direct Partners 1s to say the explanation to Partner 2s.
- Direct Partner 2s to tell Partners 1s if their explanation was correct.

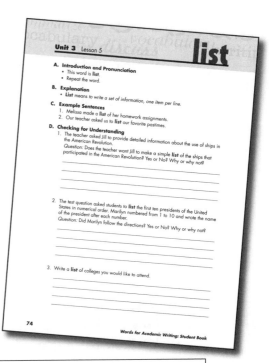

C Example Sentences
(*Student Book* page 74)

> ◆ Students chorally read example sentences with the teacher.
> ◆ Student partners answer scripted questions with provided sentence stems.

- Ask the class to chorally read the first sentence with you:
  1. Melissa made a **list** of her homework assignments.
- Ask: "When Melissa wrote down her homework assignments, what was she doing?"
- Direct students to use the word **listing** in their answer with this sentence stem:
  Melissa was **listing** _____ [homework assignments].
- Have students answer to their partners.
- Ask the class to chorally read the second sentence with you:
  2. Our teacher asked us to **list** our favorite pastimes.
- Ask: "What did your teacher ask you to do?"
- Direct students to use the word **list** in their answer with this sentence stem:
  Our teacher asked us to **list** _____ [our favorite pastimes].
- Have students answer to their partners.

D Checking for Understanding
(*Student Book* pages 74 and 75)

> ◆ Students chorally read example sentences with the teacher.
> ◆ Student partners answer scripted "Yes or No" questions with oral or written responses.

- Tell students that it is important to understand the meaning of an academic word when it is used in different forms.
- Explain to students that they will think, say, or write a response to sentences and explain the responses to their partners (e.g., say, "Partner 2s, read and respond to the first sentence. Partner 1s, tell your partner if you agree or disagree").
- Ask the class to chorally read the first sentence with you:
  1. The teacher asked Jill to provide detailed information about the use of ships in the American Revolution.
- Ask: "Does the teacher want Jill to make a simple **list** of the ships that participated in the American Revolution?" (Answer: No)
- Direct students to respond to their partners by saying "yes" or "no" and explaining the reasons for their response.
  Note: While students are responding, monitor their exchanges. Ask two or three students to share their responses with the class.
- Ask the class to chorally read the second sentence with you:
  2. The test question asked students to **list** the first ten presidents of the United States in numerical order. Marilyn numbered from 1 to 10 and wrote the name of the president after each number.
- Ask: "Did Marilyn follow the directions?" (Answer: Yes)
- Direct students to respond to their partners by saying "yes" or "no" and explaining the reasons for their response.
  Note: While students are responding, monitor their exchanges. Ask two or three students to share their responses with the class.
- Ask the class to chorally read the third sentence with you:
  3. Write a **list** of colleges you would like to attend.
- Direct partners to think, write, and share their lists with the class.
- Ask the class to chorally read the fourth sentence with you:
  4. When was the last time you made a **list** of things to do?
- Direct partners to think, write, and share their lists with the class. (A suggested sentence stem: The last time I made a **list** was _____.)

E Vocabulary Words Table
(*Student Book* page 75)

> ◆ Students add the academic word, an explanation of the word, and a usage example to the unit Vocabulary Words Table.

- Direct students to the *Unit 3 Vocabulary Words Table* on page 83 in the *Student Book*.

- Tell students to copy the explanation of the word **list** from this lesson or to write their own explanation of **list** in the second column.
- Then, direct students to write their own sentence, write another explanation, or draw a picture to represent the word **list** in the last column.

Sample Answers

Word	Explanation	Sentence/Explanation/Picture
list	To write a set of information, one item per line	Nicole will **list** her favorite amusement parks to go to.

F Word Forms Table
(*Student Book* page 75)

◆ Students add forms of the academic word to the unit Word Forms Table.

- Tell students that once a word is known, it is easy to learn other forms of the word. Adding a prefix or a suffix to a word makes a new but related word. Word forms have similar spellings, pronunciations, and meanings. They are often different parts of speech.
- Say: "It is important to understand the parts of speech: *nouns*, *verbs*, *adjectives*, and *adverbs*. We all know that a noun is a word that represents a person, place, thing, or idea. In school assignments, *nouns* are words that tell you <u>what you are asked to make</u> for an assignment or a test. A verb is a word that represents an action, an experience, or a state. In school assignments and tests, *verbs* are words that tell you <u>what you are to do</u> for the assignment. An adjective is a word that describes a noun or a pronoun. In school assignments, *adjectives* usually <u>give other information</u> about the assignment. An adverb is a word that adds meaning to a verb, an adjective, another adverb, or a sentence. In school assignments, *adverbs* tell you <u>how you should do</u> the assignment."
- Direct students to the *Unit 3 Word Forms Table* on page 84 in the *Student Book*.
- Instruct students to add these word forms of **list** to the table: **list** (n), **lists** (n), **listing** (n), **list** (v), **lists** (v), **listed** (v), **listing** (v), **unlisted** (adj).

Answer Key

NOUNS What you make or create	VERBS What you have to do for the assignment	ADJECTIVES Specific details about what you must do	ADVERBS Important information about how to do the assignment
list	list	listed	
lists	lists	unlisted	
listing	listed		
	listing		

G Cloze Exercise

(*Student Book* page 75)

> ◆ Students use word forms to complete a cloze exercise.

- Direct students to use the words **listed** and **lists** to complete this cloze exercise with their partners. Provide sufficient time for them to do so.
- Then, ask students to follow along as you read to determine if their answers to the cloze exercise are correct.

> Organized people often make **lists**. They write down assignments, chores that need to be completed, and friends they want to call or e-mail. Many people find that **lists** help them remember what needs to be done and how to organize their time. When people take care of each **listed** item, they cross it out.

H Informational Passage

(*Student Book* page 76)

> ◆ Students chorally read the informational passage with the teacher.
> ◆ Students then read the passage with their partners.

- Say: "This informational passage is designed to provide you with strategies for using the word **list** in writing assignments."
- Ask students to read the passage chorally with you and then with their partners.

Listing Information

If you know a subject, it is easy to respond to a test question or assignment that asks you to **list** information about it. All you really have to do is write down key points one by one. You may want to number each item on the **list**. You should be concise when you present a series of facts, names, events, reasons, dates, or other information.

Sometimes a test question may ask you to **list** a specific number of facts. If you can't remember all of the facts, write the ones you do know and number them. Then go on to other test questions. The additional facts may come to you when you make a connection in another part of the test. You can then go back and add the information to your numbered **list**.

I Framed Paragraph and List

(*Student Book* page 76)

(Optional, to be used in conjunction with items J and K, following.)

Note: This section may be used to support struggling students. This paragraph frame provides a sample topic sentence, a list entry, and blank lines for students to fill in to complete the list.

- Tell students that a framed paragraph is a tool to assist them in writing a list.
- Read the topic sentence and the first word in the list with students.
- Stop reading after the first listed item and assist students in filling in the remaining blank lines to complete the list.
- Once the list is completed, direct students to read it to their partners.

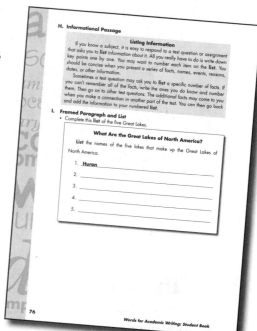

Sample List

What Are the Great Lakes of North America?

List the names of the five lakes that make up the Great Lakes of North America.

1. __Huron__
2. __Ontario__
3. __Michigan__
4. __Erie__
5. __Superior__

Note: The names of the Great Lakes can be remembered by using the acronym HOMES.

J Paragraph Starters

(*Student Book* page 77)

- To reinforce understanding of the word **list**, we suggest three related paragraph topics and topic sentences. You can assign these activities as independent practice, partner practice, or homework.

  1. **Paragraph topic:** Beginning with our current president, **list** the names of the last four presidents of the United States.

     Topic sentence: The names of the last four presidents of the United States are: _____.

     - Ask students to think about the names of the last four presidents of the United States and then **list** them.

2. **Paragraph topic: List** the three states of matter.

   Topic sentence: The three states of matter are: _____.

   - Ask students to think about how temperature affects a substance such as water and then **list** the three states.

3. **Paragraph topic: List** the names of the senators who represent your state.

   Topic sentence: The names of our state senators are: _____.

   - Ask students to **list** the names of their state senators. (Remind students that each state has only has two senators.)

K **Paragraph Topics**

(*Student Book* page 77)

- We suggest additional writing topics of general knowledge that appeal to a diverse student population. Assign these topics for additional practice in applying the academic word **list** to students' writing.

  ❏ countries of Great Britain

  ❏ reasons for going to a sporting event

  ❏ heroes

  ❏ rules for a fire drill

  ❏ books read in the past year

  ❏ housekeeping chores

  ❏ good movies

  ❏ computer games

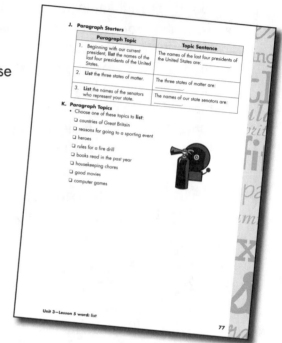

Words for Academic Writing: Teacher Guide

prove

Unit 3 Lesson 6

prove

OBJECTIVES

Students will:

1. Correctly pronounce the word **prove**.
2. Define the word **prove** in an academic context.
3. Identify examples and non-examples of the word **prove**.
4. Use the word **prove** and its word forms in an academic context as evidenced by completion of a cloze exercise.
5. Write a paragraph that appropriately **proves** a point or a result.

A Introduction and Pronunciation

(*Student Book* page 78)

- Tell students the word: "This word is **prove**."
- Say the word.
- Ask students to repeat the word.

B Explanation

(*Student Book* page 78)

- Say: "**Prove** means *to show that something is true*."
- Ask students to repeat the explanation.
- Direct Partner 1s to say the explanation to Partner 2s.
- Direct Partner 2s to tell Partner 1s if their explanation was correct.

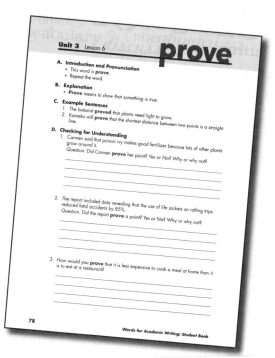

Unit 3 Lesson 6

prove

A. Introduction and Pronunciation
- This word is **prove**.
- Repeat the word.

B. Explanation
- **Prove** means to show that something is true.

C. Example Sentences
1. The botanist **proved** that plants need light to grow.
2. Kameko will **prove** that the shortest distance between two points is a straight line.

D. Checking for Understanding
1. Carmen said that poison ivy makes good fertilizer because lots of other plants grow around it.
   Question: Did Carmen **prove** *her point? Yes or No? Why or why not?*

2. The report included data revealing that the use of life jackets on rafting trips reduced fatal accidents by 85%.
   Question: Did the report **prove** *a point? Yes or No? Why or why not?*

3. How would you **prove** that it is less expensive to cook a meal at home than it is to eat at a restaurant?

78

Words for Academic Writing: Student Book

C Example Sentences

(*Student Book* page 78)

- ◆ Students chorally read example sentences with the teacher.
- ◆ Student partners answer scripted questions with provided sentence stems.

- Ask the class to chorally read the first sentence with you:
  1. The botanist **proved** that plants need light to grow.
- Ask: "When the botanist showed that plants needed light to grow, what was she doing?"
- Direct students to use the word **proving** in their answers with this sentence stem:

  The botanist was **proving** _____ [that plants need light to grow].
- Have students answer to their partners.
- Ask the class to chorally read the second sentence with you:
  2. Kameko will **prove** that the shortest distance between two points is a straight line.

- Ask: "When Kameko demonstrates on the board that the shortest distance between two points is a straight line, what will she do?"
- Direct students to use the word **prove** in their answer with this sentence stem: Kameko will **prove** _____ [that the shortest distance between two points is a straight line].
- Have students answer to their partners.

D Checking for Understanding
(*Student Book* pages 78 and 79)

> ◆ Students chorally read example sentences with the teacher.
> ◆ Student partners answer scripted "Yes or No" questions with oral or written responses.

- Tell students that it is important to understand the meaning of an academic word when it is used in different forms.
- Explain to students that they will think, say, or write a response to sentences and explain the responses to their partners (e.g., say, "Partner 2s, read and respond to the first sentence. Partner 1s, tell your partner if you agree or disagree").
- Ask the class to chorally read the first sentence with you:
  1. Carmen said that poison ivy makes good fertilizer because lots of other plants grow around it.
- Ask: "Did Carmen **prove** her point?" (Answer: No)
- Direct students to respond to their partners by saying "yes" or "no" and explaining the reasons for their response.
  Note: While students are responding, monitor their exchanges. Ask two or three students to share their responses with the class.
- Ask the class to chorally read the second sentence with you:
  2. The report included data revealing that the use of life jackets on rafting trips reduced fatal accidents by 85%.
- Ask: "Did the report **prove** a point?" (Answer: Yes)
- Direct students to respond to their partners by saying "yes" or "no" and explaining the reasons for their response.
  Note: While students are responding, monitor their exchanges. Ask two or three students to share their responses with the class.
- Ask the class to chorally read the third sentence with you:
  3. How would you **prove** that it is less expensive to cook a meal at home than it is to eat at a restaurant?
- Direct partners to think, write, and share their answers with the class. (A suggested sentence stem: We would **prove** that eating at home is less expensive by _____.)
- Ask the class to chorally read the fourth sentence with you:
  4. Tell about a time when you used data to **prove** a point.
- Direct partners to think, write, and share their answers with the class. (A suggested sentence stem: One time that I used data to **prove** my point was _____.)

E | Vocabulary Words Table

(*Student Book* page 79)

> ◆ Students add the academic word, an explanation of the word, and a usage example to the unit Vocabulary Words Table.

- Direct students to the *Unit 3 Vocabulary Words Table* on page 83 in the *Student Book*.
- Tell students to copy the explanation of the word **prove** from this lesson or to write their own explanation of **prove** in the second column.
- Then, direct students to write their own sentence, write another explanation, or draw a picture to represent the word **prove** in the last column.

Sample Answers

Word	Explanation	Sentence/Explanation/Picture
prove	To show that something is true	Antonio will **prove** that oil will float on water.

F | Word Forms Table

(*Student Book* page 79)

> ◆ Students add forms of the academic word to the unit Word Forms Table.

- Tell students that once a word is known, it is easy to learn other forms of the word. Adding a prefix or a suffix to a word makes a new but related word. Word forms have similar spellings, pronunciations, and meanings. They are often different parts of speech.
- Say: "It is important to understand the parts of speech: *nouns, verbs, adjectives,* and *adverbs*. We all know that a noun is a word that represents a person, place, thing, or idea. In school assignments, *nouns* are words that tell you <u>what you are asked to make</u> for an assignment or a test. A verb is a word that represents an action, an experience, or a state. In school assignments and tests, *verbs* are words that tell you <u>what you are to do</u> for the assignment. An adjective is a word that describes a noun or a pronoun. In school assignments, *adjectives* usually <u>give other information</u> about the assignment. An adverb is a word that adds meaning to a verb, an adjective, another adverb, or a sentence. In school assignments, *adverbs* tell you <u>how you should do</u> the assignment."
- Direct students to the *Unit 3 Word Forms Table* on page 84 in the *Student Book*.

- Instruct students to add these word forms of **prove** to the table: **proof** (n), **prove** (v), **proves** (v), **proved** (v), **proving** (v), **proven** (v), **provable** (adj), **proven** (adj).

Answer Key

NOUNS What you make or create	VERBS What you have to do for the assignment	ADJECTIVES Specific details about what you must do	ADVERBS Important information about how to do the assignment
proof	**prove**	**provable**	
	proves	**proven**	
	proved		
	proving		
	proven		

G Cloze Exercise
(*Student Book* page 79)

◆ Students use word forms to complete a cloze exercise.

- Direct students to use the words **proves**, **prove**, and **proven** to complete this cloze exercise with their partners. Provide sufficient time for them to do so.
- Then, ask students to follow along as you read to determine if their answers to the cloze exercise are correct.

> When researchers want to **prove** a point, they gather evidence to support it. They search for facts, names, dates, and places. Researchers use this information to **prove** that something is true and accurate. Then they assemble the information in a logical manner. When researchers have **proven** their point beyond a reasonable doubt, they usually publish the results and make presentations to other researchers. This **proves** to the outside world that researchers are accurate about the point they are making.

H Informational Passage
(*Student Book* page 80)

◆ Students chorally read the informational passage with the teacher.
◆ Students then read the passage with their partners.

- Say: "This informational passage is designed to provide you with strategies for using the word **prove** in writing assignments."
- Ask students to read the passage chorally with you and then with their partners. *Note: You may want to make copies of the Chain graphic organizer (Graph A-5 on the accompanying CD-ROM) for students to refer to.*

Prove Your Point

Simply making a statement does not mean that it is true. You must be able to **prove** your point. This means that you must give evidence or verification to back up your statement.

First, you must list all of the information you know about the topic. Be sure to include dates, numbers, facts, and names. Then, you must organize your **proof**. An organizer such as a Chain graphic organizer will help you put the information in a logical order.

Start writing with a topic statement that explains what you are going to **prove**. Use signal words to show your pattern of organization. Signal words such as *first*, *second*, *next*, and *finally* and signal phrases such as *on the other hand* show that you are moving from one idea to another. When in doubt, it is better to qualify a statement. For example, if you can't remember if the date was 1789 or 1798, it is better to say "near the end of the 18th century." End your paper by restating what you **proved**.

❶ Framed Paragraph and Sentence Stems
(*Student Book* pages 80 and 81)

(Optional, to be used in conjunction with items J and K, following.)

Note: This section may be used to support struggling students. A framed paragraph is a tool to assist students in writing a paragraph. The paragraph frame provides a sample topic sentence, transitional sentence stems, and a conclusion sentence.

- Tell students that a framed paragraph is a tool to assist them in writing a paragraph.
- Read the topic sentence and the first transitional sentence stem with students.
- Stop reading after the first transitional sentence stem and assist students in completing the sentence in the context of the framed paragraph.
- Continue reading each sentence stem, stopping after each one to assist students in completing the stems.
- Once the paragraph frame is completed, direct students to read both paragraphs to their partners.
- Direct students to use this information from the National Highway Traffic Safety Administration (NHTSA, 2003) to complete the framed paragraph:

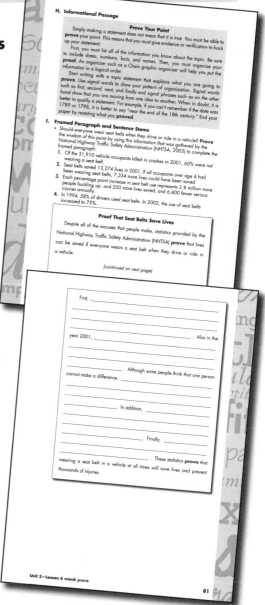

1. Of the 31,910 vehicle occupants killed in crashes in 2001, 60% were not wearing a seat belt.
2. Seat belts saved 13,274 lives in 2001. If all occupants over age 4 had been wearing seat belts, 7,334 more lives could have been saved.
3. Each percentage point increase in seat belt use represents 2.8 million more people buckling up, and 250 more lives saved, and 6,400 fewer serious injuries annually.
4. In 1994, 58% of drivers used seat belts. In 2002, the use of seat belts increased to 75%.

Sample Completed Framed Paragraph

Proof That Seat Belts Save Lives

Despite all of the excuses that people make, statistics provided by the National Highway Traffic Safety Administration (NHTSA) **prove** that lives can be saved if everyone wears a seat belt when they drive or ride in a vehicle.

First, the NHTSA reported that of the 31,910 people killed in U.S. vehicle crashes in the year 2001, more than half (60%) were not wearing a seat belt. Also in the year 2001, seat belts saved 13,274 lives, but 7,334 more lives could have been saved if more people had been wearing seat belts. Although some people think that one person cannot make a difference, each percentage point of increased seat belt use translates to 2.8 million more people buckling up. In addition, that would mean saving 250 lives and preventing 6,400 serious crash injuries in just one year. Finally, even though seat belt use increased from 58% in 1994 to 75% in 2002, we have a long way to go. These statistics **prove** that wearing a seat belt in a vehicle at all times will save lives and prevent thousands of injuries.

Topic sentence:	Despite all of the excuses that people make, statistics provided by the National Highway Traffic Safety Administration (NHTSA) **prove** that lives can be saved if everyone wears a seat belt when they drive or ride in a vehicle.
First transitional sentence stem:	First, _____.
Second transitional sentence stem:	Also in the year 2001, _____.
Third transitional sentence stem:	Although some people think that one person cannot make a difference, _____.
Fourth transitional sentence stem:	In addition, _____.
Fifth transitional sentence stem:	Finally, _____.

Conclusion sentence:	These statistics **prove** that wearing a seat belt in a vehicle at all times will save lives and prevent thousands of injuries.

J Paragraph Starters
(*Student Book* page 82)

- To reinforce understanding of the word **prove**, we suggest three related paragraph topics and topic sentences. You can assign these activities as independent practice, partner practice, or homework.

   1. **Paragraph topic:** Do you think aluminum cans and plastic bottles should be recycled? **Prove** your point.

      Topic sentence: Recycling aluminum cans and plastic bottles is _____.
      - Ask students to think about where discarded aluminum cans and plastic bottles end up. What are some other uses for these items?

   2. **Paragraph topic:** Does your school have a good athletic team? **Prove** your point.

      Topic sentence: At our school, the _____ team is _____.
      - Ask students to think about one of the school's athletic teams and its win-loss ratio.

   3. **Paragraph topic:** Does your student council do good things for your school? **Prove** your point.

      Topic sentence: Our school's student council _____.
      - Ask students to think about the various activities that the student council organizes and how it spends fund-raising money.

K Paragraph Topics
(*Student Book* page 82)

- We suggest additional writing topics of general knowledge that appeal to a diverse student population. Assign these topics for additional practice in applying the academic word **prove** to students' writing.

   ❏ the need for speed limits

   ❏ the best professional baseball/ basketball/football team

   ❏ the best cell phone service

   ❏ the most useful computer software

   ❏ the need for traffic cameras at busy intersections

   ❏ the most nutritious cereals

   ❏ the importance of career preparation

   ❏ the least expensive healthy foods

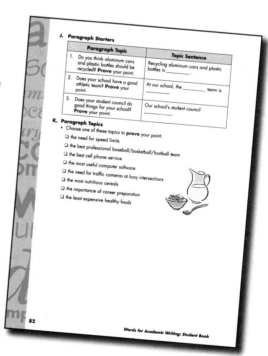

Unit 3 Posttest

Objective	To determine students' understanding of the academic words that were presented in Unit 3
Materials needed	For each student, one copy of the Unit 3 Posttest (refer to the accompanying CD-ROM) and two sheets of blank paper
Time allotment	35 minutes (Part A, 10 minutes; Part B, 10 minutes; Part C, 15 minutes)

Instructional Procedure

Step 1   Distribute Unit 3 Posttest and two sheets of blank paper to each student. Say:

- "Write your name and today's date on the lines at the top of the Posttest and at the top of each sheet of blank paper. I will collect all of them after you have finished the posttest."

Step 2   Review the directions for the Unit 3 Posttest, then administer the posttest. Say:

- "Only this Posttest score will be recorded as part of your grade. So do your very best."
- "Look at Part A. Let's read the directions together."
  (Read directions out loud with students.)
- "Place your finger on each word as I read it: **review**, **differentiate**, **interpret**, **trace**, **list**, **prove**."
- "Now, place your finger on each lowercase letter next to the explanations in the right-hand column. Listen as I read the explanation for each letter."
  a. To follow something back to its beginning
  b. To write a set of information, one item per line
  c. To personally decide the meaning of something
  d. To show or state the difference(s) between two or more people, ideas, or things
  e. To carefully examine and judge the main parts of something
  f. To show that something is true
- "Match each word with the explanation that you think is correct. Write the letter of the explanation in the middle column, next to the word."
- "You will have 10 minutes to complete Part A. Ready? Begin."
  (After 10 minutes, proceed to Part B.)
- "Now, look at Part B. It is important to know how to use academic words within the context of print."
- "Read each sentence and fill in the blank with one of the words listed in the directions."

- "You will have 10 minutes to complete Part B. Any questions? Begin."
  (After 10 minutes, proceed to Part C.)
- "Now, read the directions for Part C. Remember to make a graphic organizer on one sheet of paper to plan your answer. Then write a paragraph using a topic sentence, transitional sentences, and a conclusion sentence on the other sheet of paper. You can receive up to 15 points for this section: 5 points for the graphic organizer, 5 points for using a paragraph format, and 5 points for content."
- "You will have 15 minutes to complete Part C. Any questions? Begin."
  (After 10 minutes, tell students they have 5 minutes to finish.)
- After 5 minutes pass, say, "Please turn in your tests and papers to me."

Refer to *Appendix D* for Unit 3 Posttest Answer Key

Unit 3 Generative Assessment *(optional)*

Objective
To ensure that students are able to correctly apply Unit 3 academic words in a generalized setting

Materials needed
For each student, one copy of the Unit 3 Generative Assessment (refer to the accompanying CD-ROM) and two sheets of blank paper

Time allotment
One class period

Instructional Procedure

Step 1
Distribute Unit 3 Generative Assessment and two sheets of blank paper to each student. Say:
- "Write your name and today's date on the lines at the top of the assessment and at the top of each sheet of blank paper. I will collect all of them after you have finished the assessment."

Step 2
Review the directions for the Unit 3 Generative Assessment, then administer the assessment. Say:
- "This assessment is designed to find out how well you are able to apply the Unit 3 academic words to general situations. This assessment will ask you to demonstrate your understanding of the Unit 3 words by providing examples based on your personal knowledge and experiences."
- "Read each direction, and then use the blank paper to create your own graphic organizer to plan your answer."
- "Then, use your graphic organizer to help you write a short paragraph using a topic sentence, transitional sentences, and a conclusion sentence."
- "You can receive up to 15 points for each answer: 5 points for your graphic organizer, 5 points for using a paragraph format, and 5 points for content. You will have the whole class period to complete this assessment."
- "Any questions? When you have finished, please turn in your assessment and graphic organizers to me. Begin."

Grading Criteria

To grade a Generative Assessment, we suggest allocating a maximum of 15 points *per assessment item* as follows:
- Up to 5 points for use of a graphic organizer
- Up to 5 points for conventions (correct paragraphing; use of topic, transitional, and conclusion sentences; correct punctuation; correct spelling)
- Up to 5 points for content

Unit 4 Pretest

Objective	To determine students' prior knowledge of academic words that will be taught in Unit 4
Materials needed	For each student, one copy of the Unit 4 Pretest (refer to the accompanying CD-ROM)
Time allotment	20 minutes (Part A, 10 minutes; Part B, 10 minutes)

Instructional Procedure

Step 1 Distribute Unit 4 Pretest to students. Say:
- "Write your name and today's date on the lines at the top of the Pretest."

Step 2 Review the directions for Unit 4 Pretest, then administer the pretest. Say:
- "Look at Part A. Let's read the directions together."
(Read the directions out loud with students.)
- "Place your finger on each word as I read it: **enumerate**, **relate**, **persuade**, **defend**, **state**, **critique**."
- "Now, place your finger on each lowercase letter next to the explanations in the right-hand column. Listen as I read the explanation for each letter."
  a. To list one thing after another in a specific order; to count off
  b. To judge both the strong and weak points of something or someone
  c. To act or express to protect something
  d. To cause others to change their minds or take action
  e. To clearly give information or an opinion
  f. To tell how things, people, or events are connected or alike
- "Match each word with the explanation that you think is correct. Write the letter of the explanation in the middle column, next to the word."
- "You will have 10 minutes to complete Part A. Ready? Begin."
(After 10 minutes, proceed to Part B.)
- "Now, look at Part B. It is important to know how to use academic words within the context of print."
- "Read each of the six sentences. Then, refer back to the table in Part A. Use the words in the first column to fill in the blanks of the sentences."
- "You will have 10 minutes to complete Part B. Any questions? Begin."
- After 10 minutes, say, "Please return your tests to me."

> Refer to *Appendix D* for Unit 4 Pretest Answer Key

enumerate

Students will:

1. Correctly pronounce the word **enumerate**.
2. Define the word **enumerate** in an academic context.
3. Identify examples and non-examples of the word **enumerate**.
4. Use the word **enumerate** and its word forms in an academic context as evidenced by completion of a cloze exercise.
5. Write a paragraph that appropriately **enumerates** a series of people, places, things, or events.

A Introduction and Pronunciation
(*Student Book* page 87)

- Tell students the word: "This word is **enumerate**."
- Say the word in parts.
- Ask students to repeat the word in parts and then the whole word.

B Explanation
(*Student Book* page 87)

- Say: "**Enumerate** means *to list one thing after another in a specific order; to count off.*"
- Ask students to repeat the explanation.
- Direct Partner 1s to say the explanation to Partner 2s.
- Direct Partner 2s to tell Partner 1s if their explanation was correct.

C Example Sentences
(*Student Book* page 87)

> ◆ Students chorally read example sentences with the teacher.
> ◆ Student partners answer scripted questions with provided sentence stems.

- Ask the class to chorally read the first sentence with you:
  1. **Enumerate** the first five presidents of the United States.
- Ask: "What are you going to do with the names of the first five presidents of the United States?"
- Direct students to use the word **enumerate** in their answer with this sentence stem:
  We are going to **enumerate** _____ [the names].
- Have students answer to their partners.

- Ask the class to chorally read the second sentence with you:
  2. Vince will **enumerate** the process of evaporation.
- Ask: "When Vince lists the sequential steps in the process of evaporation, what will he be doing?"
- Direct students to use the word **enumerating** in their answer with this sentence stem:

  Vince will be **enumerating** _____ [the process of evaporation].
- Have students answer to their partners.

D Checking for Understanding
(*Student Book* pages 87 and 88)

> ◆ Students chorally read example sentences with the teacher.
> ◆ Student partners answer scripted "Yes or No" questions with oral or written responses.

- Tell students that it is important to understand the meaning of an academic word when it is used in different forms.
- Explain to students that they will think, say, or write a response to sentences and explain the responses to their partners (e.g., say, "Partner 2s, read and respond to the first sentence. Partner 1s, tell your partner if you agree or disagree").
- Ask the class to chorally read the first sentence with you:
  1. The student was asked to **enumerate** African wild animals from largest to smallest.
- Ask: "Is the student being asked to write an essay about each animal?" (Answer: No)
- Direct students to respond to their partners by saying "yes" or "no" and explaining the reasons for their response.
  Note: While students are responding, monitor their exchanges. Ask two or three students to share their responses with the class.
- Ask the class to chorally read the second sentence with you:
  2. The teacher **enumerated** famous American writers.
- Ask: "Did the teacher list the writers?" (Answer: Yes)
- Direct students to respond to their partners by saying "yes" or "no" and explaining the reasons for their response.
  Note: While students are responding, monitor their exchanges. Ask two or three students to share their responses with the class.
- Ask the class to chorally read the third sentence with you:
  3. At our school, who usually **enumerates** the school rules?
- Direct partners to think, write, and share their answers with the class. (A suggested sentence stem: The person who **enumerates** our school rules is _____.)
- Ask the class to chorally read the fourth sentence with you:
  4. **Enumerate** your best personality traits.
- Direct partners to think, write, and share their answers with the class. (A suggested sentence stem: I would **enumerate** my best personality traits as _____.)

E Vocabulary Words Table

(*Student Book* page 88)

> ◆ Students add the academic word, an explanation of the word, and a usage example to the unit Vocabulary Words Table.

- Direct students to the *Unit 4 Vocabulary Words Table* on page 111 in the *Student Book*.
- Tell students to copy the explanation of the word **enumerate** from this lesson or to write their own explanation of **enumerate** in the second column.
- Then, direct students to write their own sentence, write another explanation, or draw a picture to represent the word **enumerate** in the last column.

Sample Answers

Word	Explanation	Sentence/Explanation/Picture
enumerate	To list one thing after another in a specific order; to count off	The pilot **enumerated** the preflight check-off items.

F Word Forms Table

(*Student Book* page 88)

> ◆ Students add forms of the academic word to the unit Word Forms Table.

- Tell students that once a word is known, it is easy to learn other forms of the word. Adding a prefix or a suffix to a word makes a new but related word. Word forms have similar spellings, pronunciations, and meanings. They are often different parts of speech.
- Say: "It is important to understand the parts of speech: *nouns, verbs, adjectives,* and *adverbs*. We all know that a noun is a word that represents a person, place, thing, or idea. In school assignments, *nouns* are words that tell you <u>what you are asked to make</u> for an assignment or a test. A verb is a word that represents an action, an experience, or a state. In school assignments and tests, *verbs* are words that tell you <u>what you are to do</u> for the assignment. An adjective is a word that describes a noun or a pronoun. In school assignments, *adjectives* usually give <u>other information</u> about the assignment. An adverb is a word that adds meaning to a verb, an adjective, another adverb, or a sentence. In school assignments, *adverbs* tell you <u>how you should do</u> the assignment."
- Direct students to the *Unit 4 Word Forms Table* on page 112 in the *Student Book*.

- Instruct students to add these word forms of **enumerate** to the table: **enumeration** (n), **enumerate** (v), **enumerates** (v), **enumerated** (v), **enumerating** (v).

Answer Key

NOUNS What you make or create	VERBS What you have to do for the assignment	ADJECTIVES Specific details about what you must do	ADVERBS Important information about how to do the assignment
enumeration	enumerate		
	enumerates		
	enumerated		
	enumerating		

G Cloze Exercise
(*Student Book* page 88)

◆ Students use word forms to complete a cloze exercise.

- Direct students to use the words **enumerate** and **enumerated** to complete this cloze exercise with their partners. Provide sufficient time for them to do so.
- Then, ask students to follow along as you read to determine if their answers to the cloze exercise are correct.

Our history teacher gave us a test that asked us to **enumerate** the major battles of the Civil War. At first, Tom did not know what the word **enumerate** meant. So he studied the word. Tom noticed that if he took off the prefix "e" and the suffix "ate," the root was "numer." He figured that this meant "number." So Tom decided that **enumerate** meant "to number" or "to make an ordered list." He then **enumerated** the major Civil War battles by listing them in order. Because he was able to figure out the meaning of **enumerate**, Tom received a very good grade on the history test.

H Informational Passage
(*Student Book* page 89)

◆ Students chorally read the informational passage with the teacher.
◆ Students then read the passage with their partners.

- Say: "This informational passage is designed to provide you with strategies for using the word **enumerate** in writing assignments."
- Ask students to read the passage chorally with you and then with their partners. *Note: You may want to make copies of the Outline graphic organizer (Graph A-6 on the accompanying CD-ROM) for students to refer to.*

What Does "Enumerate" Mean?

Enumerate means "to list things one by one." When you are asked to **enumerate** something, it is expected that you will list key points or steps in order. You should be careful to restate the question. This will let your teacher know what you are **enumerating**. Your paper will probably include a numbered list or outline.

If you must **enumerate** your answer in sentences or paragraphs, use an Outline graphic organizer. Remember to use signal words that will let the reader know the sequence of events. When you **enumerate**, use words such as *first, second, third, next, also,* and *finally* or signal phrases such as *to begin with* and *at last.* You need to be very concise. You should present all of your points in a logical order.

❶ Framed Paragraph and Sentence Stems
(*Student Book* page 89)

(Optional, to be used in conjunction with items J and K, following.)

Note: This section may be used to support struggling students. A framed paragraph is a tool to assist students in writing a paragraph. The paragraph frame provides a sample topic sentence, transitional sentence stems, and a conclusion sentence.

- Tell students that a framed paragraph is a tool to assist them in writing a paragraph.
- Read the topic sentence and the first transitional sentence stem with students.
- Stop reading after the first transitional sentence stem and assist students in completing the sentence in the context of the framed paragraph.
- Continue reading each sentence stem, stopping after each one to assist students in completing the stems.
- Once the paragraph frame is completed, direct students to read the entire paragraph to their partners.

Sample Completed Framed Paragraph

Why You Don't Want to Be Late

There are a variety of reasons why students should not be tardy to class. To begin with, <u>students who are late do not get to talk to their friends before class begins</u>. Also, <u>students who are late often miss important directions from the teacher at the beginning of class</u>. Last, <u>if students are late, they may be assigned to after-school detention</u>. These are just three reasons why students should not be late to class.

Topic sentence:	There are a variety of reasons why students should not be tardy to class.
First transitional sentence stem:	To begin with, _____.
Second transitional sentence stem:	Also, _____.
Third transitional sentence stem:	Last, _____.
Conclusion sentence:	These are just three reasons why students should not be late to class.

J Paragraph Starters

(*Student Book* page 90)

- To reinforce understanding of the word **enumerate**, we suggest three related paragraph topics and topic sentences. You can assign these activities as independent practice, partner practice, or homework.

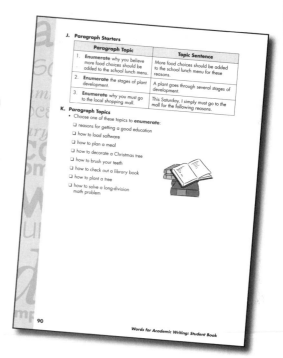

1. **Paragraph topic: Enumerate** why you believe more food choices should be added to the school lunch menu.

   Topic sentence: More food choices should be added to the school lunch menu for these reasons.

   - Ask students to think about other foods they would like to see on the school lunch menu.

2. **Paragraph topic: Enumerate** the stages of plant development.

   Topic sentence: A plant goes through several stages of development.

   - Ask students to reflect on the stages of plant life, from seed to mature plant.

3. **Paragraph topic: Enumerate** why you must go to the local shopping mall.

   Topic sentence: This Saturday, I simply must go to the mall for the following reasons.

   - Ask students to recall their last trip to a shopping mall and the reasons they needed to go.

K Paragraph Topics
(*Student Book* page 90)

- We suggest additional writing topics of general knowledge that appeal to a diverse student population. Assign these topics for additional practice in applying the academic word **enumerate** to students' writing.

  ❑ reasons for getting a good education

  ❑ how to load software

  ❑ how to plan a meal

  ❑ how to decorate a Christmas tree

  ❑ how to brush your teeth

  ❑ how to check out a library book

  ❑ how to plant a tree

  ❑ how to solve a long-division math problem

relate

OBJECTIVES

Students will:
1. Correctly pronounce the word **relate**.
2. Define the word **relate** in an academic context.
3. Identify examples and non-examples of the word **relate**.
4. Use the word **relate** and its word forms in an academic context as evidenced by completion of a cloze exercise.
5. Write a paragraph that appropriately **relates** events, ideas, or situations.

A Introduction and Pronunciation
(*Student Book* page 91)

- Tell students the word: "This word is **relate**."
- Say the word in parts.
- Ask students to repeat the word in parts and then the whole word.

B Explanation
(*Student Book* page 91)

- Say: "**Relate** means *to tell how things, people, or events are connected or alike.*"
- Ask students to repeat the explanation.
- Direct Partner 1s to give the explanation to Partner 2s.
- Direct Partner 2s to tell Partner 1s if their explanation was correct.

> **Unit 4** Lesson 2 **relate**
>
> **A. Introduction and Pronunciation**
> - This word is **relate**.
> - Say the word in parts and then the whole word.
>
> **B. Explanation**
> - **Relate** means to tell how things, people, or events are connected or alike.
>
> **C. Example Sentences**
> 1. Our teacher often **relates** lessons to real-life situations.
> 2. Koffia provided evidence that talking on a cell phone while driving is **related** to traffic accidents.
>
> **D. Checking for Understanding**
> 1. The agricultural report connected the weather to the rate of crop production.
>   *Question:* Did the report **relate** weather to crop productivity? Yes or No? Why or why not?
>
> 2. Amber was asked to accurately describe a pyramid.
>   *Question:* Should Amber be expected to **relate** the pyramids to Egyptian history? Yes or No? Why or why not?
>
> 3. How does freedom of speech **relate** to news reporting?
>
> 91

C Example Sentences
(*Student Book* page 91)

> ◆ Students chorally read example sentences with the teacher.
> ◆ Student partners answer scripted questions with provided sentence stems.

- Ask the class to chorally read the first sentence with you:
  1. Our teacher often **relates** lessons to real-life situations.
- Ask: "When your teacher connects lessons to real-life situations, what is he doing?"
- Direct students to use the word **relating** in their answer with this sentence stem:
  Our teacher is **relating** _____ [lessons to real-life situations].
- Have students answer to their partners.
- Ask the class to chorally read the second sentence with you:
  2. Koffia provided evidence that talking on a cell phone while driving is **related** to traffic accidents.

- Ask: "What was Koffia doing when she explained the link between cell phone use and traffic accidents?"
- Direct students to use the word **relating** in their answer with this sentence stem:

  Koffia was **relating** _____ [cell phone use to traffic accidents].
- Have students answer to their partners.

D Checking for Understanding
(*Student Book* pages 91 and 92)

> ◆ Students chorally read example sentences with the teacher.
> ◆ Student partners answer scripted "Yes or No" questions with oral or written responses.

- Tell students that it is important to understand the meaning of an academic word when it is used in different forms.
- Explain to students that they will think, say, or write a response to sentences and explain the responses to their partners (e.g., say, "Partner 2s, read and respond to the first sentence. Partner 1s, tell your partner if you agree or disagree").
- Ask the class to chorally read the first sentence with you:
  1. The agricultural report connected the weather to the rate of crop production.
- Ask: "Did the report **relate** weather to crop productivity?" (Answer: Yes)
- Direct students to respond to their partners by saying "yes" or "no" and explaining the reasons for their response.
  Note: While students are responding, monitor their exchanges. Ask two or three students to share their responses with the class.
- Ask the class to chorally read the second sentence with you:
  2. Amber was asked to accurately describe a pyramid.
- Ask: "Should Amber be expected to **relate** the pyramids to Egyptian history?" (Answer: No)
- Direct students to respond to their partners by saying "yes" or "no" and explaining the reasons for their response.
  Note: While students are responding, monitor their exchanges. Ask two or three students to share their responses with the class.
- Ask the class to chorally read the third sentence with you:
  3. How does freedom of speech **relate** to news reporting?
- Direct partners to think, write, and share their answers with the class. (A suggested sentence stem: Freedom of speech **relates** to news reporting by _____.)
- Ask the class to chorally read the fourth sentence with you:
  4. Tell about a book you've read or a movie you've seen that **related** to your life.
- Direct partners to think, write, and share their answers with the class. (A suggested sentence stem: One book I've read/One movie I've seen that **related** to my life was _____.)

E Vocabulary Words Table

(*Student Book* page 92)

> ◆ Students add the academic word, an explanation of the word, and a usage example to the unit Vocabulary Words Table.

- Direct students to the *Unit 4 Vocabulary Words Table* on page 111 in the *Student Book*.
- Tell students to copy the explanation of the word **relate** from this lesson or to write their own explanation of **relate** in the second column.
- Then, direct students to write their own sentence, write another explanation, or draw a picture to represent the word **relate** in the last column.

Sample Answers

Word	Explanation	Sentence/Explanation/Picture
relate	To tell how things, people, or events are connected or alike	The student showed how warm weather currents are **related** to rain.

F Word Forms Table

(*Student Book* page 92)

> ◆ Students add forms of the academic word to the unit Word Forms Table.

- Tell students that once a word is known, it is easy to learn other forms of the word. Adding a prefix or a suffix to a word makes a new but related word. Word forms have similar spellings, pronunciations, and meanings. They are often different parts of speech.
- Say: "It is important to understand the parts of speech: *nouns, verbs, adjectives,* and *adverbs*. We all know that a noun is a word that represents a person, place, thing, or idea. In school assignments, *nouns* are words that tell you <u>what you are asked to make</u> for an assignment or a test. A verb is a word that represents an action, an experience, or a state. In school assignments and tests, *verbs* are words that tell you <u>what you are to do</u> for the assignment. An adjective is a word that describes a noun or a pronoun. In school assignments, *adjectives* usually <u>give other information</u> about the assignment. An adverb is a word that adds meaning to a verb, an adjective, another adverb, or a sentence. In school assignments, *adverbs* tell you <u>how you should do</u> the assignment."
- Direct students to the *Unit 4 Word Forms Table* on page 112 in the *Student Book*.

- Then, direct students to add these word forms of **relate** to the table: **relation** (n), **relationship** (n), **relate** (v), **relates** (v), **related** (v), **relating** (v), **relative** (adj), **relatively** (adv).

Answer Key

NOUNS What you make or create	VERBS What you have to do for the assignment	ADJECTIVES Specific details about what you must do	ADVERBS Important information about how to do the assignment
relation	relate	relative	relatively
relationship	relates		
	related		
	relating		

G Cloze Exercise
(*Student Book* page 92)

◆ Students use word forms to complete a cloze exercise.

- Direct students to use the words **relationship**, **relate**, **related**, and **relatively** to complete this cloze exercise with their partners. Provide sufficient time for them to do so.
- Then, ask students to follow along as you read to determine if their answers to the cloze exercise are correct.

> Statistics show that it is possible to **relate** the use of alcohol to traffic accidents. The rate of alcohol- **related** accidents is on the increase. This is due to the fact that **relatively** large numbers of people drive while under the influence of alcohol. Studies have shown a clear **relationship** between the number of alcoholic drinks a driver has consumed and fatal car accidents. Alcohol is clearly **related** to an inability to concentrate and to be aware of potential danger. As a result, driving laws **related** to drinking and driving have been strengthened.

H Informational Passage
(*Student Book* page 93)

◆ Students chorally read the informational passage with the teacher.
◆ Students then read the passage with their partners.

- Say: "This informational passage is designed to provide you with strategies for using the word **relate** in writing assignments."
- Ask students to read the passage chorally with you and then with their partners. *Note: You may want to make copies of the Web graphic organizer (Graph A-1) on the accompanying CD-ROM for students to refer to.*

Relating Ideas

When you are asked to **relate** two or more subjects, you will need to emphasize connections, or **relationships**, between them.

Before you begin writing, use a graphic organizer such as a Web to list **relationships** between the subjects. When you begin to write, restate the question to form an introductory statement. Next, state the connections between the subjects. Tell how one is like the other or others, starting a new paragraph for each new **relationship**. Unless you know that something is absolutely true 100 percent of the time, use qualifying words to show **relationships**. Qualifying words include *usually, some, probably, might, frequently, seldom, majority, few, often, many, may,* and *mostly.* At the end of your writing assignment, remember to restate the question and tell how the subjects are **related**.

❶ Framed Paragraph and Sentence Stems

(*Student Book* page 93)

(Optional, to be used in conjunction with items J and K, following.)

Note: This section may be used to support struggling students. A framed paragraph is a tool to assist students in writing a paragraph. The paragraph frame provides a sample topic sentence, transitional sentence stems, and a conclusion sentence.

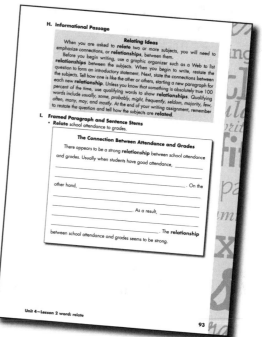

- Tell students that a framed paragraph is a tool to assist them in writing a paragraph.
- Read the topic sentence and the first transitional sentence stem with students.
- Stop reading after the first transitional sentence stem and assist students in completing the sentence in the context of the framed paragraph.
- Continue reading each sentence stem, stopping after each one to assist students in completing the stems.
- Once the paragraph frame is completed, direct students to read the entire paragraph to their partners.

Sample Completed Framed Paragraph

The Connection Between Attendance and Grades

There appears to be a strong **relationship** between school attendance and grades. Usually when students have good attendance, <u>they understand what is happening in class and they are more actively engaged in learning</u>. On the other hand, <u>students with poor school attendance miss a lot of instruction</u>. As a result, <u>they usually do not do well on tests</u>. The **relationship** between school attendance and grades seems to be strong.

Topic sentence:	There appears to be a strong **relationship** between school attendance and grades.
First transitional sentence stem:	Usually when students have good school attendance, _____.
Second transitional sentence stem:	On the other hand, _____.
Third transitional sentence stem:	As a result, _____.
Conclusion sentence:	The **relationship** between school attendance and grades seems to be strong.

J Paragraph Starters
(*Student Book* page 94)

- To reinforce understanding of the word **relate**, we suggest three paragraph topics and topic sentences. You can assign these activities as independent practice, partner practice, or homework.

    1. **Paragraph topic: Relate** snowfall measurement to river levels.

        Topic sentence: There seems to be a **relationship** between the amount of snowfall and flooding rivers.

        - Ask students to think about how melting snow can affect river levels.

    2. **Paragraph topic: Relate** advertising or commercials to spending habits.

        Topic sentence: According to marketing studies, there is a **relationship** between advertising and consumer spending.

        - Ask students to think about how advertising/commercials affect their and their parents' spending choices.

    3. **Paragraph topic: Relate** discipline to achievement.

        Topic sentence: Being disciplined and achieving goals seem to be strongly **related**.

        - Ask students to think about what they have achieved by being disciplined in thought and action.

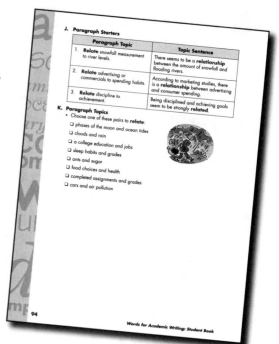

K Paragraph Topics

(*Student Book* page 94)

- We suggest additional writing topics of general knowledge that appeal to a diverse student population. Assign these topics for additional practice in applying the academic word **relate** to students' writing.

  ❑ phases of the moon and ocean tides

  ❑ clouds and rain

  ❑ a college education and jobs

  ❑ sleep habits and grades

  ❑ ants and sugar

  ❑ food choices and health

  ❑ completed assignments and grades

  ❑ cars and air pollution

persuade

OBJECTIVES

Students will:
1. Correctly pronounce the word **persuade**.
2. Define the word **persuade** in an academic context.
3. Identify examples and non-examples of the word **persuade**.
4. Use the word **persuade** and its word forms in an academic context as evidenced by completion of a cloze exercise.
5. Write a paragraph that appropriately **persuades** readers to change their minds or take action.

A Introduction and Pronunciation
(*Student Book* page 95)

- Tell students the word: "This word is **persuade**."
- Say the word in parts.
- Ask students to repeat the word in parts and then the whole word.

B Explanation
(*Student Book* page 95)

- Say: "**Persuade** means *to cause others to change their minds or take action.*"
- Ask students to repeat the explanation.
- Direct Partner 1s to give the explanation to Partner 2s.
- Direct Partner 2s to tell Partner 1s if their explanation was correct.

Unit 4 Lesson 3 **persuade**

A. **Introduction and Pronunciation**
- This word is **persuade**.
- Say the word in parts and then the whole word.

B. **Explanation**
- **Persuade** means to cause others to change their minds or take action.

C. **Example Sentences**
1. Daphne will **persuade** Kyle to collect and recycle plastic bottles and aluminum cans.
2. Ingrid will **persuade** Steve to save money for college.

D. **Checking for Understanding**
1. By pointing out that Marnisha was a good math student who attended every student council meeting, Chris convinced Alex that Marnisha would be a good school treasurer.
*Question: Did Chris **persuade** Alex to vote for Marnisha? Yes or No? Why or why not?*

2. Even though Bianca begged and pleaded, her mother would not allow her to go to the school dance.
*Question: Did Bianca **persuade** her mother to let her go to the school dance? Yes or No? Why or why not?*

3. How do student council candidates at your school **persuade** students to vote for them?

95

C Example Sentences
(*Student Book* page 95)

- ◆ Students chorally read example sentences with the teacher.
- ◆ Student partners answer scripted questions with provided sentence stems.

- Ask the class to chorally read the first sentence with you:
  1. Daphne will **persuade** Kyle to collect and recycle plastic bottles and aluminum cans.
- Ask: "When Daphne talks Kyle into collecting and recycling bottles and cans, what is she doing?"
- Direct students to use the word **persuading** in their answer with this sentence stem:
  Daphne is **persuading** _____ [Kyle into collecting and recycling].
- Have students answer to their partners.

- Ask the class to chorally read the second sentence with you:
  2. Ingrid will **persuade** Steve to save money for college.
- Ask: "When Ingrid is convincing Steve to save money for college, what is she doing?"
- Direct students to use the word **persuading** in their answer with this sentence stem:

  Ingrid is **persuading** _____ [Steve to save money].
- Have students answer to their partners.

D Checking for Understanding

(*Student Book* pages 95 and 96)

> ◆ Students chorally read example sentences with the teacher.
> ◆ Student partners answer scripted "Yes or No" questions with oral or written responses.

- Tell students that it is important to understand the meaning of an academic word when it is used in different forms.
- Explain to students that they will think, say, or write a response to sentences and explain the responses to their partners (e.g., say, "Partner 2s, read and respond to the first sentence. Partner 1s, tell your partner if you agree or disagree").
- Ask the class to chorally read the first sentence with you:
  1. By pointing out that Marnisha was a good math student who attended every student council meeting, Chris convinced Alex that Marnisha would be a good school treasurer.
- Ask: "Did Chris **persuade** Alex to vote for Marnisha?" (Answer: Yes)
- Direct students to respond to their partners by saying "yes" or "no" and explaining the reasons for their response.
  Note: While students are responding, monitor their exchanges. Ask two or three students to share their responses with the class.
- Ask the class to chorally read the second sentence with you:
  2. Even though Bianca begged and pleaded, her mother would not allow her to go to the school dance.
- Ask: "Did Bianca **persuade** her mother to let her go to the school dance?" (Answer: No)
- Direct students to respond to their partners by saying "yes" or "no" and explaining the reasons for their response.
  Note: While students are responding, monitor their exchanges. Ask two or three students to share their responses with the class.
- Ask the class to chorally read the third sentence with you:
  3. How do student council candidates at your school **persuade** students to vote for them?
- Direct partners to think, write, and share their answers with the class. (A suggested sentence stem: At our school, student council candidates **persuade** students to vote for them by _____.)

- Ask the class to chorally read the fourth sentence with you:
    4. What will you do or say the next time you want to **persuade** your parents to let you spend the night with a friend?
- Direct partners to think, write, and share their answers with the class. (A suggested sentence stem: The next time I want to **persuade** _____.)

E **Vocabulary Words Table**
(*Student Book* page 96)

> ◆ Students add the academic word, an explanation of the word, and a usage example to the unit Vocabulary Words Table.

- Direct students to the *Unit 4 Vocabulary Words Table* on page 111 in the *Student Book*.
- Tell students to copy the explanation of the word **persuade** from this lesson or to write their own explanation of **persuade** in the second column.
- Then, direct students to write their own sentence, write another explanation, or draw a picture to represent the word **persuade** in the last column.

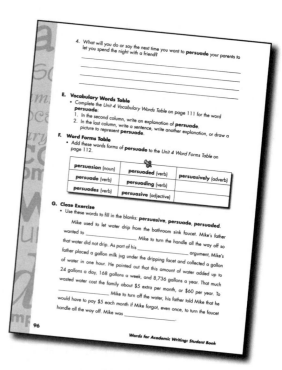

Sample Answers

Word	Explanation	Sentence/Explanation/Picture
persuade	To cause others to change their minds or take action	Maria **persuaded** Melissa to buy shoes on sale when they went shopping.

F **Word Forms Table**
(*Student Book* page 96)

> ◆ Students add forms of the academic word to the unit Word Forms Table.

- Tell students that once a word is known, it is easy to learn other forms of the word. Adding a prefix or a suffix to a word makes a new but related word. Word forms have similar spellings, pronunciations, and meanings. They are often different parts of speech.
- Say: "It is important to understand the parts of speech: *nouns*, *verbs*, *adjectives*, and *adverbs*. We all know that a noun is a word that represents a person, place, thing, or idea. In school assignments, *nouns* are words that tell you <u>what you are asked to make</u> for an assignment or a test. A verb is a word that represents an action, an experience, or a state. In school assignments and tests, *verbs* are words that tell you <u>what you are to do</u> for the assignment. An

adjective is a word that describes a noun or a pronoun. In school assignments, *adjectives* usually <u>give other information</u> about the assignment. An adverb is a word that adds meaning to a verb, an adjective, another adverb, or a sentence. In school assignments, *adverbs* tell you <u>how you should do</u> the assignment."

- Direct students to the *Unit 4 Word Forms Table* on page 112 in the *Student Book*.
- Then, direct students to add these word forms of **persuade** to the table: **persuasion** (n), **persuade** (v), **persuades** (v), **persuaded** (v), **persuading** (v), **persuasive** (adj), **persuasively** (adv).

Answer Key

NOUNS What you make or create	VERBS What you have to do for the assignment	ADJECTIVES Specific details about what you must do	ADVERBS Important information about how to do the assignment
persuasion	persuade	persuasive	persuasively
	persuades		
	persuaded		
	persuading		

G Cloze Exercise
(*Student Book* page 96)

◆ Students use word forms to complete a cloze exercise.

- Direct students to use the words **persuasive**, **persuade**, and **persuaded** to complete this cloze exercise with their partners. Provide sufficient time for them to do so.
- Then, ask students to follow along as you read to determine if their answers to the cloze exercise are correct.

Mike used to let water drip from the bathroom sink faucet. Mike's father wanted to **persuade** Mike to turn the handle all the way off so that water did not drip. As part of his **persuasive** argument, Mike's father placed a gallon milk jug under the dripping facet and collected a gallon of water in one hour. He pointed out that this amount of water added up to 24 gallons a day, 168 gallons a week, and 8,736 gallons a year. That much wasted water cost the family about $5 extra per month, or $60 per year. To **persuade** Mike to turn off the water, his father told Mike that he would have to pay $5 each month if Mike forgot, even once, to turn the faucet handle all the way off. Mike was **persuaded**.

H Informational Passage

(Student Book page 97)

> ◆ Students chorally read the informational passage with the teacher.
> ◆ Students then read the passage with their partners.

- Say: "This informational passage is designed to provide you with strategies for using the word **persuade** in writing assignments."
- Ask students to read the passage chorally with you and then with their partners. *Note: You may want to make copies of the Web graphic organizer (Graph A-1) on the accompanying CD-ROM for students to refer to.*

A Persuasive Argument

Before you begin to write a **persuasive** paper, you will need to become informed about the subject. This will allow you to choose your position and offer a solution. Go to the library or search the Internet to gather statistics, facts, quotes, and examples. You may even want to include a personal experience. Use a Web graphic organizer to sort your information into two or three topics. Decide what information you will use and the order in which you will present your evidence. You are now ready to write your **persuasive** essay.

To **persuade** readers, you need to get their attention. You may want to start with a leading question. Or, you might provide an interesting piece of information you found in your research. Then, clearly state your opinion. Let the readers know that you are going to give facts to **persuade** them to agree with you. This statement will be the foundation of your **persuasive** paper. Next, support your position with statistics, quotes, and examples. Finish your paper by restating your position **persuasively** with a powerful conclusion.

I Framed Paragraph and Sentence Stems

(Student Book page 97)

(Optional, to be used in conjunction with items J and K, following.)

Note: This section may be used to support struggling students. A framed paragraph is a tool to assist students in writing a paragraph. The paragraph frame provides a sample topic sentence, transitional sentence stems, and a conclusion sentence.

- Tell students that a framed paragraph is a tool to assist them in writing a paragraph.
- Read the topic sentences and the first transitional sentence stem with students.
- Stop reading after the first transitional sentence stem and assist students in completing the sentence in the context of the framed paragraph.

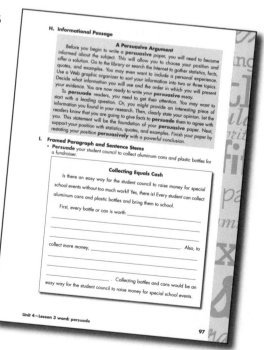

Words for Academic Writing: Teacher Guide

- Continue reading each sentence stem, stopping after each one to assist students in completing the stems.
- Once the paragraph frame is completed, direct students to read both paragraphs to their partners.

Sample Completed Framed Paragraph

Collecting Equals Cash

Is there an easy way for the student council to raise money for special school events without too much work? Yes, there is! Every student can collect aluminum cans and plastic bottles and bring them to school.

First, every bottle or can is worth <u>5 cents. There are 500 students in our school. So if every student brought only 10 bottles or cans to school each week for 5 weeks, we would earn $1,250</u>. Also, to collect more money, <u>we could encourage members of the community to donate their cans and bottles. This could be accomplished by putting up signs in town and placing recycling bins near the school parking lot</u>. Collecting bottles and cans would be an easy way for the student council to raise money for special school events.

Topic sentences: (takes a position and offers a solution)	Is there an easy way for the student council to raise money for special school events without too much work? Yes, there is! Every student can collect aluminum cans and plastic bottles and bring them to school.
First transitional sentence stem (presents evidence):	First, every bottle or can is worth _____.
Second transitional sentence stem (presents more evidence):	Also, to collect more money, _____.
Conclusion sentence:	Collecting bottles and cans would be an easy way for the student council to raise money for special school events.

J Paragraph Starters

(*Student Book* page 98)

- To reinforce understanding of the word **persuade**, we suggest three related paragraph topics and topic sentences. You can assign these activities as independent practice, partner practice, or homework.
    1. **Paragraph topic: Persuade** your classmates to start a school campus clean-up.
    Topic sentence: While our school is a good one, the grounds are often littered by the end of the school day.
    - Ask students to think about school pride and the reasons they should become involved in a clean-up campaign.

2. **Paragraph topic: Persuade** your friends to write a letter of appreciation to the school secretary.

    Topic sentences: Who is someone that most of us take for granted every day? Our school secretary, that's who.

    - Ask students to think about the many things that the school secretary does for the school every day and reasons why they should contribute to a letter of appreciation.

3. **Paragraph topic: Persuade** the principal to let you serve on a committee that will help decide which foods are offered for lunch at school.

    Topic sentence: Good food is my specialty.

    - Ask students to think about the school lunches that have been served the past few weeks. Instruct students to make a list of reasons why they would be good candidates for a food-selection committee.

K Paragraph Topics
(*Student Book* page 98)

- We suggest additional writing topics of general knowledge that appeal to a diverse student population. Assign these topics for additional practice in applying the academic word **persuade** to students' writing.

    ❏ support a school fundraiser

    ❏ participate in a charity fundraiser

    ❏ buy a certain product

    ❏ volunteer for community service

    ❏ help an elderly neighbor

    ❏ join a school club

    ❏ recycle newspapers

    ❏ write a letter to a government official about a current topic

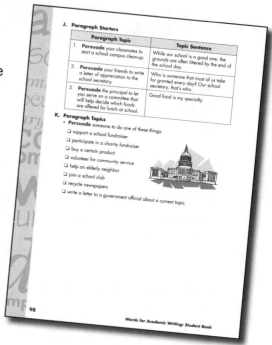

defend

Students will:

1. Correctly pronounce the word **defend**.
2. Define the word **defend** in an academic context.
3. Identify examples and non-examples of the word **defend**.
4. Use the word **defend** and its word forms in an academic context as evidenced by completion of a cloze exercise.
5. Write a paragraph that appropriately **defends** a point of view, a situation, or an action.

A Introduction and Pronunciation

(*Student Book* page 99)

- Tell students the word: "This word is **defend**."
- Say the word in parts.
- Ask students to repeat the word in parts and then the whole word.

B Explanation

(*Student Book* page 99)

- Say: "**Defend** means *to act or express to protect something.*"
- Ask the class to repeat the explanation.
- Direct Partner 1s to say the explanation to Partner 2s.
- Direct Partner 2s to tell Partner 1s if their explanation was correct.

Unit 4 Lesson 4

defend

A. **Introduction and Pronunciation**
- This word is **defend**.
- Say the word in parts and then the whole word.

B. **Explanation**
- **Defend** means to act or express to protect something.

C. **Example Sentences**
1. Using facts and statistics, Brian **defended** his opinion about the school dress code.
2. Rita **defended** her friend by using examples of his kindness.

D. **Checking for Understanding**
1. When Darnell was ask to **defend** his position, he got mad and said that his word ought to be good enough.
   Question: Did Darnell **defend** his position? Yes or No? Why or why not?

2. José presented statistics and facts to demonstrate that eating plenty of fresh food was related to a healthy lifestyle.
   Question: Did José **defend** his position? Yes or No? Why or why not?

3. How do you think television executives **defend** their position to air cartoons on Saturday mornings?

99

C Example Sentences

(*Student Book* page 99)

> - ◆ Students chorally read example sentences with the teacher.
> - ◆ Student partners answer scripted questions with provided sentence stems.

- Ask the class to chorally read the first sentence with you:
  1. Using facts and statistics, Brian **defended** his opinion about the school dress code.
- Ask: "When Bran used facts and statistics to support his opinion, what was he doing?"
- Direct students to use the word **defending** in their answer with this sentence stem:
  Brian was **defending** _____ [his opinion about the school dress code].
- Have students answer to their partners.

- Ask the class to chorally read the second sentence with you:
  2. Rita **defended** her friend by using examples of his kindness.
- Ask: "When Rita used examples of her friend's kindness, what was she doing?"
- Direct students to use the word **defending** in their answer with this sentence stem:
  Rita was **defending** _____ [her friend].
- Have students answer to their partners.

D Checking for Understanding
(*Student Book* pages 99 and 100)

> - Students chorally read example sentences with the teacher.
> - Student partners answer scripted "Yes or No" questions with oral or written responses.

- Tell students that it is important to understand the meaning of an academic word when it is used in different forms.
- Explain to students that they will think, say, or write a response to sentences and explain the responses to their partners (e.g., say, "Partner 2s, read and respond to the first sentence. Partner 1s, tell your partner if you agree or disagree").
- Ask the class to chorally read the first sentence with you:
  1. When Darnell was ask to **defend** his position, he got mad and said that his word ought to be good enough.
- Ask: "Did Darnell **defend** his position?" (Answer: No)
- Direct students to respond to their partners by saying "yes" or "no" and explaining the reasons for their response.
  Note: While students are responding, monitor their exchanges. Ask two or three students to share their responses with the class.
- Ask the class to chorally read the second sentence with you:
  2. José presented statistics and facts to demonstrate that eating plenty of fresh food was related to a healthy lifestyle.
- Ask: "Did José **defend** his position?" (Answer: Yes)
- Direct students to respond to their partners by saying "yes" or "no" and explaining the reasons for their response.
  Note: While students are responding, monitor their exchanges. Ask two or three students to share their responses with the class.
- Ask the class to chorally read the third sentence with you:
  3. How do you think television executives **defend** their position to air cartoons on Saturday mornings?
- Direct partners to think, write, and share their answers with the class. (A suggested sentence stem: I think television executives **defend** _____.)
- Ask the class to chorally read the fourth sentence with you:
  4. Describe how you would **defend** your opinion of a favorite professional athlete.
- Direct partners to think, write, and share their answers with the class. (A suggested sentence stem: I would **defend** my opinion of _____.)

E Vocabulary Words Table

(*Student Book* page 100)

> ◆ Students add the academic word, an explanation of the word, and a usage example to the unit Vocabulary Words Table.

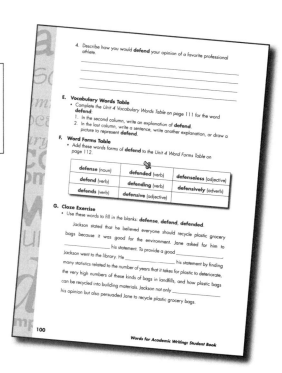

- Direct students to the *Unit 4 Vocabulary Words Table* on page 111 in the *Student Book*.
- Tell students to copy the explanation of the word **defend** from this lesson or to write their own explanation of **defend** in the second column.
- Then, direct students to write their own sentence, write another explanation, or draw a picture to represent the word **defend** in the last column.

Sample Answers

Word	Explanation	Sentence/Explanation/Picture
defend	To act or express to protect something	Pablo **defended** his point of view in class using statistics and facts.

F Word Forms Table

(*Student Book* page 100)

> ◆ Students add forms of the academic word to the unit Word Forms Table.

- Tell students that once a word is known, it is easy to learn other forms of the word. Adding a prefix or a suffix to a word makes a new but related word. Word forms have similar spellings, pronunciations, and meanings. They are often different parts of speech.
- Say: "It is important to understand the parts of speech: *nouns, verbs, adjectives,* and *adverbs*. We all know that a noun is a word that represents a person, place, thing, or idea. In school assignments, *nouns* are words that tell you <u>what you are asked to make</u> for an assignment or a test. A verb is a word that represents an action, an experience, or a state. In school assignments and tests, *verbs* are words that tell you <u>what you are to do</u> for the assignment. An adjective is a word that describes a noun or a pronoun. In school assignments, *adjectives* usually <u>give other information</u> about the assignment. An adverb is a word that adds meaning to a verb, an adjective, another adverb, or a sentence. In school assignments, *adverbs* tell you <u>how you should do</u> the assignment."
- Direct students to the *Unit 4 Word Forms Table* on page 112 in the *Student Book*.

- Then, direct students to add these word forms of **defend** to the table: **defense** (n), **defend** (v), **defends** (v), **defended** (v), **defending** (v), **defensive** (adj), **defenseless** (adj), **defensively** (adv).

Answer Key

NOUNS What you make or create	VERBS What you have to do for the assignment	ADJECTIVES Specific details about what you must do	ADVERBS Important information about how to do the assignment
defense	defend	defensive	defensively
	defends	defenseless	
	defended		
	defending		

G Cloze Exercise
(*Student Book* page 100)

> ◆ Students use word forms to complete a cloze exercise.

- Direct students to use the words **defense**, **defend**, and **defended** to complete this cloze exercise with their partners. Provide sufficient time for them to do so.
- Then, ask students to follow along as you read to determine if their answers to the cloze exercise are correct.

> Jackson stated that he believed everyone should recycle plastic grocery bags because it was good for the environment. Jane asked for him to **defend** his statement. To provide a good **defense**, Jackson went to the library. He **defended** his statement by finding many statistics related to the number of years that it takes for plastic to deteriorate, the very high numbers of these kinds of bags in landfills, and how plastic bags can be recycled into building materials. Jackson not only **defended** his opinion but also persuaded Jane to recycle plastic grocery bags.

H Informational Passage
(*Student Book* page 101)

> ◆ Students chorally read the informational passage with the teacher.
> ◆ Students then read the passage with their partners.

- Say: "This informational passage is designed to provide you with strategies for using the word **defend** in writing assignments."
- Ask students to read the passage chorally with you and then with their partners. *Note: You may want to make copies of the Chain graphic organizer (Graph A-5 on the accompanying CD-ROM) for students to refer to.*

Defend Your Position

When you are asked to **defend** your position about a topic, it is expected that you will be able to support your statements with evidence. The evidence should consist of facts and statistics. Evidence can also include quotes from knowledgeable sources of information. When you include facts, statistics, and quotes in your **defense**, you should be careful to name the sources. It is a good idea to use a Chain graphic organizer to put your evidence in logical order. Write the information you plan to use for your **defense** on index cards, and keep them available to use as references. They will help you keep your facts and quotes accurate. When you capably **defend** your position, you will gain the respect of others.

❶ Framed Paragraph and Sentence Stems
(*Student Book* pages 101 and 102)

Optional, to be used in conjunction with items J and K, following.)

Note: This section may be used to support struggling students. A framed paragraph is a tool to assist students in writing a paragraph. The paragraph frame provides a sample topic sentence, transitional sentence stems, and a conclusion sentence.

- Tell students that a framed paragraph is a tool to assist them in writing a paragraph.
- Read the topic sentence and the first transitional sentence stem with students.
- Stop reading after the first transitional sentence stem and assist students in completing the sentence in the context of the framed paragraph.
- Continue reading each sentence stem, stopping after each one to assist students in completing the stems.
- Once the paragraph frame is completed, direct students to read the entire paragraph to their partners.
- To complete the framed paragraph using the academic word defend, students may use any of this information compiled by Mothers Against Drunk Driving (MADD) and data for the year 2005 by the National Highway Traffic Safety Administration (NHTSA):

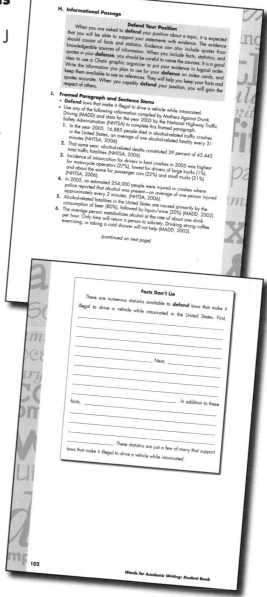

1. In the year 2005, 16,885 people died in alcohol-related traffic crashes in the United States, an average of one alcohol-related fatality every 31 minutes (NHTSA, 2006).
2. That same year, alcohol-related deaths constituted 39 percent of 43,443 total traffic fatalities (NHTSA, 2006).
3. Incidence of intoxication for drivers in fatal crashes in 2005 was highest for motorcycle operators (27%), lowest for drivers of large trucks (1%), and about the same for passenger cars (22%) and small trucks (21%) (NHTSA, 2006).
4. In 2005, an estimated 254,000 people were injured in crashes where police reported that alcohol was present—an average of one person injured approximately every 2 minutes (NHTSA, 2006).
5. Alcohol-related fatalities in the United States are caused primarily by the consumption of beer (80%), followed by liquor/wine (20%) (MADD, 2002).
6. The average person metabolizes alcohol at the rate of about one drink per hour. Only time will return a person to sobriety. Drinking strong coffee, exercising, or taking a cold shower will not help (MADD, 2002).

Sample Completed Framed Paragraph

Facts Don't Lie

There are numerous statistics available to **defend** laws that make it illegal to drive a vehicle while intoxicated in the United States. First, according to facts compiled by the National Highway Traffic Safety Administration (NHTSA), alcohol was a common factor in U.S. traffic accidents that injured more than 254,000 people in the year 2005. Next, also according to NHTSA data, it was estimated that, on average, one person died in an alcohol-related traffic accident in this country every 31 minutes in 2005. In addition to these facts, the NHTSA reported that alcohol-related fatalities accounted for 39 percent of all U.S. traffic deaths in 2005. These statistics are just a few of many that support laws that make it illegal to drive a vehicle while intoxicated.

Topic sentence:	There are numerous statistics available to defend laws that make it illegal to drive a vehicle while intoxicated in the United States.
First transitional sentence stem:	First, _____.
Second transitional sentence stem:	Next, _____.
Third transitional sentence stem:	In addition to these facts, _____.
Conclusion sentence:	These statistics are just a few of many that support laws that make it illegal to drive a vehicle while intoxicated.

J Paragraph Starters

(*Student Book* page 103)

- To reinforce understanding of the word **defend**, we suggest three related paragraph topics and topic sentences. You can assign these activities as independent practice, partner practice, or homework.

    1. **Paragraph topic:** Energy-efficient fluorescent lightbulbs cost more than regular lightbulbs. Does it make sense to use them? **Defend** your point of view.

       Topic sentence: Energy-efficient fluorescent lightbulbs cost more than regular lightbulbs. It is my belief that _____.

        - Ask students to think about the differences between the two different types of lightbulbs.

    2. **Paragraph topic:** Should students who break school rules be assigned to after-school clean-up duty? **Defend** your response.

       Topic sentence: Assigning students who break rules to after-school clean-up duty is _____.

        - Ask students to think about school rules and their opinion of being assigned to clean-up duty.

    3. **Paragraph topic:** State a **defense** for or against professional athletes' salaries.

       Topic sentence: The salaries made by professional athletes are _____.

        - Ask students to think about why professional athletes make millions of dollars. Are athletes worth what they are paid? Why or why not?

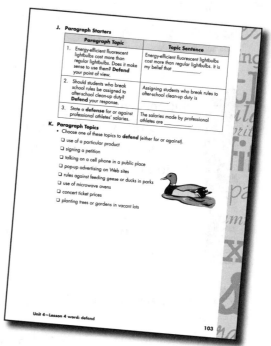

K Paragraph Topics

(*Student Book* page 103)

- We suggest additional writing topics of general knowledge that appeal to a diverse student population. Assign these topics for additional practice in applying the academic word **defend** to students' writing.

    ❑ use of a particular product

    ❑ signing a petition

    ❑ talking on a cell phone in a public place

    ❑ pop-up advertising on Web sites

    ❑ rules against feeding geese or ducks in parks

    ❑ use of microwave ovens

    ❑ concert ticket prices

    ❑ planting trees or gardens in vacant lots

state

Students will:
1. Correctly pronounce the word **state**.
2. Define the word **state** in an academic context.
3. Identify examples and non-examples of the word **state**.
4. Use the word **state** and its word forms in an academic context as evidenced by completion of a cloze exercise.
5. Write a paragraph that appropriately **states** key points of a topic or event.

A Introduction and Pronunciation
(*Student Book* page 104)

- Tell students: "This word is **state**."
- Say the word.
- Ask students to repeat the word.

B Explanation
(*Student Book* page 104)

- Say: "**State** means *to clearly give information or an opinion*."
- Ask students to repeat the explanation.
- Direct Partner 1s to give the explanation to Partner 2s.
- Direct Partner 2s to tell Partner 1s if their explanation was correct.

C Example Sentences
(*Student Book* page 104)

> ◆ Students chorally read example sentences with the teacher.
> ◆ Student partners answer scripted questions with provided sentence stems.

- Ask the class to chorally read the first sentence with you:
  1. The science teacher **stated** the characteristics of a volcano.
- Ask: "When the science teacher talked about the characteristics of a volcano, what was she doing?"
- Direct students to use the word **stating** in their answer with this sentence stem:
  The science teacher was **stating** _____ [the characteristics].
- Have students answer to their partners.
- Ask the class to chorally read the second sentence with you:
  2. The vice principal precisely **stated** the consequences of poor school attendance.

- Ask: "What was the vice principal doing?"
- Direct students to use the word **stating** in their answer with this sentence stem: The vice principal was **stating** _____ [the consequences].
- Have students answer to their partners.

D Checking for Understanding
(*Student Book* pages 104 and 105)

> ◆ Students chorally read example sentences with the teacher.
> ◆ Student partners answer scripted "Yes or No" questions with oral or written responses.

- Tell students that it is important to understand the meaning of an academic word when it is used in different forms.
- Explain to students that they will think, say, or write a response to sentences and explain the responses to their partners (e.g., say, "Partner 2s, read and respond to the first sentence. Partner 1s, tell your partner if you agree or disagree").
- Ask the class to chorally read the first sentence with you:
  1. The teacher asked Philip to compare and contrast oceans with freshwater lakes.
- Ask: "Should Philip **state** only the names of freshwater lakes?" (Answer: No)
- Direct students to respond to their partners by saying "yes" or "no" and explaining the reasons for their response.
  Note: While students are responding, monitor their exchanges. Ask two or three students to share their responses with the class.
- Ask the class to chorally read the second sentence with you:
  2. Steve clearly reported the key points of First Amendment rights.
- Ask: "Did Steve **state** key points?" (Answer: Yes)
- Direct students to respond to their partners by saying "yes" or "no" and explaining the reasons for their response.
  Note: While students are responding, monitor their exchanges. Ask two or three students to share their responses with the class.
- Ask the class to chorally read the third sentence with you:
  3. The student handbook clearly **states** the types of footwear that are acceptable at school.
- Ask: "Can students find out in the handbook if it's OK to wear flip-flops to school?" (Answer: Yes)
- Direct partners to think, write, and share their answers with the class. (A suggested sentence stem: The school handbooks **states** _____.)
- Ask the class to chorally read the fourth sentence with you:
  4. When was the last time your parents **stated** your curfew?
- Direct partners to think, write, and share their answers with the class. (A suggested sentence stem: The last time my parents **stated** my curfew was when _____.)

E Vocabulary Words Table

(Student Book page 105)

> ◆ Students add the academic word, an explanation of the word, and a usage example to the unit Vocabulary Words Table.

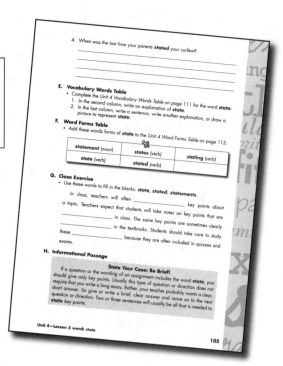

- Direct students to the *Unit 4 Vocabulary Words Table* on page 111 in the *Student Book*.
- Tell students to copy the explanation of the word **state** from this lesson or to write their own explanation of **state** in the second column.
- Then, direct students to write their own sentence, write another explanation, or draw a picture to represent the word **state** in the last column.

Sample Answers

Word	Explanation	Sentence/Explanation/Picture
state	To clearly give information or an opinion	Kim will **state** the names of the seven continents.

F Word Forms Table

(Student Book page 105)

> ◆ Students add forms of the academic word to the unit Word Forms Table.

- Tell students that once a word is known, it is easy to learn other forms of the word. Adding a prefix or a suffix to a word makes a new but related word. Word forms have similar spellings, pronunciations, and meanings. They are often different parts of speech.
- Say: "It is important to understand the parts of speech: *nouns, verbs, adjectives,* and *adverbs.* We all know that a noun is a word that represents a person, place, thing, or idea. In school assignments, *nouns* are words that tell you <u>what you are asked to make</u> for an assignment or a test. A verb is a word that represents an action, an experience, or a state. In school assignments and tests, *verbs* are words that tell you <u>what you are to do</u> for the assignment. An adjective is a word that describes a noun or a pronoun. In school assignments, *adjectives* usually <u>give other information</u> about the assignment. An adverb is a word that adds meaning to a verb, an adjective, another adverb, or a sentence. In school assignments, *adverbs* tell you <u>how you should do</u> the assignment."
- Direct students to the *Unit 4 Word Forms Table* on page 112 in the *Student Book.*

Words for Academic Writing: Teacher Guide

- Then, direct students to add these word forms of **state** to the table: **statement** (n), **state** (v), **states** (v), **stated** (v), **stating** (v).

Answer Key

NOUNS What you make or create	VERBS What you have to do for the assignment	ADJECTIVES Specific details about what you must do	ADVERBS Important information about how to do the assignment
statement	state		
	states		
	stated		
	stating		

G Cloze Exercise
(*Student Book* page 105)

- ◆ Students use word forms to complete a cloze exercise.

- Direct students to use the words **state**, **stated**, and **statements** to complete this cloze exercise with their partners. Provide sufficient time for them to do so.
- Then, ask students to follow along as you read to determine if their answers to the cloze exercise are correct.

> In class, teachers will often __**state**__ key points about a topic. Teachers expect that students will take notes on key points that are __**stated**__ in class. The same key points are sometimes clearly __**stated**__ in the textbooks. Students should take care to study these __**statements**__ because they are often included in quizzes and exams.

H Informational Passage
(*Student Book* page 105)

- ◆ Students chorally read the informational passage with the teacher.
- ◆ Students then read the passage with their partners.

- Say: "This informational passage is designed to provide you with strategies for using the word **state** in writing assignments."
- Ask students to read the passage chorally with you and then with their partners.

State Your Case: Be Brief!
If a question or the wording of an assignment includes the word **state**, you should give only key points. Usually this type of question or direction does not require that you write a long essay. Rather, your teacher probably wants a clear, short answer. So give or write a brief, clear answer and move on to the next question or direction. Two or three sentences will usually be all that is needed to **state** key points.

I Framed Paragraph and Sentence Stems

(Student Book page 106)

Optional, to be used in conjunction with items J and K, following.)

Note: This section may be used to support struggling students. A framed paragraph is a tool to assist students in writing a paragraph. The paragraph frame provides a sample topic sentence, transitional sentence stems, and a conclusion sentence.

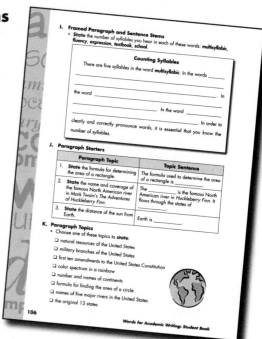

- Tell students that a framed paragraph is a tool to assist them in writing a paragraph.
- Read the topic sentence and the first transitional sentence stem with students.
- Stop reading after the first transitional sentence stem and assist students in completing the sentence in the context of the framed paragraph.
- Continue reading each sentence stem, stopping after each one to assist students in completing the stems.
- Once the paragraph frame is completed, direct students to read the entire paragraph to their partners.
- The direction to students is: "**State** the number of syllables you hear in each of these words: **multisyllabic, fluency, expression, textbook, school**."

Sample Completed Framed Paragraph

Counting Syllables

There are five syllables in the word **multisyllabic**. In the words **<u>fluency</u> and <u>expression</u>, <u>there are three syllables</u>**. In the word **<u>textbook</u>, <u>there are two syllables</u>**. In the word **<u>school</u>, <u>there is only one syllable</u>**. In order to clearly and correctly pronounce words, it is essential that you know the number of syllables.

Topic sentence:	There are five syllables in the word **multisyllabic**.
First transitional sentence stem:	In the words _____.
Second transitional sentence stem:	In the word _____.
Third transitional sentence stem:	In the word _____.
Conclusion sentence:	In order to clearly and correctly pronounce words, it is essential that you know the number of syllables.

J Paragraph Starters

(*Student Book* page 106)

- To reinforce understanding of the word **state**, we suggest three related paragraph topics and topic sentences. You can assign these activities as independent practice, partner practice, or homework.

  1. **Paragraph topic: State** the formula for determining the area of a rectangle.

     Topic sentence: The formula used to determine the area of a rectangle is _____.

     - Ask students to **state** what they know about how to determine the area of a rectangle (Answer: width x length).

  2. **Paragraph topic: State** the name and coverage of the famous North American river in Mark Twain's *The Adventures of Huckleberry Finn*.

     Topic sentence: The _____ is the famous North American river in *Huckleberry Finn*. It flows through the states of _____.

     - Encourage students to look up this information in a reference book or on the Internet. (Answers: Mississippi River, which flows through Minnesota, Wisconsin, Iowa, Illinois, Missouri, Kentucky, Tennessee, Arkansas, Mississippi, and Louisiana).

  3. **Paragraph topic: State** the distance of the sun from Earth.

     Topic sentence: Earth is _____.

     - Encourage students to look up this information in a reference book or on the Internet. (Answer: Average distance is about 93 million miles. The sun is closest to Earth in January and farthest from Earth in early July.)

K Paragraph Topics

(*Student Book* page 106)

- We suggest additional writing topics of general knowledge that appeal to a diverse student population. Assign these topics for additional practice in applying the academic word **state** to students' writing.

  ❑ natural resources of the United States

  ❑ military branches of the United States

  ❑ first ten amendments to the United States Constitution

  ❑ color spectrum in a rainbow

  ❑ number and names of continents

  ❑ formula for finding the area of a circle

  ❑ names of five major rivers in the United States

  ❑ the original 13 states

critique

OBJECTIVES

Students will:

1. Correctly pronounce the word **critique**.
2. Define the word **critique** in an academic context.
3. Identify examples and non-examples of the word **critique**.
4. Use the word **critique** and its word forms in an academic context as evidenced by completion of a cloze exercise.
5. Write a paragraph that appropriately **critiques** a product, an event, or an activity.

A Introduction and Pronunciation
(*Student Book* page 107)

- Tell students the word: "This word is **critique**."
- Say the word in parts.
- Ask students to repeat the word in parts and then the whole word.

B Explanation
(*Student Book* page 107)

- Say: "**Critique** means *to judge both the strong and weak points of something or someone.*"
- Ask the class to repeat the explanation.
- Direct Partner 1s to give the explanation to Partner 2s.
- Direct Partner 2s to tell Partner 1s if their explanation was correct.

Unit 4 Lesson 6 **critique**

A. Introduction and Pronunciation
- This word is **critique**.
- Say the word in parts and then the whole word.

B. Explanation
- **Critique** means *to judge both the strong and weak points of something or someone.*

C. Example Sentences
1. Humberto was asked to **critique** the new computer software.
2. When Jan was asked to **critique** the school play, she wrote about its strong and weak points.

D. Checking for Understanding
1. Joe was asked to **critique** the school's basketball team, so he wrote about only those things he disliked about it.
   *Question: Did Joe fairly **critique** the basketball team? Yes or No? Why or why not?*

2. When you write a **critique**, you should include both strengths and weaknesses.
   Question: Is this statement true or false? Why?

3. **Critique** the last TV program you watched.

107

C Example Sentences
(*Student Book* page 107)

> ◆ Students chorally read example sentences with the teacher.
> ◆ Student partners answer scripted questions with provided sentence stems.

- Ask the class to chorally read the first sentence with you:
  1. Humberto was asked to **critique** the new computer software.
- Ask: "What was Humberto asked to **critique**?"
- Direct students to use the word **critique** in their answer with this sentence stem:
  Humberto was asked to **critique** _____ [the new computer software].
- Have students answer to their partners.
- Ask the class to chorally read the second sentence with you:
  2. When Jan was asked to **critique** the school play, she wrote about its strong and weak points.

- Ask: "When Jan stated the good and bad points of the school play, what was she doing?"
- Direct students to use the word **critiquing** in their answer with this sentence stem:

  Jan was **critiquing** _____ [the school play].
- Have students answer to their partners.

D Checking for Understanding
(*Student Book* pages 107 and 108)

> ◆ Students chorally read example sentences with the teacher.
> ◆ Student partners answer scripted "Yes or No" questions with oral or written responses.

- Tell students that it is important to understand the meaning of an academic word when it is used in different forms.
- Explain to students that they will think, say, or write a response to sentences and explain the responses to their partners (e.g., say, "Partner 2s, read and respond to the first sentence. Partner 1s, tell your partner if you agree or disagree").
- Ask the class to chorally read the first sentence with you:
  1. Joe was asked to **critique** the school's basketball team, so he wrote about only those things he disliked about it.
- Ask: "Did Joe fairly **critique** the basketball team?" (Answer: No)
- Direct students to respond to their partners by saying "yes" or "no" and explaining the reasons for their response.
  Note: While students are responding, monitor their exchanges. Ask two or three students to share their responses with the class.
- Ask the class to chorally read the second sentence with you:
  2. When you write a **critique**, you should include both strengths and weaknesses.
- Ask: "Is this statement true or false?" (Answer: True)
- Direct students to respond to their partners by saying "true" or "false" and explaining the reasons for their response.
  Note: While students are responding, monitor their exchanges. Ask two or three students to share their responses with the class.
- Ask the class to chorally read the third sentence with you:
  3. **Critique** the last TV program you watched.
- Direct partners to think, write, and share their answers with the class. (A suggested sentence stem: My **critique** of [program name]_____.)
- Ask the class to chorally read the fourth sentence with you:
  4. **Critique** your school library.
- Direct partners to think, write, and share their answers with the class. (A suggested sentence stem: My **critique** of our school library would include _____.)

E Vocabulary Words Table

(*Student Book* page 108)

Students add the academic word, an explanation of the word, and a usage example to the unit Vocabulary Words Table.

- Direct students to the *Unit 4 Vocabulary Words Table* on page 111 in the *Student Book*.

- Tell students to copy the explanation of the word **critique** from this lesson or to write their own explanation of **critique** in the second column.

- Then, direct students to write their own sentence, write another explanation, or draw a picture to represent the word **critique** in the last column.

Sample Answers

Word	Explanation	Sentence/Explanation/Picture
critique	To judge both the strong and weak points of something or someone	Jackson will **critique** the student council's efforts in fundraising for a school garden.

F Word Forms Table

(*Student Book* page 108)

- ◆ Students add forms of the academic word to the unit Word Forms Table.

- Tell students that once a word is known, it is easy to learn other forms of the word. Adding a prefix or a suffix to a word makes a new but related word. Word forms have similar spellings, pronunciations, and meanings. They are often different parts of speech.

- Say: "It is important to understand the parts of speech: *nouns, verbs, adjectives,* and *adverbs*. We all know that a noun is a word that represents a person, place, thing, or idea. In school assignments, *nouns* are words that tell you <u>what you are asked to make</u> for an assignment or a test. A verb is a word that represents an action, an experience, or a state. In school assignments and tests, *verbs* are words that tell you <u>what you are to do</u> for the assignment. An adjective is a word that describes a noun or a pronoun. In school assignments, *adjectives* usually <u>give other information</u> about the assignment. An adverb is a word that adds meaning to a verb, an adjective, another adverb, or a sentence. In school assignments, *adverbs* tell you <u>how you should do</u> the assignment."

- Direct students to the *Unit 4 Word Forms Table* on page 112 in the *Student Book*.

- Then, direct students to add these word forms of **critique** to the table: **critique** (n), **critiques** (n), **critique** (v), **critiques** (v), **critiqued** (v), **critiquing** (v), **critical** (adj), **critically** (adv).

NOUNS What you make or create	VERBS What you have to do for the assignment	ADJECTIVES Specific details about what you must do	ADVERBS Important information about how to do the assignment
critique	**critique**	**critical**	**critically**
critiques	**critiques**		
	critiqued		
	critiquing		

G Cloze Exercise

(*Student Book* page 108)

◆ Students use word forms to complete a cloze exercise.

- Direct students to use the words **critique** and **critiqued** to complete this cloze exercise with their partners. Provide sufficient time for them to do so.

- Then, ask students to follow along as you read to determine if their answers to the cloze exercise are correct.

> Vince was asked to __**critique**__ the use of coal for heating homes. In his __**critique**__, Vince was careful to include both the plusses and minuses of using this energy source. Vince also clearly stated his opinion on this issue. Because Vince __**critiqued**__ both sides of the issue, his __**critique**__ was well received by his teacher.

H Informational Passage

(*Student Book* pages 108 and 109)

◆ Students chorally read the informational passage with the teacher.

◆ Students then read the passage with their partners.

- Say: "This informational passage is designed to provide you with strategies for using the word **critique** in writing assignments."

- Ask students to read the passage chorally with you and then with their partners. *Note: You may want to make copies of the T-Chart graphic organizer (Graph A-3 on the accompanying CD-ROM) for students to refer to.*

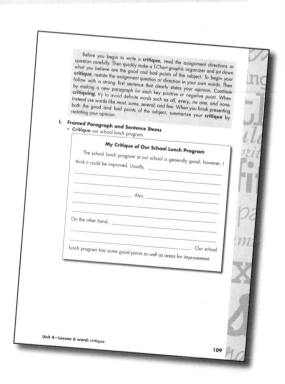

"Critique" Does Not Mean "Negative"

Oftentimes when students are asked to write a **critique**, they think it means to be negative about the subject. This is not so. When you are asked to **critique**, you should judge something carefully by looking at both its positive and negative aspects. A **critique** is an opinion.

Before you begin to write a **critique**, read the assignment directions or question carefully. Then quickly make a T-Chart graphic organizer and jot down what you believe are the good and bad points of the subject. To begin your **critique**, restate the assignment question or direction in your own words. Then follow with a strong first sentence that clearly states your opinion. Continue by making a new paragraph for each key positive or negative point. When **critiquing**, try to avoid definite words such as *all, every, no one,* and *none.* Instead use words like *most, some, several,* and *few.* When you finish presenting both the good and bad points of the subject, summarize your **critique** by restating your opinion.

❶ Framed Paragraph and Sentence Stems
(*Student Book* page 109)

Optional, to be used in conjunction with items J and K, following.)

Note: This section may be used to support struggling students. A framed paragraph is a tool to assist students in writing a paragraph. The paragraph frame provides a sample topic sentence, transitional sentence stems, and a conclusion sentence.

- Tell students that a framed paragraph is a tool to assist them in writing a paragraph.
- Read the topic sentence and the first transitional sentence stem with students.
- Stop reading after the first transitional sentence stem and assist students in completing the sentence in the context of the framed paragraph.
- Continue reading each sentence stem, stopping after each one to assist students in completing the stems.
- Once the paragraph frame is completed, direct students to read the entire paragraph to their partners.
- The direction to students is: "**Critique** our school lunch program."

Sample Completed Framed Paragraph

My Critique of Our School Lunch Program

The school lunch program at our school is generally good; however, I think it could be improved. Usually, <u>the food is nutritious and tastes good</u>. Also, <u>prices are fair. Most kids choose to buy their lunch at school</u>. On the other hand, <u>the program could be improved with a greater selection of food items. The lines could move faster, too</u>. Our school lunch program has some good points as well as areas for improvement.

Topic sentence:	The school lunch program at our school is generally good; however, I think it could be improved.
First transitional sentence stem:	Usually, _____.
Second transitional sentence stem:	Also, _____.
Third transitional sentence stem:	On the other hand, _____.
Conclusion sentence:	Our school lunch program has some good points as well as areas for improvement.

J Paragraph Starters

(*Student Book* page 110)

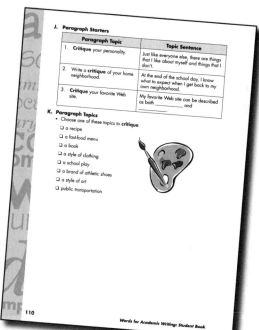

- To reinforce understanding of the word **critique**, we suggest three related paragraph topics and topic sentences. You can assign these activities as independent practice, partner practice, or homework.

1. **Paragraph topic: Critique** your personality.

   Topic sentence: Just like everyone else, there are things that I like about myself and things that I don't.

   - Ask students to think about how they may come across to other people.

2. **Paragraph topic:** Write a **critique** of your home neighborhood.

   Topic sentence: At the end of the school day, I know what to expect when I get back to my own neighborhood.

   - Ask students to think about how they feel about their home neighborhood. What things do they like and what things do they want to change?

3. **Paragraph topic: Critique** your favorite Web site.

   Topic sentence: My favorite Web site can be described as both _____ and _____.

   - Ask students to think about what they like about the Web site and how they would change it.

K Paragraph Topics

(*Student Book* page 110)

- We suggest additional writing topics of general knowledge that appeal to a diverse student population. Assign these topics for additional practice in applying the academic word **critique** to students' writing.

  ❑ a recipe

  ❑ a fast-food menu

  ❑ a book

  ❑ a style of clothing

  ❑ a school play

  ❑ a brand of athletic shoes

  ❑ a style of art

  ❑ public transportation

Unit 4 Posttest

Objective	To determine students' understanding of the academic words that were presented in Unit 4
Materials needed	For each student, one copy of the Unit 4 Posttest (refer to the accompanying CD-ROM) and two sheets of blank paper
Time allotment	35 minutes (Part A, 10 minutes; Part B, 10 minutes; Part C, 15 minutes)

Instructional Procedure

Step 1 Distribute Unit 4 Posttest and two sheets of blank paper to each student. Say:
- "Write your name and today's date on the lines at the top of the Posttest and at the top of each sheet of blank paper. I will collect all of them after you have finished the posttest."

Step 2 Review the directions for the Unit 4 Posttest, then administer the posttest. Say:
- "Only this Posttest score will be recorded as part of your grade. So do your very best."
- "Look at Part A. Let's read the directions together." *(Read directions out loud with students.)*
- "Place your finger on each word as I read it: **enumerate**, **relate**, **persuade**, **defend**, **state**, **critique**."
- "Now, place your finger on each lowercase letter next to the explanations in the right-hand column. Listen as I read the explanation for each letter."
  a. To list one thing after another in a specific order; to count off
  b. To judge both the strong and weak points of something or someone
  c. To act or express to protect something
  d. To cause others to change their minds or take action
  e. To clearly give information or an opinion
  f. To tell how things, people, or events are connected or alike
- "Match each word with the explanation that you think is correct. Write the letter of the explanation in the middle column, next to the word."
- "You will have 10 minutes to complete Part A. Ready? Begin." *(After 10 minutes, proceed to Part B.)*
- "Now, look at Part B. It is important to know how to use academic words within the context of print."
- "Read each sentence and fill in the blank with one of the words listed in the directions."
- "You will have 10 minutes to complete Part B. Any questions? Begin." *(After 10 minutes, proceed to Part C.)*

- "Now, read the directions for Part C. Remember to make a graphic organizer on one sheet of paper to plan your answer. Then write a paragraph using a topic sentence, transitional sentences, and a conclusion sentence on the other sheet of paper. You can receive up to 15 points for this section: 5 points for the graphic organizer, 5 points for using a paragraph format, and 5 points for content."
- "You will have 15 minutes to complete Part C. Any questions? Begin." *(After 10 minutes, tell students they have 5 minutes to finish.)*
- After 5 minutes pass, say, "Please turn in your tests and papers to me."

Refer to *Appendix D* for Unit 4 Posttest Answer Key

Unit 4 Generative Assessment *(optional)*

Objective	To ensure that students are able to correctly apply Unit 4 academic words in a generalized setting
Materials needed	For each student, one copy of the Unit 4 Generative Assessment (refer to the accompanying CD-ROM) and two sheets of blank paper
Time allotment	One class period

Instructional Procedure

Step 1 Distribute Unit 4 Generative Assessment and two sheets of blank paper to each student. Say:
- "Write your name and today's date on the lines at the top of the assessment and at the top of each sheet of blank paper. I will collect all of them after you have finished the assessment."

Step 2 Review the directions for the Unit 4 Generative Assessment, then administer the assessment. Say:
- "This assessment is designed to find out how well you are able to apply the Unit 4 academic words to general situations. This assessment will ask you to demonstrate your understanding of the Unit 4 words by providing examples based on your personal knowledge and experiences."
- "Read each direction, and then use the blank paper to create your own graphic organizer to plan your answer."
- "Then, use your graphic organizer to help you write a short paragraph using a topic sentence, transitional sentences, and a conclusion sentence."
- "You can receive up to 15 points for each answer: 5 points for your graphic organizer, 5 points for using a paragraph format, and 5 points for content. You will have the whole class period to complete this assessment."
- "Any questions? When you have finished, please turn in your assessment and graphic organizers to me. Begin."

Grading Criteria

To grade a Generative Assessment, we suggest allocating a maximum of 15 points *per assessment item* as follows:
- Up to 5 points for use of a graphic organizer
- Up to 5 points for conventions (correct paragraphing; use of topic, transitional, and conclusion sentences; correct punctuation; correct spelling)
- Up to 5 points for content

Unit 5 *(Optional)*—Unit 5 is designed to ensure that students understand academic writing terms that are commonly used to evaluate writing. Since writing terms are concept vocabulary, Unit 5 does not include a Vocabulary Words Table, Word Forms Table, framed paragraph and sentence stems, paragraph starters, or additional writing topics.

Unit 5 Pretest

Objective	To determine students' prior knowledge of academic writing terms that will be taught in Unit 5
Materials needed	For each student, one copy of the Unit 5 Pretest (refer to the accompanying CD-ROM)
Time allotment	20 minutes (Part A, 10 minutes; Part B, 10 minutes)

Instructional Procedure

Step 1   Distribute Unit 5 Pretest to students. Say:
- "Write your name and today's date on the lines at the top of the Pretest."

Step 2   Review the directions for Unit 5 Pretest, then administer the pretest. Say:
- "Look at Part A. Let's read the directions together."
  (Read the directions out loud with students.)
- "Place your finger on each writing term as I read it: **ideas and content**, **conventions**, **sentence fluency**, **word choice**, **organization**, **voice**."
- "Now, place your finger on each lowercase letter next to the explanations in the right-hand column. Listen as I read the explanation for each letter."
  - **a.** The selection of words to create a specific message
  - **b.** Sentences that start with different words, are of different lengths, and are easy to understand
  - **c.** The use of words that lets the reader know the writer's personality and feelings
  - **d.** The state of being well arranged in a logical manner
  - **e.** Standards that are applied to writing, including correct capitalization, punctuation, spelling, and choice of words
  - **f.** Reasons for writing a paper that conveys a message
- "Match each writing term with the explanation that you think is correct. Write the letter of the explanation in the middle column, next to the writing term."
- "You will have 10 minutes to complete Part A. Ready? Begin."
  (After 10 minutes, proceed to Part B.)

- "Now, look at Part B. It is important to know how to use academic writing terms within the context of print."
- "Read each sentence and fill in the blank with one of the writing terms according to the directions."
- "You will have 10 minutes to complete Part B. Any questions? Begin."
- After 10 minutes, say, "Please return your tests to me."

Refer to *Appendix D* for Unit 5 Pretest Answer Key

ideas and content

Students will:
1. Define the writing term **ideas and content**.
2. Identify examples and non-examples of the writing term **ideas and content**.

A Introduction and Pronunciation
(*Student Book* page 115)

• Introduce the writing term to students: "This writing term is **ideas and content**."
• Ask students to repeat the writing term.

B Explanation
(*Student Book* page 115)

• Say: "In writing, **ideas and content** refer to *the reasons for writing a paper*. **Ideas and content** *provide a message that is easy to follow*."
• Ask the class to repeat the explanation.
• Direct Partner 1s to give the explanation to Partner 2s.
• Direct Partner 2s to tell Partner 1s if their explanation was correct.

ideas and content
Unit 5   Lesson 1

A. Introduction and Pronunciation
• This writing term is **ideas and content**.
• Say the writing term.

B. Explanation
• In writing, **ideas and content** refer to the reasons for writing a paper. **Ideas and content** provide a message that is easy to follow.

C. Example Sentences
1. The **ideas and content** of Teresa's paper focus on reasons why she wants to protect the wild geese in the park.
2. When Vince wrote about whales, he made sure that the **ideas and content** were easy to follow.

D. Checking for Understanding
1. In his paper about the life cycle of butterflies, Max was careful to explain how each stage contributed to the environment.
   Question: Do you think that the **ideas and content** of Max's paper conveyed a message that was easy to follow? Yes or No? Why or why not?

2. Betty filled five pages with interesting but unrelated facts about insects in no specific order.
   Question: Do you think that the **ideas and content** of Betty's paper conveyed a message that was easy to follow? Yes or No? Why or why not?

115

C Example Sentences
(*Student Book* page 115)

◆ Students chorally read example sentences with the teacher.
◆ Student partners answer scripted questions with provided sentence stems.

• Ask the class to chorally read the first sentence with you:
  1. The **ideas and content** of Teresa's paper focus on reasons why she wants to protect the wild geese in the park.
• Ask: "When Teresa focuses on reasons that the wild geese should be protected, what writing term is she applying?"

- Direct students to use the writing term **ideas and content** in their answer with this sentence stem:
  Teresa is applying the writing term **ideas and content** when _____ [she focuses on reasons for protecting the wild geese in the park].
- Have students answer to their partners.
- Ask the class to chorally read the second sentence with you:
  2. When Vince wrote about whales, he made sure that the **ideas and content** were easy to follow.
- Ask: "What did Vince make easy to follow when he wrote about whales?"
- Direct students to use the writing term **ideas and content** in their answer with this sentence stem:
  Vince made sure that the _____ [**ideas and content** were easy to follow].
- Have students answer to their partners.

D Checking for Understanding
(*Student Book* pages 115 and 116)

> ◆ Students chorally read example sentences with the teacher.
> ◆ Student partners answer scripted "Yes or No" questions with oral or written responses.

- Explain to students that they will think, say, or write a response to sentences and explain the responses to their partners (e.g., say, "Partner 2s, read and respond to the first sentence. Partner 1s, tell your partner if you agree or disagree").
- Ask the class to chorally read the first sentence with you:
  1. In his paper about the life cycle of butterflies, Max was careful to explain how each stage contributed to the environment.
- Ask: "Do you think that the **ideas and content** of Max's paper conveyed a message that was easy to follow?" (Answer: Yes)
- Direct students to respond to their partners by saying "yes" or "no" and explaining the reasons for their response.
  Note: While students are responding, monitor their exchanges. Ask two or three students to share their responses with the class.
- Ask the class to chorally read the second sentence with you:
  2. Betty filled five pages with interesting but unrelated facts about insects in no specific order.
- Ask: "Do you think that the **ideas and content** of Betty's paper conveyed a message that was easy to follow?" (Answer: No)
- Direct students to respond to their partners by saying "yes" or "no" and explaining the reasons for their response.
  Note: While students are responding, monitor their exchanges. Ask two or three students to share their responses with the class.
- Ask the class to chorally read the third sentence with you:
  3. If you were a teacher, what would you look for when grading papers for **ideas and content**?

- Direct partners to think, write, and share their answers with the class. (A suggested sentence stem: If I were a teacher, _____.)
- Ask the class to chorally read the fourth sentence with you:

  4. Were the **ideas and content** of the last article you read clear and focused?

- Direct partners to think, write, and share their answers with the class. (A suggested sentence stem: The **ideas and content** of the last article I read _____.)

E Writing Terms Table
(*Student Book* page 116)

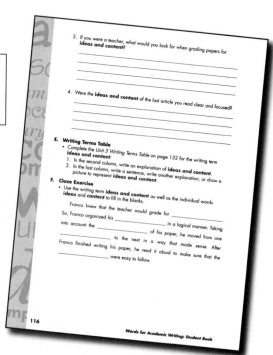

> ◆ Students add the academic writing term, an explanation of the term, and a usage example to the unit Writing Terms Table.

- Direct students to the *Unit 5 Writing Terms Table* on page 132 in the *Student Book*.
- Tell students to copy the explanation of the writing term **ideas and content** from this lesson or to write their own explanation of **ideas and content** in the second column.
- Then, direct students to write their own sentence, write another explanation, or draw a picture to represent the writing term **ideas and content** in the last column.

Sample Answers

Word	Explanation	Sentence/Explanation/Picture
ideas and content	Reasons for writing a paper that conveys a message	The **ideas and content** of the article on sleep allowed readers to better understand why everyone should get eight hours of sleep every night.

F Cloze Exercise
(*Student Book* page 116)

> ◆ Students use the writing term to complete a cloze exercise.

*Note: To help students better comprehend the meaning of the writing term **ideas and content**, the individual words **ideas** and **content** are included in the Cloze Exercise.*

- Direct students to use the writing term **ideas and content** as well as the individual words **ideas** and **content** to complete this cloze exercise with their partners. Provide sufficient time for them to do so.

- Then, ask students to follow along as you read to determine if their answers to the cloze exercise are correct.

> Franco knew that the teacher would grade for __**ideas and content**__. So, Franco organized his __**ideas**__ in a logical manner. Taking into account the __**content**__ of his paper, he moved from one __**idea**__ to the next in a way that made sense. After Franco finished writing his paper, he read it aloud to make sure that the __**ideas and content**__ were easy to follow.

G Informational Passage

(Student Book page 117)

> ◆ Students chorally read the informational passage with the teacher.
> ◆ Students then read the passage with their partners.

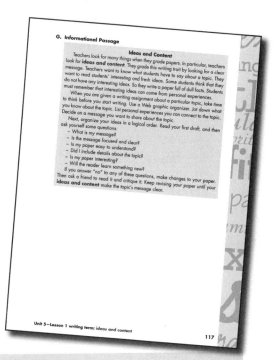

- Say: "This informational passage is designed to provide you with strategies for applying the concept of **ideas and content** to your writing assignments."
- Ask students to read the passage chorally with you and then with their partners. *Note: You may want to make copies of the Web graphic organizer (Graph A-1 on the accompanying CD-ROM) for students to refer to.*

Ideas and Content

Teachers look for many things when they grade papers. In particular, teachers look for **ideas and content**. They grade this writing trait by looking for a clear message. Teachers want to know what students have to say about a topic. They want to read students' interesting and fresh ideas. Some students think that they do not have any interesting ideas. So they write a paper full of dull facts. Students must remember that interesting ideas can come from personal experiences.

When you are given a writing assignment about a particular topic, take time to think before you start writing. Use a Web graphic organizer. Jot down what you know about the topic. List personal experiences you can connect to the topic. Decide on a message you want to share about the topic.

(continued)

Next, organize your ideas in a logical order. Read your first draft, and then ask yourself some questions:

– What is my message?
– Is the message focused and clear?
– Is my paper easy to understand?
– Did I include details about the topic?
– Is my paper interesting?
– Will the reader learn something new?

If you answer "no" to any of these questions, make changes to your paper. Then ask a friend to read it and critique it. Keep revising your paper until your **ideas and content** make the topic's message clear.

OBJECTIVES

Students will:
1. Define the writing term **conventions**.
2. Identify examples and non-examples of the writing term **conventions**.

A Introduction and Pronunciation
(*Student Book* page 118)

*   Introduce the writing term to students: "This writing term is **conventions**."
*   Ask students to repeat the writing term.

B Explanation
(*Student Book* page 118)

*   Say: "**Conventions** is a writing term that means *standards that are applied to writing, including correct capitalization, punctuation, spelling, and choice of words*."
*   Ask the class to repeat the explanation.
*   Direct Partner 1s to give the explanation to Partner 2s.
*   Direct Partner 2s to tell Partner 1s if their explanation was correct.

Unit 5   Lesson 2   conventions

A. Introduction and Pronunciation
  • This writing term is **conventions**.
  • Say the writing term.

B. Explanation
  • **Conventions** is a writing term that means *standards that are applied to writing, including correct capitalization, punctuation, spelling, and choice of words*.

C. Example Sentences
  1. Jackson knew that the proper use of **conventions** such as correct spelling and capitalization of proper nouns would make his writing easy for others to understand.
  2. After Stefano finished writing his first draft, he carefully edited his paper to make sure he followed **conventions** such as correct word usage and sentence punctuation.

D. Checking for Understanding
  1. Because Tanya writes very creatively, she did not think it was necessary to check the spelling and punctuation in her assignment paper. *Question: Did Tanya check her writing for* **conventions**? *Yes or No? Why or why not?*
  _____
  _____
  _____

  2. Roberto wanted to get a good grade. After he wrote his first draft, he proofread his paper for correct spelling, grammar, capitalization, and punctuation. *Question: Did Roberto edit for* **conventions**? *Yes or No? Why or why not?*
  _____
  _____
  _____

118   *Words for Academic Writing: Student Book*

C Example Sentences
(*Student Book* page 118)

> ◆ Students chorally read example sentences with the teacher.
> ◆ Student partners answer scripted questions with provided sentence stems.

*   Ask the class to chorally read the first sentence with you:
    1. Jackson knew that the proper use of **conventions** such as correct spelling and capitalization of proper nouns would make his writing easy for others to understand.
*   Ask: "What did Jackson know about making his writing easy for others to understand?"
*   Direct students to use the writing term **conventions** in their answer with this sentence stem:
    Jackson knew that _____ [properly using these **conventions** would make his writing easy to understand.]
*   Have students answer to their partners.

- Ask the class to chorally read the second sentence with you:
  2. After Stefano finished writing his first draft, he carefully edited his paper to make sure he followed **conventions** such as correct word usage and sentence punctuation.
- Ask: "When Stefano finished writing his first draft, what did he do?"
- Direct students to use the writing term **conventions** in their answer with this sentence stem:

  Stefano edited for **conventions** such as _____ [correct word usage and sentence punctuation.]
- Have students answer to their partners.

D Checking for Understanding
(*Student Book* pages 118 and 119)

> ◆ Students chorally read example sentences with the teacher.
> ◆ Student partners answer scripted "Yes or No" questions with oral or written responses.

- Explain to students that they will think, say, or write a response to sentences and explain the responses to their partners (e.g., say, "Partner 2s, read and respond to the first sentence. Partner 1s, tell your partner if you agree or disagree").
- Ask the class to chorally read the first sentence with you:
  1. Because Tanya writes very creatively, she did not think it was necessary to check the spelling and punctuation in her assignment paper.
- Ask: "Did Tanya check her writing for **conventions**?" (Answer: No)
- Direct students to respond to their partners by saying "yes" or "no" and explaining the reasons for their response.
  Note: While students are responding, monitor their exchanges. Ask two or three students to share their responses with the class.
- Ask the class to chorally read the second sentence with you:
  2. Roberto wanted to get a good grade. After he wrote his first draft, he proofread his paper for correct spelling, grammar, capitalization, and punctuation.
- Ask: "Did Roberto edit for **conventions**?" (Answer: Yes)
- Direct students to respond to their partners by saying "yes" or "no" and explaining the reasons for their response.
  Note: While students are responding, monitor their exchanges. Ask two or three students to share their responses with the class.
- Ask the class to chorally read the third sentence with you:
  3. What does it mean when a teacher grades a paper for **conventions**?
- Direct partners to think, write, and share their answers with the class. (A suggested sentence stem: When a teacher grades for _____.)
- Ask the class to chorally read the fourth sentence with you:
  4. If your teacher gave you a checklist titled "Editing for **Conventions**," what items would the checklist include?
- Direct partners to think, write, and share their answers with the class. (A suggested sentence stem: If I received a checklist titled _____.)

E Writing Terms Table

(*Student Book* page 119)

> ◆ Students add the academic writing term, an explanation of the term, and a usage example to the unit Writing Terms Table.

- Direct students to the *Unit 5 Writing Terms Table* on page 132 in the *Student Book*.
- Tell students to copy the explanation of the writing term **conventions** from this lesson or to write their own explanation of **conventions** in the second column.
- Then, direct students to write their own sentence, write another explanation, or draw a picture to represent the writing term **conventions** in the last column.

Sample Answers

Word	Explanation	Sentence/Explanation/Picture
conventions	Standards that are applied to writing, including correct capitalization, punctuation, spelling, and choice of words	Good writers make an effort to use writing **conventions** that reflect excellence.

F Cloze Exercise

(*Student Book* page 119)

> ◆ Students use the writing term to complete a cloze exercise.

Note: To help students better comprehend the meaning of the writing term **conventions**, *a different form (i.e.,* **conventional***) and meaning of the term is included in the Cloze Exercise. You may need to scaffold this exercise by explaining that the word* **conventional** *means "in an accepted or traditional way."*

- Direct students to use the words **conventions** and **conventional** to complete this cloze exercise with their partners. Provide sufficient time for them to do so.
- Then, ask students to follow along as you read to determine if their answers to the cloze exercise are correct.

> Esther quickly wrote her paper. She did not pay attention to writing **conventions**. In her paper, she did not use **conventional** spellings. She did not capitalize city names. She wrote many run-on sentences. As a result, she received a poor grade for **conventions**.

G Informational Passage

(*Student Book* page 120)

> ◆ Students chorally read the informational passage with the teacher.
>
> ◆ Students then read the passage with their partners.

- Say: "This informational passage is designed to provide you with strategies for applying the concept of **conventions** to your writing assignments."

- Ask students to read the passage chorally with you and then with their partners.

Conventions Are Standards for Writing

Writing **conventions** include correct spelling, punctuation, capitalization, and word usage. Your time is well spent when you use a dictionary to make sure you have spelled words correctly. Correct punctuation helps the reader read with expression and rhythm. The first word of every sentence should be capitalized. Also, proper nouns such as people's names and names of cities and countries should be capitalized. Using the right words will help the reader clearly understand what you are saying. To mark a new idea or section in your writing, begin with an indented paragraph.

Sometimes students use a writing rubric to edit their work. A writing rubric is a checklist for proofreading what you have written. Ask yourself:

- Did I write a title for my paper?
- Did I indent each paragraph?
- Did I check the spelling of words?
- Did I use capital letters at the beginning of sentences?
- Did I use capital letters for names of people and places?
- Is my word usage correct?
- Did I add spaces between words and sentences?

It is important to check your paper for **conventions**. You do not want to write a creative paper and then lose points because you did not take time to proofread and make corrections.

sentence fluency

OBJECTIVES

Students will:
1. Define the writing term **sentence fluency**.
2. Identify examples and non-examples of the writing term **sentence fluency**.

A Introduction and Pronunciation
(*Student Book* page 121)

- Introduce the writing term to students: "This writing term is **sentence fluency**."
- Ask students to repeat the writing term.

B Explanation
(*Student Book* page 121)

- Say: "**Sentence fluency** means *sentences that start with different words, are of different lengths, and are easy to understand.*"
- Ask the class to repeat the explanation.
- Direct Partner 1s to give the explanation to Partner 2s.
- Direct Partner 2s to tell Partner 1s if their explanation was correct.

sentence fluency

Unit 5 Lesson 3

A. Introduction and Pronunciation
- This writing term is **sentence fluency**.
- Say the writing term.

B. Explanation
- **Sentence fluency** means sentences that start with different words, are of different lengths, and are easy to understand.

C. Example Sentences
1. Good writers make sure that their **sentence fluency** includes both long and short sentences.
2. Daphne read her paper aloud to check for **sentence fluency**, especially to make sure that her sentences were easy to understand.

D. Checking for Understanding
1. Steve checked to make sure that each sentence in his paper began differently. *Question:* Was Steve concerned about **sentence fluency**? Yes or No? Why or why not?
_____
_____
_____

2. Anita did not like to worry about punctuation, so she wrote long sentences and used the word "**and**" often. *Question:* Do you think Anita received a high score for **sentence fluency**? Yes or No? Why or why not?
_____
_____
_____

121

C Example Sentences
(*Student Book* page 121)

> ◆ Students chorally read example sentences with the teacher.
> ◆ Student partners answer scripted questions with provided sentence stems.

- Ask the class to chorally read the first sentence with you:
  1. Good writers make sure that their **sentence fluency** includes both long and short sentences.
- Ask: "Why do good writers use both long and short sentences?"
- Direct students to use the writing term **sentence fluency** in their answer with this sentence stem:
  Good writers _____ [use both long and short sentences for **sentence fluency**].
- Have students answer to their partners.

- Ask the class to chorally read the second sentence with you:
  2. Daphne read her paper aloud to check for **sentence fluency**, especially to make sure that her sentences were easy to understand.
- Ask: "Why did Daphne read her paper aloud?"
- Direct students to use the writing term **sentence fluency** in their answer with this sentence stem:

  Daphne read her paper aloud to _____ [check for **sentence fluency** and to make sure that her sentences were easy to understand].
- Have students answer to their partners.

D Checking for Understanding
(*Student Book* pages 121 and 122)

> ◆ Students chorally read example sentences with the teacher.
> ◆ Student partners answer scripted "Yes or No" questions with oral or written responses.

- Explain to students that they will think, say, or write a response to sentences and explain the responses to their partners (e.g., say, "Partner 2s, read and respond to the first sentence. Partner 1s, tell your partner if you agree or disagree").
- Ask the class to chorally read the first sentence with you:
  1. Steve checked to make sure that each sentence in his paper began differently.
- Ask: "Was Steve concerned about **sentence fluency**?" (Answer: Yes)
- Direct students to respond to their partners by saying "yes" or "no" and explaining the reasons for their response.
  Note: While students are responding, monitor their exchanges. Ask two or three students to share their responses with the class.
- Ask the class to chorally read the second sentence with you:
  2. Anita did not like to worry about punctuation, so she wrote long sentences and used the word "**and**" often.
- Ask: "Do you think Anita received a high score for **sentence fluency**?" (Answer: No)
- Direct students to respond to their partners by saying "yes" or "no" and explaining the reasons for their response.
  Note: While students are responding, monitor their exchanges. Ask two or three students to share their responses with the class.
- Ask the class to chorally read the third sentence with you:
  3. When Marc read his paper aloud to his mother, she told him that she was confused because his sentences did not follow in a logical order.
- Ask: "What should Marc do about this problem?"
- Direct partners to think, write, and share their answers with the class. (A suggested sentence stem: Marc should _____.)
- Ask the class to chorally read the fourth sentence with you:
  4. When was the last time you rewrote sentences to make your paper read smoothly?

- Direct partners to think, write, and share their answers with the class. (A suggested sentence stem: The last time I rewrote sentences _____.)

E Writing Terms Table
(*Student Book* page 122)

♦ Students add the academic writing term, an explanation of the term, and a usage example to the unit Writing Terms Table.

- Direct students to the *Unit 5 Writing Terms Table* on page 132 in the *Student Book*.
- Tell students to copy the explanation of the writing term **sentence fluency** from this lesson or to write their own explanation of **sentence fluency** in the second column.
- Then, direct students to write their own sentence, write another explanation, or draw a picture to represent the writing term **sentence fluency** in the last column.

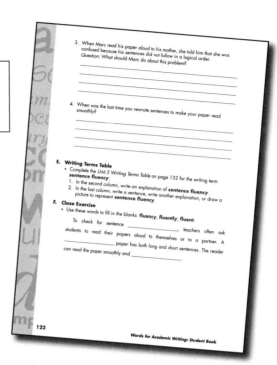

Sample Answers

Word	Explanation	Sentence/Explanation/Picture
sentence fluency	Sentences that start with different words, are of different lengths, and are easy to understand	To check for **sentence fluency**, it is a good idea to read your paper out loud.

F Cloze Exercise
(*Student Book* page 122)

♦ Students use the writing term to complete a cloze exercise.

Note: To help students better comprehend the meaning of the writing term **sentence fluency**, *different forms of the word* **fluent** *are included in the Cloze Exercise. You may need to scaffold this exercise by explaining that the word* **fluent** *means "to speak, read, and write a language easily and correctly" and that the word* **fluently** *means "in an easy and accurate manner."*

- Direct students to use the words **fluency**, **fluently**, and **fluent** to complete this cloze exercise with their partners. Provide sufficient time for them to do so.
- Then, ask students to follow along as you read to determine if their answers to the cloze exercise are correct.

> To check for sentence **fluency**, teachers often ask students to read their papers aloud to themselves or to a partner. A **fluent** paper has both long and short sentences. The reader can read the paper smoothly and **fluently**.

G Informational Passage

(*Student Book* page 123)

> ◆ Students chorally read the informational passage with the teacher.
>
> ◆ Students then read the passage with their partners.

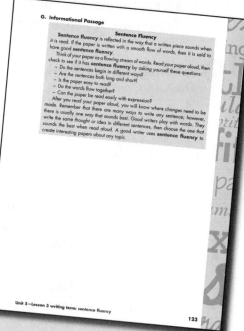

- Say: "This informational passage is designed to provide you with strategies for applying the concept of **sentence fluency** to your writing assignments."

- Ask students to read the passage chorally with you and then with their partners.

Sentence Fluency

Sentence fluency is reflected in the way that a written piece sounds when it is read. If the paper is written with a smooth flow of words, then it is said to have good **sentence fluency**.

Think of your paper as a flowing stream of words. Read your paper aloud, then check to see if it has **sentence fluency** by asking yourself these questions:

- Do the sentences begin in different ways?
- Are the sentences both long and short?
- Is the paper easy to read?
- Do the words flow together?
- Can the paper be read easily with expression?

After you read your paper aloud, you will know where changes need to be made. Remember that there are many ways to write any sentence; however, there is usually one way that sounds best. Good writers play with words. They write the same thought or idea in different sentences, then choose the one that sounds the best when read aloud. A good writer uses **sentence fluency** to create interesting papers about any topic.

word choice

Unit 5   Lesson 4

word choice

A. Introduction and Pronunciation
- This writing term is **word choice**.
- Say the writing term.

B. Explanation
- **Word choice** means the selection of words to create a specific message.

C. Example Sentences
1. Since Jessica used many descriptive adjectives in her paper, she received high marks for **word choice**.
2. A paper is more interesting when a writer uses creative **word choice** to build a clear mental picture for the reader.

D. Checking for Understanding
1. Wayne wanted to watch TV, so he quickly wrote his paper using lots of common words, which he repeated often.
   Question: Did Wayne use good **word choice**? Yes or No? Why or why not?

2. Teri wanted a good grade on her paper, so she focused on carefully selecting very descriptive words about her topic.
   Question: Do you think that Teri received a high mark for **word choice** on her paper? Yes or No? Why or why not?

124

Words for Academic Writing: Student Book

OBJECTIVES

Students will:
1. Define the writing term **word choice**.
2. Identify examples and non-examples of the writing term **word choice**.

A Introduction and Pronunciation
(*Student Book* page 124)

- Introduce the writing term to students: "This writing term is **word choice**."
- Ask students to repeat the writing term.

B Explanation
(*Student Book* page 124)

- Say: "**Word choice** means *the selection of words to create a specific message.*"
- Ask the class to repeat the explanation.
- Direct Partner 1s to give the explanation to Partner 2s.
- Direct Partner 2s to tell Partner 1s if their explanation was correct.

C Example Sentences
(*Student Book* page 124)

> ◆ Students chorally read example sentences with the teacher.
> ◆ Student partners answer scripted questions with provided sentence stems.

- Ask the class to chorally read the first sentence with you:
  1. Since Jessica used many descriptive adjectives in her paper, she received high marks for **word choice**.
- Ask: "Why did Jessica receive high marks for **word choice** on her paper?"
- Direct students to use the writing term **word choice** in their answer with this sentence stem:

  Jessica received high marks _____ [for **word choice** because she used many descriptive adjectives in her paper.]
- Have students answer to their partners.

- Ask the class to chorally read the second sentence with you:
  2. A paper is more interesting when a writer uses creative **word choice** to build a clear mental picture for the reader.
- Ask: "What does a writer use to effectively build a clear mental picture for the reader?"
- Direct students to use the writing term **word choice** in their answer with this sentence stem:

  A writer effectively uses _____ [**word choice** to build a clear mental picture for the reader.]
- Have students answer to their partners.

D Checking for Understanding
(*Student Book* pages 124 and 125)

> ◆ Students chorally read example sentences with the teacher.
> ◆ Student partners answer scripted "Yes or No" questions with oral or written responses.

- Explain to students that they will think, say, or write a response to sentences and explain the responses to their partners (e.g., say, "Partner 2s, read and respond to the first sentence. Partner 1s, tell your partner if you agree or disagree").
- Ask the class to chorally read the first sentence with you:
  1. Wayne wanted to watch TV, so he quickly wrote his paper using lots of common words, which he repeated often.
- Ask: "Did Wayne use good **word choice**?" (Answer: No)
- Direct students to respond to their partners by saying "yes" or "no" and explaining the reasons for their response.
  Note: While students are responding, monitor their exchanges. Ask two or three students to share their responses with the class.
- Ask the class to chorally read the second sentence with you:
  2. Teri wanted a good grade on her paper, so she focused on carefully selecting very descriptive words about her topic.
- Ask: "Do you think that Teri received a high mark for **word choice** on her paper?" (Answer: Yes)
- Direct students to respond to their partners by saying "yes" or "no" and explaining the reasons for their response.
  Note: While students are responding, monitor their exchanges. Ask two or three students to share their responses with the class.
- Ask the class to chorally read the third sentence with you:
  3. Our English teacher presented a lengthy lesson on the importance of **word choice** in writing.
- Ask: "Why do you think the English teacher presented this particular topic?"
- Direct partners to think, write, and share their answers with the class. (A suggested sentence stem: I think the English teacher _____)
- Ask the class to chorally read the fourth sentence with you:
  4. Describe how you pay attention to **word choice** when you write a paper.
- Direct partners to think, write, and share their answers with the class. (A suggested sentence stem: When it comes to **word choice**, I _____.)

E Writing Terms Table
(*Student Book* page 125)

◆ Students add the academic writing term, an explanation of the term, and a usage example to the unit Writing Terms Table.

- Direct students to the *Unit 5 Writing Terms Table* on page 132 in the *Student Book*.
- Tell students to copy the explanation of the writing term **word choice** from this lesson or to write their own explanation of **word choice** in the second column.
- Then, direct students to write their own sentence, write another explanation, or draw a picture to represent the writing term **word choice** in the last column.

Sample Answers

Word	Explanation	Sentence/Explanation/Picture
word choice	The selection of words to create a specific message	Good authors develop **word choice** skills by carefully selecting words to precisely describe events.

F Cloze Exercise
(*Student Book* page 125)

◆ Students use the writing term to complete a cloze exercise.

Note: To help students better comprehend the meaning of the writing term **word choice**, *different forms of the word* **choice** *(i.e.,* **choose**, **choosing**, *and* **chose***) are included in the Cloze Exercise. You may need to scaffold this exercise by reviewing the definitions of the three word forms.*

- Direct students to use the writing term **word choice** as well as the words **choose**, **choosing**, and **chose** to complete this cloze exercise with their partners. Provide sufficient time for them to do so.
- Then, ask students to follow along as you read to determine if their answers to the cloze exercise are correct.

Eduardo knows that __**choosing**__ powerful verbs is necessary to keep the reader's attention. He wants to __**choose**__ creative words that give specific meanings. So when he wrote his essay, instead of using "ran," he __**chose**__ the word "dashed." Instead of using "yelled," he __**chose**__ the word "screeched." Because his __**word choice**__ gave the reader a very clear mental picture of the essay topic, Eduardo received a high grade.

G Informational Passage

(Student Book page 126)

◆ Students chorally read the informational passage with the teacher.

◆ Students then read the passage with their partners.

- Say: "This informational passage is designed to provide you with strategies for applying the concept of **word choice** to your writing assignments."

- Ask students to read the passage chorally with you and then with their partners.

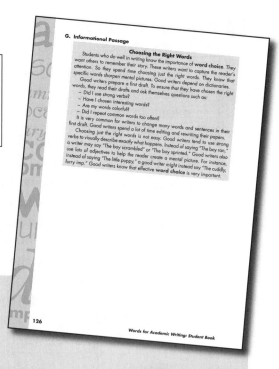

Choosing the Right Words

Students who do well in writing know the importance of **word choice**. They want others to remember their story.

These writers want to capture the reader's attention.

So they spend time choosing just the right words. They know that specific words sharpen mental pictures. Good writers depend on dictionaries.

Good writers prepare a first draft. To ensure that they have chosen the right words, they read their drafts and ask themselves questions such as:

- – Did I use strong verbs?
- – Have I chosen interesting words?
- – Are my words colorful?
- – Did I repeat common words too often?

It is very common for writers to change many words and sentences in their first draft. Good writers spend a lot of time editing and rewriting their papers.

Choosing just the right words is not easy. Good writers tend to use strong verbs to visually describe exactly what happens. Instead of saying "The boy ran," a writer may say "The boy scrambled" or "The boy sprinted." Good writers also use lots of adjectives to help the reader create a mental picture. For instance, instead of saying "The little puppy," a good writer might instead say "The cuddly, furry imp." Good writers know that effective **word choice** is very important.

Students will:
1. Define the writing term **organization**.
2. Identify examples and non-examples of the writing term **organization**.

(A) Introduction and Pronunciation
(*Student Book* page 127)

- Introduce the writing term to students: "This writing term is **organization**."
- Ask students to repeat the writing term.

(B) Explanation
(*Student Book* page 127)

- Say: "In writing, **organization** refers to *the state of being well arranged in a logical manner.*"
- Ask the class to repeat the explanation.
- Direct Partner 1s to give the explanation to Partner 2s.
- Direct Partner 2s to tell Partner 1s if their explanation was correct.

Unit 5 Lesson 5 **organization**

A. **Introduction and Pronunciation**
- This writing term is **organization**.
- Say the writing term.

B. **Explanation**
- In writing, **organization** refers to the state of being well arranged in a logical manner.

C. **Example Sentences**
1. Pam wanted to present herself as a logical thinker, so she carefully planned the **organization** of her paper.
2. An **organized** paper presents information in a way that makes sense.

D. **Checking for Understanding**
1. Bill's paper about penguins was **organized** in a logical manner.
   Question: Do you think Bill received a high mark for **organization**? Yes or No? Why or why not?

2. Janice began her assigned paper about penguins with one interesting fact, but continued her writing with facts about polar bears, elk, and walruses.
   Question: Do you think Janice received a high mark for **organization**? Yes or No? Why or why not?

3. What are some ways that you have been taught to **organize** papers?

127

(C) Example Sentences
(*Student Book* page 127)

- Students chorally read example sentences with the teacher.
- Student partners answer scripted questions with provided sentence stems.

Note: To help students better comprehend the meaning of the writing term **organization**, *the word form* **organized** *("in a structured, logical manner") is used in both Example Sentences. You may need to scaffold this exercise by reviewing definitions of the word forms* **organized**, **organizes**, **organizing**, **organization**, *and* **organizational**.

- Ask the class to chorally read the first sentence with you:
  1. Pam wanted to present herself as a logical thinker, so she carefully planned the **organization** of her paper.
- Ask: "When Pam wanted her teacher to see that she was a logical thinker, what did she focus on?"

Chapter 3, Unit 5—Lesson 5 writing term: organization   **217**

- Direct students to use the writing term **organization** in their answer with this sentence stem:

  Pam focused on _____ [the **organization** of her paper].
- Have students answer to their partners.
- Ask the class to chorally read the second sentence with you:

  2. An **organized** paper presents information in a way that makes sense.
- Ask: "What kind of a paper presents information in a way that makes sense?"
- Direct students to use the word **organized** in their answer with this sentence stem:

  An **organized** paper _____ [presents information in a way that makes sense.]
- Have students answer to their partners.

D Checking for Understanding
(*Student Book* pages 127 and 128)

- ◆ Students chorally read example sentences with the teacher.
- ◆ Student partners answer scripted "Yes or No" questions with oral or written responses.

Note: To help students better comprehend the meaning of the writing term **organization**, *the word forms* **organize** *and* **organized** *are used in two sentences. You may need to scaffold this exercise by reviewing the definitions of the two word forms.*

- Explain to students that they will think, say, or write a response to sentences and explain the responses to their partners (e.g., say, "Partner 2s, read and respond to the first sentence. Partner 1s, tell your partner if you agree or disagree").
- Ask the class to chorally read the first sentence with you:

  1. Bill's assigned paper about penguins was **organized** in a logical manner.
- Ask: "Do you think Bill received a high mark for **organization**?" (Answer: Yes)
- Direct students to respond to their partners by saying "yes" or "no" and explaining the reasons for their response.
  Note: While students are responding, monitor their exchanges. Ask two or three students to share their responses with the class.
- Ask the class to chorally read the second sentence with you:

  2. Janice began her assigned paper about penguins with one interesting fact, but continued her writing with facts about polar bears, elk, and walruses.
- Ask: "Do you think Janice received a high mark for **organization**?" (Answer: No)
- Direct students to respond to their partners by saying "yes" or "no" and explaining the reasons for their response.
  Note: While students are responding, monitor their exchanges. Ask two or three students to share their responses with the class.
- Ask the class to chorally read the third sentence with you:

  3. What are some ways that you have been taught to **organize** papers?

- Direct partners to think, write, and share their answers with the class.
- Ask the class to chorally read the fourth sentence with you:
    4. Describe the best **organized** paper you have ever read or written.
- Direct partners to think, write, and share their answers with the class.

E Writing Terms Table
(*Student Book* page 128)

> ◆ Students add the academic writing term, an explanation of the term, and a usage example to the unit Writing Terms Table.

- Direct students to the *Unit 5 Writing Terms Table* on page 132 in the *Student Book*.
- Tell students to copy the explanation of the writing term **organization** from this lesson or to write their own explanation of **organization** in the second column.
- Then, direct students to write their own sentence, write another explanation, or draw a picture to represent the writing term **organization** in the last column.

Sample Answers

Word	Explanation	Sentence/Explanation/Picture
organization	The state of being well arranged in a logical manner	Good reporters make **organization** their top priority when writing news stories.

F Cloze Exercise
(*Student Book* page 128)

> ◆ Students use the writing term to complete a cloze exercise.

Note: To help students better comprehend the meaning of the writing term **organization**, *the word forms* **organize**, **organized**, **organizing**, *and* **organizational** *are used in the Cloze Exercise. You may need to scaffold this exercise by reviewing the definitions of the four word forms.*

- Direct students to use the words **organize**, **organizing**, **organized**, and **organizational** to complete this cloze exercise with their partners. Provide sufficient time for them to do so.
- Then, ask students to follow along as you read to determine if their answers to the cloze exercise are correct.

> **Organizing** a paper takes planning. You must decide on a topic and then **organize** the material in a logical and interesting manner. To get **organized**, you need a plan. An **organizational** plan is like a road map. It guides you, the writer, about where to begin, where to be in the middle, and where to end.

Ⓖ Informational Passage
(*Student Book* page 128)

◆ Students chorally read the informational passage with the teacher.
◆ Students then read the passage with their partners.

- Say: "This informational passage is designed to provide you with strategies for applying the concept of **organization** to your writing assignments."
- Ask students to read the passage chorally with you and then with their partners.

Get Organized

Organization is the key to good writing. This writing term refers to the order in which information or facts are written. The order should be logical, meaning that the information or facts should be presented in a way that is easy to follow. Your paper should make sense to the reader.

Begin with a statement that makes the reader want to find out more. This type of opening statement is often called a lead or a "hook." At the very start, you should make a point. Next, include facts and details. Link ideas together, allowing the reader to see how one idea relates to the next. At the end of the paper, tie everything together. This helps the reader understand the point of your paper. Once you know what **organization** means and how to create it, you are on your way to becoming an effective writer.

voice

OBJECTIVES

Students will:
1. Define the writing term **voice**.
2. Identify examples and non-examples of the writing term **voice**.

(A) Introduction and Pronunciation
(*Student Book* page 129)

- Introduce the writing term to students: "This writing term is **voice**."
- Ask students to repeat the writing term.

(B) Explanation
(*Student Book* page 129)

- Say: "**Voice** refers to *the use of words that lets the reader know the writer's personality and feelings.*"
- Ask the class to repeat the explanation.
- Direct Partner 1s to give the explanation to Partner 2s.
- Direct Partner 2s to tell Partner 1s if their explanation was correct.

Unit 5 Lesson 6 **voice**

A. **Introduction and Pronunciation**
- This writing term is **voice**.
- Say the writing term.

B. **Explanation**
- **Voice** refers to the use of words that lets the reader know the writer's personality and feelings.

C. **Example Sentences**
1. The **voice** of Ralph's paper revealed that he was upset about the plan to build a road through a national forest.
2. **Voice** reveals a writer's personality and feelings about a topic.

D. **Checking for Understanding**
1. Jack checked his paper to make sure that his feelings about saving whales were clearly stated.
   Question: Do you think Jack received a high score for using **voice** in his paper? Yes or No? Why or why not?

2. Loren's paper was full of facts and information about whales.
   Question: Do you think Loren's paper revealed her feelings about saving whales? Yes or No? Why or why not?

3. What do you think is the most important thing to remember about using **voice** in a paper?

129

(C) Example Sentences
(*Student Book* page 129)

> ◆ Students chorally read example sentences with the teacher.
> ◆ Student partners answer scripted questions with provided sentence stems.

- Ask the class to chorally read the first sentence with you:
  1. The **voice** of Ralph's paper revealed that he was upset about the plan to build a road through a national forest.
- Ask: "What writing term is used to describe the tone of Ralph's paper?"
- Direct students to use the writing term **voice** in their answer with this sentence stem:
  The tone of Ralph's paper _____ [is revealed through **voice**].
- Have students answer to their partners.
- Ask the class to chorally read the second sentence with you:
  2. **Voice** reveals a writer's personality and feelings about a topic.
- Ask: "In a good paper, what quality lets the reader experience the writer's personality and feelings?"

- Direct students to use the writing term **voice** in their answer with this sentence stem:

  In a good paper, _____ [**voice** reveals the writer's personality and feelings].
- Have students answer to their partners.

Ⓓ Checking for Understanding
(*Student Book* pages 129 and 130)

> ◆ Students chorally read example sentences with the teacher.
> ◆ Student partners answer scripted "Yes or No" questions with oral or written responses.

- Explain to students that they will think, say, or write a response to sentences and explain the responses to their partners (e.g., say, "Partner 2s, read and respond to the first sentence. Partner 1s, tell your partner if you agree or disagree").
- Ask the class to chorally read the first sentence with you:
  1. Jack checked his paper to make sure that his feelings about saving whales were clearly stated.
- Ask: "Do you think Jack received a high score for using **voice** in his paper?" (Answer: Yes)
- Direct students to respond to their partners by saying "yes" or "no" and explaining the reasons for their response.
  Note: While students are responding, monitor their exchanges. Ask two or three students to share their responses with the class.
- Ask the class to chorally read the second sentence with you:
  2. Loren's paper was full of facts and information about whales.
- Ask: "Do you think Loren's paper revealed her feelings about saving whales?" (Answer: No)
- Direct students to respond to their partners by saying "yes" or "no" and explaining the reasons for their response.
  Note: While students are responding, monitor their exchanges. Ask two or three students to share their responses with the class.
- Ask the class to chorally read the third sentence with you:
  3. What do you think is the most important thing to remember about using **voice** in a paper?
- Direct partners to think, write, and share their answers with the class.
- Ask the class to chorally read the fourth sentence with you:
  4. Write a sentence that shows **voice**.
- Direct partners to think, write, and share their answers with the class.

E Writing Terms Table

(*Student Book* page 130)

◆ Students add the academic writing term, an explanation of the term, and a usage example to the unit Writing Terms Table.

- Direct students to the *Unit 5 Writing Terms Table* on page 132 in the *Student Book*.
- Tell students to copy the explanation of the writing term **voice** from this lesson or to write their own explanation of **voice** in the second column.
- Then, direct students to write their own sentence, write another explanation, or draw a picture to represent the writing term **voice** in the last column.

Sample Answers

Word	Explanation	Sentence/Explanation/Picture
voice	The use of words that lets the reader know the writer's personality and feelings	When you read an essay, you will hear the writer's **voice**.

F Cloze Exercise

(*Student Book* page 130)

◆ Students use word forms to complete a cloze exercise.

Note: To help students better comprehend the meaning of the writing term **voice**, *the word forms* **voices** *and* **voiced** *are used in the Cloze Exercise. You may need to scaffold this exercise by reviewing the definitions of the two word forms.*

- Direct students to use the words **voices**, **voiced**, and **voice** to complete this cloze exercise with their partners. Provide sufficient time for them to do so.
- Then, ask students to follow along as you read to determine if their answers to the cloze exercise are correct.

The teacher told the class that she wanted students' essays to express **voice**. Tania thought that meant the teacher wanted lots of dialogue in the essays. So she wrote a cute play about her friends. The characters in Tania's play used different **voices**. When she received a poor grade on her essay, Tania was upset and **voiced** her opinion. Then the teacher told Tania that she did not understand the meaning of **voice** as it related to writing.

G Informational Passage

(*Student Book* page 131)

> ◆ Students chorally read the informational passage with the teacher.
>
> ◆ Students then read the passage with their partners.

- Say: "This informational passage is designed to provide you with strategies for applying the concept of **voice** to your writing assignments."
- Ask students to read the passage chorally with you and then with their partners.

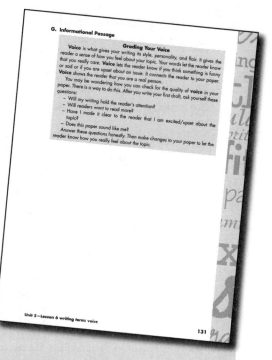

Grading Your Voice

Voice is what gives your writing its style, personality, and flair. It gives the reader a sense of how you feel about your topic. Your words let the reader know that you really care. **Voice** lets the reader know if you think something is funny or sad or if you are upset about an issue. It connects the reader to your paper. **Voice** shows the reader that you are a real person.

You may be wondering how you can check for the quality of **voice** in your paper. There is a way to do this. After you write your first draft, ask yourself these questions:

- Will my writing hold the reader's attention?
- Will readers want to read more?
- Have I made it clear to the reader that I am excited/upset about the topic?
- Does this paper sound like me?

Answer these questions honestly. Then make changes to your paper to let the reader know how you really feel about the topic.

Objective	To determine students' understanding of the academic writing terms that were presented in Unit 5
Materials needed	For each student, one copy of the Unit 5 Posttest (refer to the accompanying CD-ROM) and two sheets of blank paper
Time allotment	35 minutes (Part A, 10 minutes; Part B, 10 minutes; Part C, 15 minutes)

Instructional Procedure

Step 1 Distribute Unit 5 Posttest and two sheets of blank paper to each student. Say:

- "Write your name and today's date on the lines at the top of the Posttest and at the top of each sheet of blank paper. I will collect all of them after you have finished the posttest."

Step 2 Review the directions for the Unit 5 Posttest, then administer the posttest. Say:

- "Only this Posttest score will be recorded as part of your grade. So do your very best."
- "Look at Part A. Let's read the directions together." *(Read directions out loud with students.)*
- "Place your finger on each writing term as I read it: **ideas and content**, **conventions**, **sentence fluency**, **word choice**, **organization**, **voice**."
- "Now, place your finger on each lowercase letter next to the explanations in the right-hand column. Listen as I read the explanation for each letter."
    - **a.** The selection of words to create a specific message
    - **b.** Sentences that start with different words, are of different lengths, and are easy to understand
    - **c.** The use of words that lets the reader know the writer's personality and feelings
    - **d.** The state of being well arranged in a logical manner
    - **e.** Standards that are applied to writing, including correct capitalization, punctuation, spelling, and choice of words
    - **f.** Reasons for writing a paper that conveys a message
- "Match each writing term with the explanation that you think is correct. Write the letter of the explanation in the middle column, next to the writing term."
- "You will have 10 minutes to complete Part A. Ready? Begin." *(After 10 minutes, proceed to Part B.)*

- "Now, look at Part B. It is important to know how to use academic writing terms within the context of print."
- "Read the first six sentences. Use the writing terms in the first column of the table in Part A to fill in the blanks of the sentences."
- "Then, read the last three sentences and fill in the blanks with one of the words listed in the directions."
- "You will have 10 minutes to complete Part B. Any questions? Begin." *(After 10 minutes, proceed to Part C.)*
- "Now, read the directions for Part C. Remember to make a graphic organizer on one sheet of paper to plan your answer. Then write a paragraph using a topic sentence, transitional sentences, and a conclusion sentence on the other sheet of paper. You can receive up to 15 points for this section: 5 points for the graphic organizer, 5 points for using a paragraph format, and 5 points for content."
- "You will have 15 minutes to complete Part C. Any questions? Begin." *(After 10 minutes, tell students they have 5 minutes to finish.)*
- After 5 minutes pass, say, "Please turn in your tests and papers to me."

> Refer to *Appendix D* for Unit 5 Posttest Answer Key

Unit 5　Generative Assessment *(optional)*

Objective	To ensure that students are able to correctly apply Unit 5 academic writing terms in a generalized setting
Materials needed	For each student, one copy of the Unit 5 Generative Assessment (refer to the accompanying CD-ROM) and two sheets of blank paper
Time allotment	One class period

Instructional Procedure

Step 1:　Distribute Unit 5 Generative Assessment and two sheets of blank paper to each student. Say:
- "Write your name and today's date on the lines at the top of the assessment and at the top of each sheet of blank paper. I will collect all of them after you have finished the assessment."

Step 2:　Review the directions for the Unit 5 Generative Assessment, then administer the assessment. Say:
- "This assessment is designed to find out how well you are able to apply the Unit 5 academic writing terms to general situations. This assessment will ask you to demonstrate your understanding of the Unit 5 writing terms by providing examples based on your personal knowledge and experiences."
- "Read each direction, and then use the blank paper to create your own graphic organizer to plan your answer."
- "Then, use your graphic organizer to help you write a short paragraph using a topic sentence, transitional sentences, and a conclusion sentence."
- "You can receive up to 15 points for each answer: 5 points for your graphic organizer, 5 points for using a paragraph format, and 5 points for content. You will have the whole class period to complete this assessment."
- "Any questions? When you have finished, please turn in your assessment and graphic organizers to me. Begin."

Grading Criteria

To grade a Generative Assessment, we suggest allocating a maximum of 15 points *per assessment item* as follows:
- Up to 5 points for use of a graphic organizer
- Up to 5 points for conventions (correct paragraphing; use of topic, transitional, and conclusion sentences; correct punctuation; correct spelling)
- Up to 5 points for content

appendices

Sample Unit 2 Pretest

Name _____ Date _____

Part A: Match each word with its explanation. Write the letter of the explanation in the second column.

Word	Match Letter	Explanation
define		**a.** To write main points in an order using only headings and subheadings, not details
outline		**b.** To give an opinion of worth or value
justify		**c.** To make an idea or statement very clear or easy to understand with examples
evaluate		**d.** To show or tell what something is or means
illustrate		**e.** To prove or show why something is right or acceptable
clarify		**f.** To create a mental picture by clearly explaining or giving examples

Part B: Use the words listed in the first column of the table above to complete the following sentences.

1. The student was asked to _____ the meaning of the word

   "**glanced**."

2. Using words, not pictures, John was asked to _____ the phases

   of the life cycle of an insect.

3. To determine grades, the teacher used a checklist of instructions to

   _____ the essays.

4. When Mel came home late, he made an effort to _____ his

   actions by telling his parents all of the reasons he was delayed.

(continued)

5. To organize her essay, Janet will first _____ the book's main points.

6. Jackson was asked to _____ his answers by adding more

specific information and some examples.

Score

Part A	_____	/ **6**
Part B	_____	/ **6**
TOTAL	_____	/ **12**

Sample Unit 2 Posttest

Name _____ Date _____

Part A: Match each word with its explanation. Write the letter of the explanation in the second column.

Word	Match Letter	Explanation
define		**a.** To write main points in an order using only headings and subheadings, not details
outline		**b.** To give an opinion of worth or value
justify		**c.** To make an idea or statement very clear or easy to understand with examples
evaluate		**d.** To show or tell what something is or means
illustrate		**e.** To prove or show why something is right or acceptable
clarify		**f.** To create a mental picture by clearly explaining or giving examples

Part B: Use the words **compare**, **define**, **outline**, **justify**, **explain**, **evaluate**, **illustrate**, **contrast**, and **clarify** to complete the following sentences.

1. Jack plans to buy a new cell phone. He will look at the ways that many cell phones are alike and will check out all of their features. He will _____ the different cell phones before he decides which one to buy.

2. The student was asked to _____ the meaning of the word **glanced**.

3. Using words, not pictures, John was asked to _____ the phases of the life cycle of an insect.

4. Sean knows that there are many differences between lions and tigers. He will make a _____ between them.

(continued)

5. To determine grades, the teacher used a checklist of instructions to _____ the essays.

6. To help her sister understand long division, Tanika will _____ each step clearly.

7. When Mel came home late, he made an effort to _____ his actions by telling his parents all of the reasons he was delayed.

8. To organize her essay, Janet will first _____ the book's main points.

9. Jackson was asked to _____ his answers by adding more specific information and some examples.

Part C: On a separate sheet of paper, **compare** the last two television shows you watched.

Score _____

Part A	_____ / **6**
Part B	_____ / **9**
Part C	_____ / **15**
TOTAL	_____ / **30**

Name _____ Date _____

1. **define**: *Define* friendship.

_____

_____

_____

2. **outline**: *Outline* your class schedule.

_____

_____

_____

3. **justify**: Tell how you might *justify* getting a poor grade on a test.

_____

_____

_____

4. **evaluate**: *Evaluate* the last lunch you ate at school.

_____

_____

_____

5. **illustrate**: *Illustrate* how people can be kind to one another.

_____

_____

_____

(continued)

6. **clarify**: *Clarify* your school's dress code as it relates to shirts.

_____

_____

_____

Score

#1	_____	/ **15**
#2	_____	/ **15**
#3	_____	/ **15**
#4	_____	/ **15**
#5	_____	/ **15**
#6	_____	/ **15**
TOTAL	_____	/ **90**

Extension Activities

Extension activities are designed for students to use and think about the definitions of academic words within a game-like structure. Conduct these extension activities following the completion of the units as follows:

- After Unit 2: "I'm Thinking of a Word"
- After Unit 3: "Concentration"
- After Unit 4: "Jeopardy!®"

"I'm Thinking of a Word" extension activity
(to be played at the conclusion of Unit 2)

Preparation

- On a whiteboard or an overhead transparency sheet, draw a T scoring chart. Label one side "Team 1" and the other side "Team 2."
- Create two student teams.
- Ask each team to select a captain, who will give answers for the team.
- Flip a coin to determine which team goes first.

Activity Rules

- Teams may not look up the answers to the clues; however, team members may consult with each other and discuss their answers before the captain announces them.
- If the first team's answer to the first clue is correct, that team receives 30 points. If the first team's answer is incorrect, the second team gets to guess the answer word.
- If the second team gives the correct answer word, the team receives 20 points, and that team is given the first chance to identify the next word.
- If the second team does not come up with the correct answer word for the second clue, the other team (i.e., the first team) is allowed give the answer. If the first team is correct, it receives 10 points, and that team is given the first chance to identify the next word.
- Teacher records each team's points and totals their scores.

Activity Clues and Questions

Word 1 (**evaluate**)
- I am thinking of a word that rhymes with **calculate**. (30 points)
- This word means "to give an opinion of worth or value." (20 points)
- Teachers often do this when they grade papers. (10 points)

Word 2 (**clarify**)
- I am thinking of word that rhymes with **mystify**. (30 points)
- This word means "to make an idea or statement very clear or easy to understand with examples." (20 points)
- Teacher often do this by giving examples or reasons so that everyone understands. (10 points)

Word 3 (**compare**)

- I am thinking of a word that rhymes with **despair**. (30 points)
- This word means "to tell or show how two or more people, ideas, or things are alike and not alike." (20 points)
- Shoppers often do this when they look at similar items. (10 points)

Word 4 (**outline**)

- I am thinking of a word that rhymes with **skyline**. (30 points)
- This word means "to write main points in an order using only headings and subheadings, not details." (20 points)
- Students often do this when they study a chapter in a textbook. (10 points)

Word 5 (**summarize**)

- This word rhymes with **sanitize**. (30 points)
- This word means "to write or say a short statement about main points of information." (20 points)
- Teachers often ask students to do this when they want an answer that is short and to the point. (10 points)

Word 6 (**justify**)

- This word rhymes with **amplify**. (30 points)
- This word means "to prove or show why something is right or acceptable." (20 points)
- Students often do this when they explain why they took a certain action. (10 points)

Word 7 (**contrast**)

- This word rhymes with **broadcast**. (30 points)
- This word means "to show or state the difference(s) between two people, ideas, or things." (20 points)
- People often do this when they talk about a book and a movie with the same title. (10 points)

Word 8 (**illustrate**)

- This word rhymes with **demonstrate**. (30 points)
- This word means "to create a mental picture by clearly explaining or giving examples." (20 points)
- People do this by describing, clarifying, or explaining something. (10 points)

Word 9 (**explain**)

- This word begins with the letter "**e**." (30 points)
- This word means "to give a reason for something; to make something easy to understand." (20 points)
- Parents often ask their children to do this when they have done something wrong. (10 points)

Word 10 (**define**)

- This word rhymes with **alpine**. (30 points)
- This word means "to show or tell what something is or means." (20 points)
- Students are often assigned to do this with particular words. (10 points)

Word 11 (**analyze**)

- This word rhymes with **finalize**. (30 points)
- This word means "to study something carefully." (20 points)
- Scientists do this when they want to find out what something is made of. (10 points)

Word 12 (**discuss**)

- This word begins with the letter "**d**." (30 points)
- This word means "to talk about something; to consider different points of view." (20 points)
- People often do this before they make a decision. (10 points)

"Concentration" extension activity
(to be played at the conclusion of Unit 3)

Preparation

- Make one copy of the game sheet (next page) for each pair of vocabulary partners.
- Cut apart the words and definitions, and place all pieces in an envelope. (Each piece will serve as a playing card.)
- Distribute one envelope to each pair of vocabulary partners.
- Designate the student partners as Partner A and Partner B.

Activity Rules

- Both students shuffle the cards and lay them on a desk facedown in a 3-piece by 6-piece pattern.
- Partner B goes first. Partner B turns over two cards—one at a time—and keeps the cards if a word and a definition match. If they match, Partner B gets another turn. If the two cards do not match, those cards are turned facedown again and Partner A takes a turn.
- The game continues until all of the cards have been matched by word and definition. The partner with the most matches is considered the winner.
  Note: Students may check the accuracy of their answers by referring to the Glossary section in the back of the Student Book.

"Concentration" Game Sheet

analyze	to study something carefully
clarify	to make an idea or statement very clear or easy to understand with examples
compare	to tell or show how two or more people, ideas, or things are alike and not alike
contrast	to show or state the difference(s) between two people, ideas, or things
define	to show or tell what something is or means
differentiate	to show or state the difference(s) between two or more people, ideas, or things
discuss	to talk about something; to consider different points of view
evaluate	to give an opinion of worth or value
explain	to give a reason for something; to make something easy to understand
illustrate	to create a mental picture by clearly explaining or giving examples
interpret	to personally decide the meaning of something
justify	to prove or show why something is right or acceptable
list	to write a set of information, one item per line
outline	to write main points in an order using only headings and subheadings, not details
prove	to show that something is true
review	to carefully examine and judge the main parts of something
summarize	to write or say a short statement about main points of information
trace	to follow something back to its beginning

"Jeopardy!" extension activity
(to be played at the conclusion of Unit 4)

Preparation
- Draw a "Jeopardy!" game board as illustrated below.
- Select one student to be the scorekeeper, who will keep score for each team and erase each cell point value on the game board as the question related to the cell value is correctly answered.
- Divide the remaining students in the class into teams of six each.
- Assign students a number from 1–6 within their teams.
- Tell students that all of the questions are related to the 24 academic words they have studied in the past four units.

Unit 1	Unit 2	Unit 3	Unit 4
10 points	10 points	10 points	10 points
20 points	20 points	20 points	20 points
30 points	30 points	30 points	30 points
40 points	40 points	40 points	40 points
50 points	50 points	50 points	50 points
60 points	60 points	60 points	60 points

Activity Rules
- Call out a random number between 1 and 6 and say, "This answer is for (#2) students." Begin the game by reading the 10-point answer for Unit 1 (following). The first #2 student who correctly phrases the related question wins the points for his/her team, and that student selects the next cell-point value.
- Then call out another random number between 1 and 6, and clarify that you are addressing only those students with that assigned number. The game ends when all of the cells have been erased and, consequently, all of the answers. The team with the most points wins the game.
- Accept any derivations of a correct answer (e.g., if the answer word is **explain** and the student replies "**explained**" or "**explanation**," you may consider either answer to be correct).

UNIT 1

10 points
Answer: The counselor told the student how the three classes were alike and not alike.
Question: What is **compared**?

20 points
Answer: The class talked about various aspects of recent political campaigns.
Question: What is **discussed**?

30 points
Answer: The teacher condensed the story to make it short and to the point.
Question: What is **summarized**?

40 points
Answer: The players carefully watched the baseball game video to figure out why the team was losing.
Question: What is **analyzed**?

50 points
Answer: The girls looked at both dresses to identify the differences between them.
Question: What is **contrasted**?

60 points
Answer: It was a complicated math problem; however, the teacher made it easy to understand.
Question: What is **explained**?

UNIT 2

10 points
Answer: Students were assigned to review the chapter and then list the main points in an order using headings but no details.
Question: What is **outlined**?

20 points
Answer: Students were assigned to explain the meanings of six phrases.
Question: What is **defined**?

30 points
Answer: The teacher made the author's goal very clear by using lots of examples.
Question: What is **clarified**?

40 points
Answer: The student gave reasons as to why it is appropriate to stand at attention for the national anthem.
Question: What is **justified**?

50 points
Answer: The principal judged the science fair projects by awarding first, second, and third places.
Question: What is **evaluated**?

60 points
Answer: The chef created mental pictures with words to describe his fancy desserts.
Question: What is **illustrated**?

UNIT 3

10 points
Answer: The question asked that students write a set of names in order.
Question: What is **listed**?

20 points
Answer: The differences between Arizona, New Hampshire, and Alaska were shown.
Question: What is **differentiated**?

30 points
Answer: After students read the book, they summarized and judged the main plot of the story.
Question: What is **reviewed**?

40 points
Answer: Ron presented his version of the meaning of the popular song.
Question: What is **interpreted**?

50 points
Answer: Linda wrote down the developmental life cycle of a butterfly.
Question: What is **traced**?

60 points
Answer: All students were responsible for explaining why their own answer was true.
Question: What is **proved**?

UNIT 4

10 points
Answer: In class, Jamal protected his essay from challenges by carefully explaining each section.
Question: What is **defended**?

20 points
Answer: Sandy clearly presented statistics and her opinions about her favorite football team
Question: What is **stated**?

30 points
Answer: The school nurse was able to show to how eating a healthy breakfast is linked to good health.
Question: What is **related**?

40 points
Answer: The vice principal was able to convince the basketball team to paint the walls of the gym blue.
Question: What is **persuaded**?

50 points
Answer: After reading the article, Tanya wrote about its strong and weak points and then told everyone that she thought the article was lacking in content.
Question: What is **critiqued**?

60 points
Answer: Students listed the planets in the solar system from largest to smallest.
Question: What is **enumerated**?

100-Point Bonus Question

For this final "Jeopardy!" activity, each team may select one person to be the team representative. Teams may wager as many points as they have accumulated. The team representative has 30 seconds to come up with the correct question.

100 points   *Answer:* This is the type of language or words we use in the classroom, see in textbooks, and are often included in test directions.

Question: What is **academic language** (or **academic words**)?

Graphic Organizers

Graphic organizers are valuable tools for writing. They allow students to quickly organize thoughts and information they want to include on a test or an assignment. Graphic organizers are flexible and endless in application. Although there are basically four main types of graphic organizers, there are many variations. Reference to the use of graphic organizers is often found in informational passages.

The first of the four types is a **Web** organizer (refer to *Graph A-1*, following). This type of organizer is excellent for single-topic assignments that ask students to *define*, *interpret*, or *relate* a particular issue.

The second type of graphic organizer is a chart or matrix organizer such as a **Venn diagram** (refer to *Graph A-2*, following) or a **T-Chart** (refer to *Graph A-3*, following). These organizers are most useful for *comparing*, *contrasting*, *evaluating*, or *differentiating* information. Students may find that a T-Chart organizer is also helpful when asked to *critique* an issue, idea, or suggestion.

A third type of organizer uses a **Tree/Map** format (refer to *Graph A-4*, following). This graphic organizer is most effective for illustrating a main event with a variety of possible outcomes. This type of organizer is usually used when assignment directions include words such as *analyze*, *discuss*, *justify*, or *clarify*.

A **Chain** graphic organizer is best for showing processes, sequences, and chronology (refer to *Graph A-5*, following). This organizer is best used when students are asked to *illustrate*, *trace*, *prove*, or *defend* an assignment topic.

Finally, an **Outline** organizer (refer to *Graph A-6*, following) is most useful for students when they are asked to *outline*, *review*, or *enumerate* a topic, or to use with short, simple text. Its straightforward linear format makes this type of organizer perhaps the easiest for students to learn and process among other types of graphic organizers.

All of these graphic organizers can also be found on the accompanying CD-ROM for duplication purposes.

Graph A-1. Web graphic organizer

This type of graphic organizer is most useful for students to use when you ask them to *define*, *interpret*, or *relate* a single-topic assignment. This organizer may also be helpful for students to use when you are presenting the academic writing term *ideas and content*.

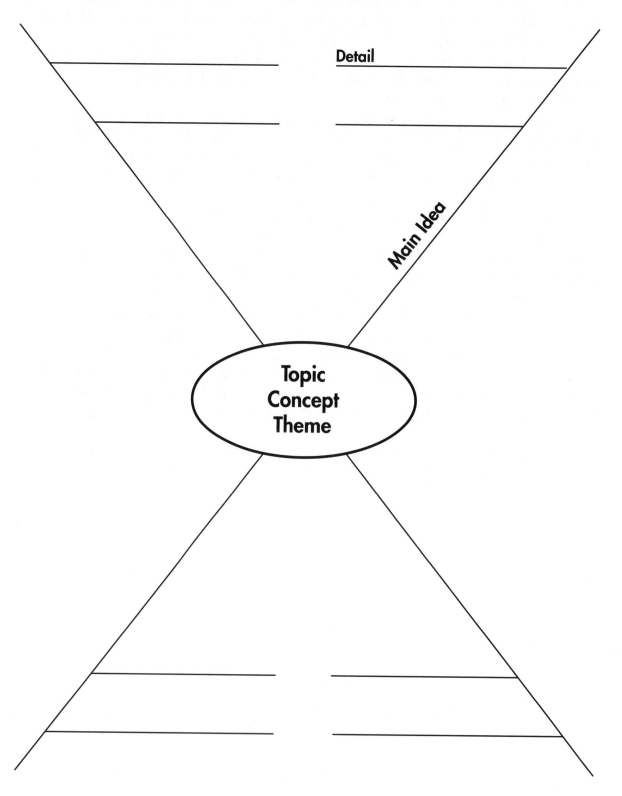

Words for Academic Writing: Teacher Guide

Graph A-2. Venn diagram graphic organizer
This type of graphic organizer is most useful for students to use when you ask them to *compare*, *contrast*, *evaluate*, or *differentiate* information.

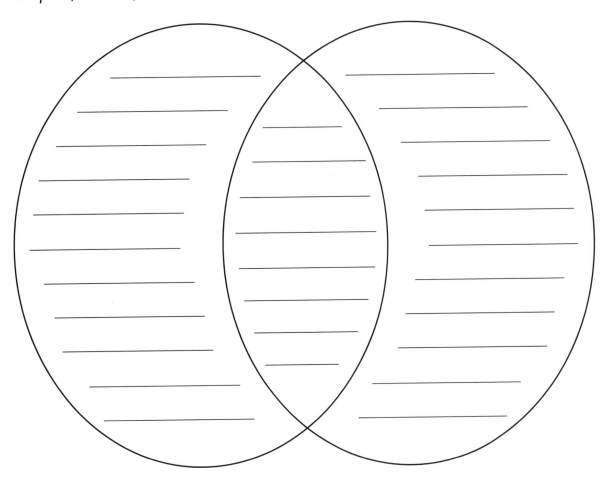

Graph A-3. T-Chart graphic organizer

This type of graphic organizer is most useful for students to use when you ask them to *compare, contrast, evaluate, differentiate,* or *critique* information.

+ item	– item

Graph A-4. Tree/Map graphic organizer

This type of graphic organizer is most useful for students to use when you ask them to illustrate a main event with a variety of possible outcomes. This type of organizer is usually used when assignment directions include words such as *analyze*, *discuss*, *justify*, or *clarify*.

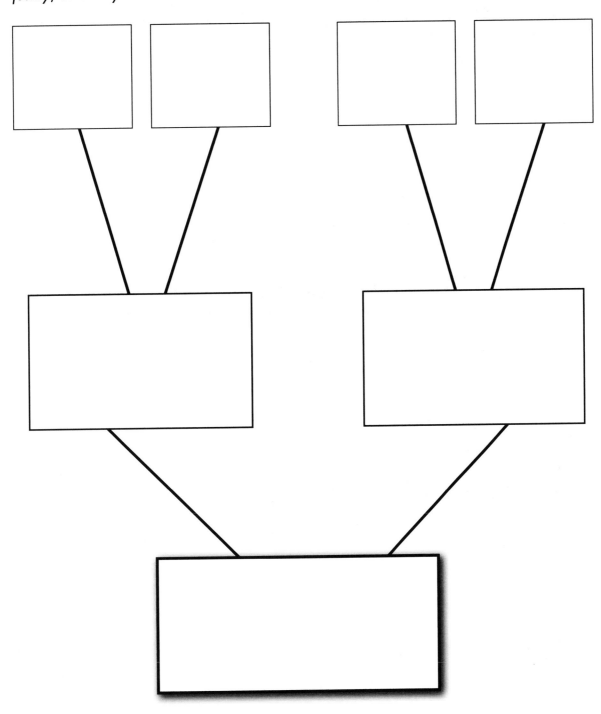

Graph A-5. Chain graphic organizer

This type of graphic organizer is most useful for students to use when you ask them to *illustrate*, *trace*, *prove*, or *defend* a topic. This type of organizer is best for showing processes, sequences, and chronology.

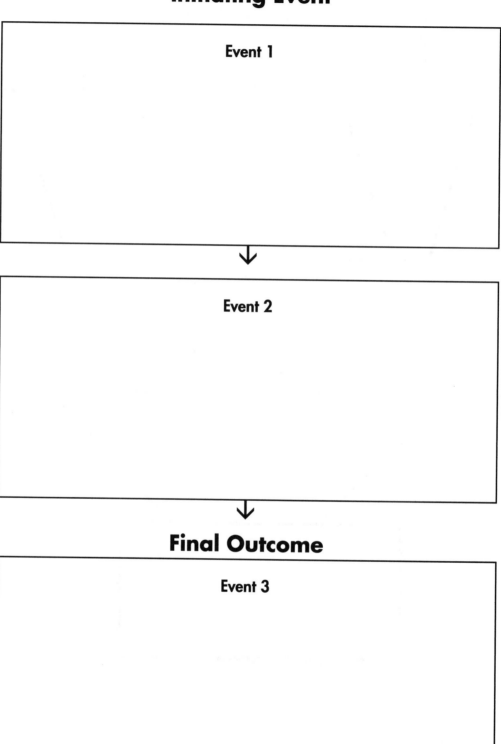

Initiating Event

Event 1

↓

Event 2

↓

Final Outcome

Event 3

Graph A-6. Outline graphic organizer

This type of graphic organizer is most useful for students to use when you ask them to *outline*, *review*, or *enumerate* a single-topic assignment or to use with short, simple text. Outlines are sometimes easier and quicker to process than other graphic organizers. In an outline, topics are listed with their subtopics in a linear format.

I. (Topic) _____
    A. (Subtopic or detail) _____
       1. (Supporting information) _____
       2. (Supporting information) _____
    B. (Subtopic or detail) _____
       1. (Supporting information) _____
       2. (Supporting information) _____
    C. (Subtopic or detail) _____
       1. (Supporting information) _____
       2. (Supporting information) _____

II. (Topic) _____
    A. (Subtopic or detail) _____
       1. (Supporting information) _____
       2. (Supporting information) _____
    B. (Subtopic or detail) _____
       1. (Supporting information) _____
       2. (Supporting information) _____
    C. (Subtopic or detail) _____
       1. (Supporting information) _____
       2. (Supporting information) _____

III. (Topic) _____
    A. (Subtopic or detail) _____
       1. (Supporting information) _____
       2. (Supporting information) _____
    B. (Subtopic or detail) _____
       1. (Supporting information) _____
       2. (Supporting information) _____
    C. (Subtopic or detail) _____
       1. (Supporting information) _____
       2. (Supporting information) _____

Unit 1   Pretest Answer Key

Part A: Match each word with its explanation. Write the letter of the explanation in the second column.

Word	Match Letter	Explanation
contrast	e	**a.** To give a reason for something; to make something easy to understand
compare	c	**b.** To study something carefully
summarize	f	**c.** To tell or show how two or more people, ideas, or things are alike and not alike
explain	a	**d.** To talk about something; to consider different points of view
analyze	b	**e.** To show or state the difference(s) between two people, ideas, or things
discuss	d	**f.** To write or say a short statement about main points of information

Part B: Use the words listed in the first column of the table above to complete the following sentences.

1. The teacher asked the students to tell the similarities and differences among three Native American tribes. The teacher wanted the students to **compare** the three tribes.

2. The student arrived at school 15 minutes after the start of the first class. The student was asked to **explain** the reason for her tardiness.

3. Alberto often volunteers to answer questions in class, while John does not. The **contrast** between the two students is noticeable.

4. In biology class, we often perform experiments. We study them carefully and **analyze** the results.

5. The history teacher will lecture for an hour about the causes of the American Revolution. At the very end of the lecture, the teacher will **summarize** the main points.

6. My friend Juan is trying to decide whether or not to try out for the track team. He wants to talk about the advantages and disadvantages before making a decision. Juan wants to **discuss** his choices.

Part A: Match each word with its explanation. Write the letter of the explanation in the second column.

Word	Match Letter	Explanation
contrast	e	**a.** To give a reason for something; to make something easy to understand
compare	c	**b.** To study something carefully
summarize	f	**c.** To tell or show how two or more people, ideas, or things are alike and not alike
explain	a	**d.** To talk about something; to consider different points of view
analyze	b	**e.** To show or state the difference(s) between two people, ideas, or things
discuss	d	**f.** To write or say a short statement about main points of information

Part B: Use the words listed in the first column of the table above to complete the following sentences.

1. The teacher asked the students to tell the similarities and differences among three Native American tribes. The teacher wanted the students to **compare** the three tribes.

2. The student arrived at school 15 minutes after the start of the first class. The student was asked to **explain** the reason for her tardiness.

3. Alberto often volunteers to answer questions in class, while John does not. The **contrast** between the two students is noticeable.

4. In biology class, we often perform experiments. We study them carefully and **analyze** the results.

5. The history teacher will lecture for an hour about the causes of the American Revolution. At the very end of the lecture, the teacher will **summarize** the main points.

6. My friend Juan is trying to decide whether or not to try out for the track team. He wants to talk about the advantages and disadvantages before making a decision. Juan wants to **discuss** his choices.

(continued)

Part C: Students are asked to **contrast** dogs and cats.

Grading Criteria for Part C

To grade a generative response, we suggest allocating a maximum of 15 points as follows:

- Up to 5 points for use of a graphic organizer
- Up to 5 points for conventions (correct paragraphing; use of topic, transitional, and conclusion sentences; correct punctuation; correct spelling)
- Up to 5 points for content

Part A: Match each word with its explanation. Write the letter of the explanation in the second column.

Word	Match Letter	Explanation
define	d	**a.** To write main points in an order using only headings and subheadings, not details
outline	a	**b.** To give an opinion of worth or value
justify	e	**c.** To make an idea or statement very clear or easy to understand with examples
evaluate	b	**d.** To show or tell what something is or means
illustrate	f	**e.** To prove or show why something is right or acceptable
clarify	c	**f.** To create a mental picture by clearly explaining or giving examples

Part B: Use the words listed in the first column of the table above to complete the following sentences.

1. The student was asked to **define** the meaning of the word "**glanced**."

2. Using words, not pictures, John was asked to **illustrate** the phases of the life cycle of an insect.

3. To determine grades, the teacher used a checklist of instructions to **evaluate** the essays.

4. When Mel came home late, he made an effort to **justify** his actions by telling his parents all of the reasons he was delayed.

5. To organize her essay, Janet will first **outline** the book's main points.

6. Jackson was asked to **clarify** his answers by adding more specific information and some examples.

Part A: Match each word with its explanation. Write the letter of the explanation in the second column.

Word	Match Letter	Explanation
define	d	a. To write main points in an order using only headings and subheadings, not details
outline	a	b. To give an opinion of worth or value
justify	e	c. To make an idea or statement very clear or easy to understand with examples
evaluate	b	d. To show or tell what something is or means
illustrate	f	e. To prove or show why something is right or acceptable
clarify	c	f. To create a mental picture by clearly explaining or giving examples

Part B: Use the words **compare**, **define**, **outline**, **justify**, **explain**, **evaluate**, **illustrate**, **contrast**, and **clarify** to complete the following sentences.

1. Jack plans to buy a new cell phone. He will look at the ways that many cell phones are alike and will check out all of their features. He will **compare** the different cell phones before he decides which one to buy.

2. The student was asked to **define** the meaning of the word "**glanced**."

3. Using words, not pictures, John was asked to **illustrate** the phases of the life cycle of an insect.

4. Sean knows that there are many differences between lions and tigers. He will make a **contrast** between them.

5. To determine grades, the teacher used a checklist of instructions to **evaluate** the essays.

6. To help her sister understand long division, Tanika will **clarify** each step.

7. When Mel came home late, he made an effort to **justify** his actions by telling his parents all of the reasons he was delayed.

8. To organize her essay, Janet will first **outline** the book's main points.

9. Jackson was asked to **explain** his answers by adding more specific information and some examples.

(continued)

Part C: Students are asked to **compare** the last two television shows they watched.

Grading Criteria for Part C

To grade a generative response, we suggest allocating a maximum of 15 points as follows:

- Up to 5 points for use of a graphic organizer
- Up to 5 points for conventions (correct paragraphing; use of topic, transitional, and conclusion sentences; correct punctuation; correct spelling)
- Up to 5 points for content

Part A: Match each word with its explanation. Write the letter of the explanation in the second column.

Word	Match Letter	Explanation
review	e	a. To follow something back to its beginning
differentiate	d	b. To write a set of information, one item per line
interpret	c	c. To personally decide the meaning of something
trace	a	d. To show or state the difference(s) between two or more people, ideas, or things
list	b	e. To carefully examine and judge the main parts of something
prove	f	f. To show that something is true

Part B: Use the words listed in the first column of the table above to complete the following sentences.

1. Barbara used evidence to **prove** her point that the girls' sports program could be improved.

2. Barry was asked to **trace** the historical issues in the development of the Pony Express.

3. Anita will **list** all the types of birds in her home state on a chart.

4. The assignment was that all students **review** their favorite book.

5. Jackson was asked to read the school dress code and to **interpret** its meaning as it related to wearing hats in class.

6. LeMai was assigned to **differentiate** between the life cycle of an insect and a mammal.

Part A: Match each word with its explanation. Write the letter of the explanation in the second column.

Word	Match Letter	Explanation
review	e	a. To follow something back to its beginning
differentiate	d	b. To write a set of information, one item per line
interpret	c	c. To personally decide the meaning of something
trace	a	d. To show or state the difference(s) between two or more people, ideas, or things
list	b	e. To carefully examine and judge the main parts of something
prove	f	f. To show that something is true

Part B: Use the words **review**, **differentiate**, **illustrate**, **interpret**, **trace**, **list**, **summarize**, **justify**, and **prove** to complete the following sentences.

1. Barbara used evidence to **prove** her point that the girls' sports program could be improved.
2. Carmen will **justify** why her behavior at the assembly was acceptable.
3. Barry was asked to **trace** the historical issues in the development of the Pony Express.
4. Anita will **list** all the types of birds in her home state on a chart.
5. When Arturo wants to **illustrate** a point, he uses lots of colorful words to create a mental picture.
6. The assignment was that all students **review** their favorite book.
7. Jackson was asked to read the school dress code and to **interpret** its meaning as it related to wearing hats in class.
8. LeMai was assigned to **differentiate** between the life cycle of an insect and a mammal.
9. At the end of her paper, Concha wrote a short statement to **summarize** her report.

Part C: Students are asked to **evaluate** the last meal they ate.

Grading Criteria for Part C

To grade a generative response, we suggest allocating a maximum of 15 points as follows:

- Up to 5 points for use of a graphic organizer
- Up to 5 points for conventions (correct paragraphing; use of topic, transitional, and conclusion sentences; correct punctuation; correct spelling)
- Up to 5 points for content

Part A: Match each word with its explanation. Write the letter of the explanation in the second column.

Word	Match Letter	Explanation
enumerate	a	a. To list one thing after another in a specific order; to count off
relate	f	b. To judge both the strong and weak points of something or someone
persuade	d	c. To act or express to protect something
defend	c	d. To cause others to change their minds or take action
state	e	e. To clearly give information or an opinion
critique	b	f. To tell how things, people, or events are connected or alike

Part B: Use the words listed in the first column of the table above to complete the following sentences.

1. Ellen can **enumerate** the names of all presidents of the United States in sequential order.

2. Anne was able to **persuade** Bob to go to the library to study.

3. Cheryl uses many facts to **defend** her opinion about the protection of wildlife.

4. The form asked students to **state** their name, address, and phone number.

5. Roberto explained how heavy rainfalls could **relate** to flooding.

6. Lenny will **critique** the school lunch program by pointing out that the food is good, but the service is poor.

Part A: Match each word with its explanation. Write the letter of the explanation in the second column.

Word	Match Letter	Explanation
enumerate	a	a. To list one thing after another in a specific order; to count off
relate	f	b. To judge both the strong and weak points of something or someone
persuade	d	c. To act or express to protect something
defend	c	d. To cause others to change their minds or take action
state	e	e. To clearly give information or an opinion
critique	b	f. To tell how things, people, or events are connected or alike

Part B: Use the words **enumerate**, **relate**, **discuss**, **state**, **trace**, **defend**, **persuade**, **prove**, and **critique** to complete the following sentences.

1. Ellen can **enumerate** the names of all presidents of the United States in sequential order.
2. Juan will **prove** his point when he shows that his facts are true and accurate.
3. Anne was able to **persuade** Bob to go to the library to study.
4. Jackie and Armeda will **discuss** the strong and weak points of the gymnastic meet.
5. Cheryl uses many facts to **defend** her opinion about the protection of wildlife.
6. Marc will **trace** the history of car racing in Baja, California.
7. The form asked students to **state** their name, address, and phone number.
8. Roberto explained how heavy rainfalls could **relate** to flooding.
9. Lenny will **critique** the school lunch program by pointing out that the food is good, but the service is poor.

Part C: Students are asked to **define** the word "recycle" and **explain** why it's a good idea.

Grading Criteria for Part C

To grade a generative response, we suggest allocating a maximum of 15 points as follows:

- Up to 5 points for use of a graphic organizer
- Up to 5 points for conventions (correct paragraphing; use of topic, transitional, and conclusion sentences; correct punctuation; correct spelling)
- Up to 5 points for content

Part A: Match each writing term with its explanation. Write the letter of the explanation in the second column.

Writing Term	Match Letter	Explanation
ideas and content	f	a. The selection of words to create a specific message
conventions	e	b. Sentences that start with different words, are of different lengths, and are easy to understand
sentence fluency	b	c. The use of words that lets the reader know the writer's personality and feelings
word choice	a	d. The state of being well arranged in a logical manner
organization	d	e. Standards that are applied to writing, including correct capitalization, punctuation, spelling, and choice of words
voice	c	f. Reasons for writing a paper that conveys a message

Part B: Use the writing terms listed in the first column of the table above to complete the following sentences.

1. To make sure that he would receive a high score for **conventions**, Roberto checked to make sure that his spelling, word usage, and punctuation were correct.

2. When Jill carefully selected words to create a mental picture, she was concerned about **word choice**.

3. To check for **sentence fluency**, Jake reviewed his paper to see if some sentences were longer and some were shorter.

4. When Alex used words to reveal his personality, his teacher said his paper had **voice**.

5. The **organization** of the paper was exceptional because the topic was presented in a logical manner.

6. To receive a high score for **ideas and content**, Joe made sure that he stated the reasons for writing his paper and that he conveyed a message.

Part A: Match each writing term with its explanation. Write the letter of the explanation in the second column.

Writing Term	Match Letter	Explanation
ideas and content	f	a. The selection of words to create a specific message
conventions	e	b. Sentences that start with different words, are of different lengths, and are easy to understand
sentence fluency	b	c. The use of words that lets the reader know the writer's personality and feelings
word choice	a	d. The state of being well arranged in a logical manner
organization	d	e. Standards that are applied to writing, including correct capitalization, punctuation, spelling, and choice of words
voice	c	f. Reasons for writing a paper that conveys a message

Part B: Use the writing terms listed in the first column of the table above to complete the following sentences.

1. To make sure that he would receive a high score for **conventions**, Roberto checked to make sure that his spelling, word usage, and punctuation were correct.

2. When Jill carefully selected words to create a mental picture, she was concerned about **word choice**.

3. To check for **sentence fluency**, Jake reviewed his paper to see if some sentences were longer and some were shorter.

4. When Alex used words to reveal his personality, his teacher said his paper had **voice**.

5. The **organization** of the paper was exceptional because the topic was presented in a logical manner.

6. To receive a high score for **ideas and content**, Joe made sure that he stated the reasons for writing his paper and that he conveyed a message.

(continued)

Now, use the words **interpret**, **defend**, and **enumerate** to complete the following sentences.

7. Robin will **<u>defend</u>** her paper by backing up statements with research and personal examples.

8. Roberto will **<u>enumerate</u>** the five steps necessary for completing the science experiment.

9. Students are sometimes asked to **<u>interpret</u>** the meaning of a painting.

Part C: Students are asked to **critique** the last movie they saw.

Grading Criteria for Part C

To grade a generative response, we suggest allocating a maximum of 15 points as follows:

- Up to 5 points for use of a graphic organizer
- Up to 5 points for conventions (correct paragraphing; use of topic, transitional, and conclusion sentences; correct punctuation; correct spelling)
- Up to 5 points for content

Glossary

Academic Words

analyze	to study something carefully
clarify	to make an idea or statement very clear or easy to understand with examples
compare	to tell or show how two or more people, ideas, or things are alike and not alike
contrast	to show or state the difference(s) between two people, ideas, or things
critique	to judge both the strong and weak points of something or someone
defend	to act or express to protect something
define	to show or tell what something is or means
differentiate	to show or state the difference(s) between two or more people, ideas, or things
discuss	to talk about something; to consider different points of view
enumerate	to list one thing after another in a specific order; to count off
evaluate	to give an opinion of worth or value
explain	to give a reason for something; to make something easy to understand
illustrate	to create a mental picture by clearly explaining or giving examples
interpret	to personally decide the meaning of something
justify	to prove or show why something is right or acceptable
list	to write a set of information, one item per line
outline	to write main points in an order using only headings and subheadings, not details
persuade	to cause others to change their minds or take action
prove	to show that something is true
relate	to tell how things, people, or events are connected or alike
review	to carefully examine and judge the main parts of something
state	to clearly give information or an opinion
summarize	to write or say a short statement about main points of information
trace	to follow something back to its beginning

Academic Writing Terms

conventions   standards that are applied to writing, including correct capitalization, punctuation, spelling, and choice of words

ideas and content   reasons for writing a paper that conveys a message

organization   the state of being well arranged in a logical manner

sentence fluency   sentences that start with different words, are of different lengths, and are easy to understand

voice   the use of words that lets the reader know the writer's personality and feelings

word choice   the selection of words to create a specific message

References

Adams, G. N., & Brown, S. (2007). *The six-minute solution: A reading fluency program (Intermediate)*. Longmont, CO: Sopris West Educational Services.

Adams, G. N., & Brown, S. (2007). *The six-minute solution: A reading fluency program (Primary)*. Longmont, CO: Sopris West Educational Services.

Adams, G. N., & Brown, S. (2007). *The six-minute solution: A reading fluency program (Secondary)*. Longmont, CO: Sopris West Educational Services.

Anderson, R. C., & Nagy, W. E. (1991). Word meanings. In R. Barr, M. L. Kamil, P. B. Mosenthal, & P. D. Pearson (Eds.), *Handbook of reading research* (Vol. 2, pp. 690–724). New York: Longman.

Baumann, J. F., & Kame'enui, F. J. (1991). Research on vocabulary instruction: Ode to Voltaire. In J. Flood, D. Lapp, & J. R. Squire (Eds.), *Handbook of research on teaching the English language arts* (pp. 604–632). New York: Macmillan.

Beck, I. L., & McKeown, M. C. (1991). Conditions of vocabulary acquisition. In R. Barr, M. Kamil, P. Mosenthal, & P. D. Pearsons (Eds.), *Handbook of reading research* (Vol. 2, pp. 789–814). New York: Longman.

Beck, I. L., McKeown, M. C., & Kucan, L. (2002). *Bringing words to life: Robust vocabulary instruction*. New York: Guilford.

Beck, I. L., McKeown, M. G., & Omanson, R. (1987). The effects and uses of diverse vocabulary instructional techniques. In M. G. McKeown & M. E. Curtis (Eds.), *The nature of vocabulary acquisition* (pp. 147–163). Hillsdale, NJ: Lawrence Erlbaum.

Becker, W. C. (1977). Teaching reading and language to the disadvantaged—What we have learned from field research. *Harvard Educational Review, 47,* 518–543.

Carlo, M. S., August, D., McLaughlin, B., Snow, C. E., Dressler, C., Lipman, D. N., et al. (2004, April/May/June). Closing the gap: Addressing the vocabulary needs of English language learners in bilingual and mainstream classrooms. *Reading Research Quarterly, 39*(2), 188–215.

Chall, J. S., Jacobs, V., & Baldwin, L. (1990). *The reading crisis: Why poor children fall behind*. Cambridge, MA: Harvard University Press.

Coxhead, A. (2000). A new academic word list. *TESOL Quarterly, 34*(2), 213–238.

Hirsch, E. D. (2003, Spring). Scientific insights into the fourth-grade slump and the nation's stagnant comprehension scores. *American Educator,* 10–44.

McIntosh, R., Vaughn, S., Schumm, J., Haager, D., & Lee, O. (1993). Observations of students with learning disabilities in general education classrooms. *Exceptional Children, 60*(3), 249–261.

McKeown, M. G., Beck, I. L., Omanson, R. C., & Pople, M. T. (1985). Some effects of the nature and frequency of vocabulary instruction on the knowledge and use of words. *Reading Research Quarterly, 20,* 533–535.

McTighe, J., & Lyman, F. (1988). Cueing thinking in the classroom: The promise of theory-embedded tools. *Educational Leadership, 45*, 18–24.

Mothers Against Drunk Driving (MADD) General Statistics. (2002). Retrieved July 20, 2007, from http://www.madd.org/stats/1789

National Highway Traffic Safety Administration (NHTSA), National Center for Statistics and Analysis (NCSA). Traffic Safety Facts—2005 Data. (2006). Retrieved July 20, 2007, from http://www-nrd.nhtsa.dot.gov/pdf/nrd-30/NCSA/TSF2005/810616.pdf

National Highway Traffic Safety Administration (NHTSA), U.S. Department of Transportation (DOT). Fact Sheet (2003). Retrieved July 20, 2007, from http://www.nhtsa.dot.gov/people/injury/airbags/buckleplan/mayplanner2003/factsheet.html

Nagy, W. E. (1988). *Teaching vocabulary to improve reading comprehension.* Newark, DE: International Reading Association.

Scarborough, H. S. (1998). Early identification of children at risk for reading disabilities: Phonological awareness and some other promising predictors. In B. K. Shapiro, P. J. Accardo, & A. J. Capute (Eds.), *Specific reading disability: A view of the spectrum* (pp. 75–119). Timonium, MD: York Press.

Scarcella, R. (2003). Academic English: A conceptual framework (The University of California Linguistic Minority Research Institute Tech. Rep. No. 2003-1). Retrieved July 20, 2007, from http://lmri.ucsb.edu/publications/03_scarcella.pdf

Stahl, S. A., & Fairbanks, M. (1986). The effects of vocabulary instruction: A model-based meta-analysis. *Review of Educational Research, 56*(1), 72–110.

Stanovich, K. E. (1986). Matthew effects in reading: Some consequences of individual differences in the acquisition of literacy. *Reading Research Quarterly, 24*, 360–407.

White, T. G., Graves, M. F., & Slater, W. H. (1990). Growth of reading vocabulary in diverse elementary schools: Decoding and word meaning. *Journal of Educational Psychology, 82*(2), 281–290.

Wolfe, P. (2001). *Brain matters: Translating research into classroom practice.* Alexandria, VA: Association for Supervision and Curriculum Development.